Argentina
a travel survival kit

Alan Samagalski

Argentina – a travel survival kit
  1st edition

Published by
  Lonely Planet Publications
  Head Office: PO Box 617, Hawthorn, Victoria 3122, Australia
  US Office: PO Box 2001A, Berkeley, CA 94702, USA

Printed by
  Colorcraft, Hong Kong

Photographs by
  Alan Samagalski
  Embassy of Argentina (EA)
  Nicholas De Vore III – Photographers Aspen
  Front Cover: Lakes District – Nicholas De Vore III
  Back Cover: La Boca, Buenos Aires – Alan Samalgaski

Published
  July 1989

National Library of Australia Cataloguing in Publication Data

Samagalski, Alan.
  Argentina, a travel survival kit.

  Includes index.
  ISBN 0 86442 030 7.

  1. Argentina – Description and travel –
  1981- – Guide-books. I. Title.

918.2'0464

Alan Samagalski

Alan's career started to look checkered when he left Melbourne University's Genetics Deparment for mixed receptions at some legendary Melbourne comedy venues. After 'The Last Laugh', he fled to the Indian sub-continent for a lengthy stay. He eventually returned home and formed a symbiotic relationship with Lonely Planet, who sent him to some of the more obscure parts of the country to research *Australia – a travel survival kit*. After several missions to help update *travel survival kits* for *Hong Kong, Macau & Canton* and *Bali & Lombok*, and co-writing our guides to *China* and *Indonesia*, it seemed he was feeling too much at home in Asia, so we sent him to South America. By the time he'd researched and written *Chile – a travel survival kit* he'd learned to like the Latin way of life, and they had learned to live with his Spanish. After Argentina, he was so disoriented that he went to live in Adelaide, where he stays between updating forays to Asia and South America.

Lonely Planet Credits

Production Editor	James Lyon
Maps	Ralph Roob
Design, cover design & illustrations	Greg Herriman
Typesetting	Ann Jeffree

Thanks also to Lindy Cameron and Peter Turner for editorial direction, Vicki Beale and Valerie Tellini for help with the paste-up, Gaylene Miller for extra typesetting and Margaret Jung for the title page.

A Warning & a Request

Things change – prices go up, schedules change, good places go bad and bad places go bankrupt – nothing stays the same. So if you find things better or worse, recently opened or long since closed, please write and tell us and help make the next edition better! All information is greatly appreciated and the best letters will receive a free copy of the next edition, or any other Lonely Planet book of your choice.

Extracts from the best letters are also included in the *Lonely Planet Update*. The *Update* helps us make useful information available to you as soon as possible – it's like reading an up-to-date noticeboard or postcards from a friend. Each edition contains hundreds of useful tips, and advice from the best possible source of information – other travellers. The *Lonely Planet Update* is published quarterly in paperback and is available from bookshops and by subscription. Turn to the back pages of this book for more details.

Contents

Introduction

The story of Argentina is one of conquest, the subjugation of an indigenous people, and the mass settlement of Europeans. Some 450 years ago the Spanish entered Argentina and began to reshape it in the image of their homeland. Few of Argentina's indigenous Indians survived the conquest. Most were wiped out in the extermination campaigns of the 19th century. Others inter-married with the early Spanish settlers to produce *mestizo* offspring, neither Indian nor European. Argentina became a European outpost in South America, a male-dominated society where events were made and recorded by men. Women, with some exceptions like the 'Mothers of the Plaza de Mayo' and Evita Perón, are curiously absent from the scene.

Like the North American 'wild west' and the Australian 'outback' the history of Argentina is a confused mixture of historical fact and romantic fiction. It has produced the *gaucho*, the flamboyantly dressed gentleman-cowboy, the one image which foreigners instantly identify with Argentina. It has produced a menagerie of famous and infamous men like San Martín, Perón and Videla, who either coaxed or jackbooted Argentina into line before losing their momentum and falling by the wayside. It has also produced the mystery : how has a country, which a century ago seemed destined for greatness, slipped into a permanent state of economic depression and political instability, stumbling from one crisis to another with no apparent end to the cycle?

Argentina is tucked away in the cone of South America. The capital, Buenos Aires, is 9000 km from New York and over 11,000 km from Paris. Partly because of this isolation Argentina is one of the least known countries of Latin America. It has long been a stamping ground for British and North American capitalists but, in comparison to the Latin American countries to the north, relatively few tourists find their way there. Unlike Brazil with its carnivals and Peru with its Inca ruins, the tourist attractions of Argentina are natural ones. They include the awesome Iguazú Falls (which formed the backdrop to the film *The Mission*), the huge Moreno Glacier near Calafate, and the largest penguin colonies outside Antarctica.

The majority of Argentines regard their country as European, though to an outsider its blend of southern Europe with outback Australia defies simple categorisation. It's easy to imagine that Argentina is what Australia or the USA would be like if those countries had been settled initially by the

Spanish rather than the British. In *The Old Patagonian Express*, the North American author Paul Theroux writes that Argentina permits a restful anonymity, the ability to disappear into a crowd because the faces are the same as those you see in the USA or Europe. The opportunity to mingle with familiar faces in a vibrant Latin culture makes Argentina a unique travel experience.

Argentina

0   200   400 km

Facts About the Country

HISTORY

For all practical purposes the history of Argentina begins in 1494. In that year a treaty between Spain and Portugal drew a line which divided the world between them. All the land east of the line was granted to Portugal and all the land west of the line was granted to Spain. By chance, this placed the coast of Brazil (then unknown to Europeans) within the Portuguese sphere and the rest of America within the Spanish sphere.

The Spanish accomplished the task of discovery and conquest with astonishing speed. Christopher Columbus first landed in the Caribbean Islands in 1492. By 1550 the Spanish presided over most of the land from central Chile to the southern USA, and had founded many of what are now Latin America's largest cities such as Lima, Santiago, Asunción and La Paz. Yet the motivation behind the Spanish conquests had not been empire building but plunder. When the first Aztec treasure was unveiled in Europe in 1520 one witness, the German Albrecht Dürer, wrote:

I saw the things which were brought to the King from the New Lands. There was a sun made entirely of gold a whole fathom broad. There was a moon made entirely of silver and just as big. There were many curiosities from their weapons, arms and missiles . . . I have never seen such things which made my heart rejoice as much as these.

The New World came to be known as the land of *El Dorado* (the Golden Man), a reference to a legendary Indian king of the Colombian highlands who was said to be ritually anointed with oil and smeared with gold dust so that he resembled a piece of brilliantly crafted gold. In time, Europeans came to think of El Dorado as a place rather than a person, perhaps a lost city in the South American jungle. The

Major Indian Groups in South America before the Spanish conquest

Spanish *conquistadores* who sought this fantastic city were not empire-builders but a rabble of adventurers and fortune-seekers. They were small in numbers, but they were ruthless and determined, had horses and firearms which terrified the Indians, and the good luck to enter America when the Indian civilisations were vulnerable to attack.

The Collapse of the Indian Empires

The American Indians first arrived in the continent over 20,000 years ago. They came overland from Siberia when the Bering Straits were still dry land. Some 17,000 years ago, many of these semi-nomadic hunters and gatherers developed permanent settlements based on corn (maize) farming.

In Mexico, Central America and northern South America, sophisticated Indian civilisations arose. By 300 AD the Mayan tribes of Central America had developed calendars and hieroglyphic writing, and had constructed massive stone temples. Around 1200 AD the Aztecs made their appearance in Mexico. The Incas, who appeared in the 11th century, carved out a formidable civilisation in the Andes of present-day Peru, expanding into what is now Bolivia, Ecuador and northern Chile and Argentina.

The Aztec empire was overthrown by the Spanish in just two years by an army of 550 men, with a few horses and cannon, commanded by Hernán Cortés. In 1531, Francisco Pizarro and his band of 180 men entered the Inca Empire. They exploited the dissension caused by a civil war and used deceit and treachery to capture and murder the Inca emperor. For the most part the Spanish conquest was brief, bloody and brutal.

The first Spanish colonisers in America were soldiers. Since they knew little about building, agriculture or mining it was the Indians who had to do the work. A soldier would receive an *encomienda* which meant that the Indians of a certain area were 'commended' to him to work. This system was used all through Latin America, so the success of Spanish colonisation relied on their ability to subdue large numbers of agrarian Indians.

South of the Inca Empire were Indians who lived as hunters and gatherers. In the 16th century there were about 300,000 Indians in Argentina. However, because it had no large populations of agrarian Indians, Argentina never provided the Spanish with quite the same incentive for conquest as Peru and Mexico had. Nevertheless the first attempt by the Spanish to gain a toe-hold on the Argentine coast was made quite early, partly to find a southern route around the American continent, partly to prevent the Portuguese from expanding their territory by moving down the coast from Brazil, and partly to lay their hands on the silver which Argentina was said to possess in abundance.

Araucanian Indians

The Invasion of Argentina

In 1536 a Spanish expedition under the command of Pedro de Mendoza (with a phenomenal 14 ships and 1500 men) established a colony on the bank of the Río de la Plata estuary, now the site of Buenos Aires. Hostile Indians and the constant threat of starvation forced the Spanish to shift upriver into the interior the following year. They established the city of Asunción, now the capital of Paraguay, and were joined four years later by the remaining Spanish from the Río de la Plata settlement.

Having failed to find mineral wealth or agrarian Indians on the coast, the Spanish conquest of Argentina actually began inland where the agrarian Indians lived. Spanish expeditions, launched from Peru and Chile, resulted in the foundation of Argentina's oldest cities including Jujuy (1592), Salta (1582), Tucumán (1565), Mendoza (1561) and Córdoba (1573).

Warfare, interbreeding, exploitation by whites and the ravages of European-introduced diseases such as smallpox and measles all helped to diminish the Indian population.

The northern Argentine towns gradually developed as suppliers to the mining towns of Peru and Bolivia. Santiago del Estero supplied cloth. Córdoba supplied mules, cloth and food. Mendoza and San Juan supplied wine, brandy and cereals. Tucumán provided rice, cotton, mules and the ox carts which carried these goods into Peru. In these towns the original settlers and a few of their *mestizo* (mixed Spanish and Indian) offspring formed the upper classes. They considered themselves *criollos*, people of Spanish descent born in Latin America and distinct from the Spanish born in Spain.

Argentina's first southern and coastal towns were established by settlers from Asunción. After failing to make any headway against the natural obstacles and hostile Indians of the interior they turned down river and founded settlements such as Santa Fe (1573), Buenos Aires (1580) and Corrientes (1588). Though cattle, horses and mules could be raised, the labour shortage on the coast prevented the development of textile and handicraft industries or extensive crop farming. With Spanish power concentrated in Peru, Mexico and Panama, the Argentine settlers found themselves on the remote flank of the the empire, where isolation and the peculiar conditions of this land would lead to the development of a distinctive Argentine character.

16th century map of South America

The Rise of the Estancia & Buenos Aires

In the first years of the Spanish empire in Latin America a man's wealth was directly connected to the mining of precious metals or to the number of Indians under his control. The encomienda system allowed Spain to maintain control of the land and prevent the rise of an independently-minded class of landed gentry.

However, during the 17th century the Spanish government began to sell or grant large areas of land in Latin America to private owners, partly to meet the demands of the criollos and partly because of the Spanish government's need for money. In Argentina this led to the establishment of the *estancias*, vast estates consisting of thousands of hectares of land, paid for by wealthy criollos.

Initially Spain forbade the export of Argentine goods via Buenos Aires. To enable taxes to be collected all trade had to pass through Panama or Mexico. This was an extraordinarily cumbersome system since goods exported from Argentina first had to be sent to Peru. In the middle of the 18th century the Spanish government accepted the inevitable and removed restrictions on the export of Latin American goods out of Buenos Aires. From then on, the Río de la Plata ceased to be the frontier of the Spanish empire and took on new importance. Measures were undertaken to encourage the development and settlement of the coast. Thus the stage was set for Buenos Aires to become the predominant urban centre of Argentina in the 19th century.

The Independence Movements

The empire which lasted for some 300 years was suddenly swept away in the early years of the 19th century. In 1808 Spain controlled an area stretching from California to Cape Horn. Seventeen years later she retained only Puerto Rico and Cuba.

There were many factors involved in the development of the independence movements in Latin America. One was the rise of the *criollo* elite who considered themselves American rather than Spanish. Another was their resentment of the rigid control of trade by the Spanish Government.

The influx of gold and silver from the New World into Spain encouraged extravagance, stimulated inflation and discouraged industry. Eventually Spain could no longer provide the manufactured goods which the American colonies demanded. By the later part of the 18th century the colonies were becoming increasingly self-sufficient, maintaining their own administrations, defence forces and economies.

Spain also had to contend with interloping European nations. The British, Dutch and French all acquired minor bases in Latin America. By the 18th century the British, in order to advance their own commercial ventures in Latin America, were encouraging the Spanish colonies to acquire independence.

Other factors which inspired the Latin Americans included the successful North American War of Independence against Britain, the overthrow of the French monarchy at the end of the 18th century, Napoleon's seizure of Spain (which allowed a period of temporary self-government for the colonies), and the influence of a liberal intellectual trend in Europe. Since the colonial armies were made up mainly of criollos and mestizos, and not Spanish troops, it was possible for the Latin Americans to fight Spain.

The Revolutionary Wars

Argentine independence came about not so much as a result of dissatisfaction with Spain but more because of British military and commercial intervention during the Napoleonic Wars. In 1806 a British naval squadron, which had just taken part in the annexation of the Cape of Good Hope, sailed for Buenos Aires and took the city. Several months later the *porteños* (as inhabitants of Buenos Aires are known) threw the British out. The

British reinforcements which arrived shortly after were unable to recapture the city.

When Napoleon occupied most of Spain in 1807-08, England suddenly became an ally of Spain. British merchants stationed in Portuguese Río de Janeiro, with the support of the criollos, took the opportunity to break the Spanish commercial blockade on Argentina. Faced with the need for some form of outlet for its produce the Spanish administrators in Buenos Aires partially opened the region to foreign trade. When the Spanish government in southern Spain dissolved in 1810 the overseas possessions were left without any formal link to the Spanish crown. Under pressure from the criollos of Buenos Aires (backed up by the criollo militia) the Spanish viceroy surrendered power to a criollo junta. The junta was to rule in the name of the Spanish crown but, clearly, the link with Spain had finally been cut and the Spanish commercial monopoly broken. The 25 May 1810 represents Argentina's break with Spain, though independence was not formally declared until 1816.

Latin America was thrown into turmoil following the end of the Napoleonic Wars and Spain's subsequent attempts to reassert authority over its overseas possessions. Revolutionary movements arose and ferocious wars of independence were fought. Spain attempted to retake Argentina by blockading the estuary of the Río de la Plata and sending in an army from Peru. The Spanish forces were soundly defeated and from these battles emerged one of Latin America's great heroes, General José San Martín.

From Venezuela, a revolutionary army under Simon Bolívar fought its way to the Pacific and marched south towards Peru. Meanwhile, in 1817, an army under the command of San Martín marched from Argentina over the mountains into Chile, occupied Santiago, and then sailed northward along the coast to Lima.

San Martín's troops were transported in ships either seized from the Spanish, or bought from British or North American owners, often with the aid of British and North American finance. British and North American merchants also financed the purchase of arms and ammunition,

Declaration of Independence, Tucumán, 1816

knowing that the removal of the Spanish would allow them to set up their own businesses on the continent. By 1825 Spain had been pushed out of all its Latin American colonies, except Cuba and Puerto Rico. The Spanish administrative divisions provided the political framework for the new countries and Latin America broke up into some 17 independent republics.

Economic & Political Change

Tyrants will rise from my tomb.

Simón Bolívar

Though Argentina and the other newly independent Latin American countries had won political independence they had not yet undergone a social revolution. The essential structure of society remained the same. The criollos and other members of the Latin American upper-classes stepped into the shoes of the Spanish.

The revolution left most of the newly established Latin American republics in shambles. Since the army provided the only strong organisation the generals stepped into the power vacuum. The Venezuelan revolutionary Simon Bolívar became Latin America's first military dictator, and while he is said to have ruled justly he essentially laid the foundations for future military dictatorships. Since then Latin America has been plagued by an endless string of *caudillos* – strongmen.

Argentina soon came under the rule of a caudillo, a situation brought about by a shift in the economic makeup of the country. When independence from Spain was attained the cattle interests of the coast demanded free international trade in order to open up the export market. The provinces of the interior demanded protectionist policies to guard their industries from imported goods.

Buenos Aires opened up to international trade. Foreign imports soon displaced the inferior quality and higher-priced products of the Argentine provinces. The construct-

ion of meat-salting plants (*saladeros*) on the coast and along the main rivers increased the number of cattle slaughtered for consumption from around 7000 in the 1790s to 350,000 by the end of the 1820s. The profits from meat and hide exports increased dramatically.

These developments sealed the economic supremacy of the coastal cattle interests over the towns of the interior. Progressive leaders such as Bernardino Rivadavia (who was briefly president of Argentina in the 1820s) sought to encourage the development of small farms on the the pampas which would have created a large class of small landholders. But when he was overthrown in 1827 the titles to huge areas of land, originally intended to be divided into small farms, were transferred to a few hundred *estancieros* (cattlemen).

The Rise of Rosas

By now Argentina was dominated by Juan Manuel de Rosas whose successful meat-salting business had allowed him to establish political and economic leadership of Buenos Aires.

Under Rosas the easy availability of cheap land to those in political favour allowed the estancias to grow larger and larger. Minimal taxation increased profits for the wealthy. Minimal duties on the export of hides and salted meat, and on the import of consumer goods, favoured the coastal cattle interests at the expense of the industry and agriculture of the interior.

By 1835 Rosas had established himself as the caudillo of Argentina. The naturalist, Charles Darwin, who visited Argentina in 1833 gave a first-hand account of the coup which brought Rosas to power:

This revolution was supported by scarcely any pretext of grievances: but in a state which, in the course of nine months [from February to October, 1820] underwent fifteen changes in its government – each governor, according to the constitution, being elected for three years – it would be very unreasonable to ask for pretexts.

In this case, a party of men – who, being attached to Rosas, were disgusted with the governor Balcarce – to the number of seventy left the city [Buenos Aires], and with the cry of Rosas the whole country took up arms. The city was then blockaded, no provisions, cattle or horses, were allowed to enter; besides this, there was only a little skirmishing, and a few men daily killed. The outside party knew well that by stopping the supply of meat they would certainly be victorious ... the Governor, ministers, and part of the military, to the number of some hundreds, fled from the city. The rebels entered, elected a new governor, and were paid for their services ... From these proceedings, it was clear that Rosas ultimately would become the dictator .... Since leaving South America, we have heard that Rosas has been elected, with powers and for a time altogether opposed to the constitutional principles of the republic.

Rosas' power rested on the support of the cattlemen, merchants, military officers and churchmen, and on persecution and murder of his political enemies. Internal revolts in the 1840s, an unsuccessful 12 year campaign (1839-51) to crush political opposition at Montevideo, and French and British blockades of Buenos Aires (1838-40 and 1845-48) threatened his regime.

During the French and British blockades, the estancias and saladeros on other parts of the coast started trading directly with the outside world rather than through Buenos Aires. When the blockade was lifted, Buenos Aires reasserted itself as Argentina's only port, sparking a revolt amongst the estancieros of the outer provinces. Justo José de Urquiza, governor of Entre Ríos, its leading estanciero and once Rosas' chief field commander, united with forces at Montevideo. Backed by the Brazilian army he overthrew Rosas in 1851. Rosas fled to England and lived there until his death in 1877.

Agricultural Diversification
The fall of Rosas coincided with the first major shift of the Argentine economy away from cattle, estancias and saladeros.

Sheep farming became increasingly important, with the number of sheep in the coastal regions rising from a quarter million in 1810 to five million by 1850. By the 1880s wool exports contributed half the value of Argentina's exports.

Sheep grazing was more labour intensive. It increased the size of the rural population and also encouraged Basque, Scottish, Irish and English immigration. Many estancia owners turned their less profitable cattle runs over to sheep. The expansion of sheep raising around Buenos Aires forced cattle grazing to shift further south and westward. The pressure for space and grazing land led to the Indian Wars of the late 1870s and early 1880s. In this Argentine version of the North American wild west the tribes that occupied the Pampas and Patagonia were ruthlessly exterminated and their lands taken over by the officers who had led the campaign.

By the 1880s crop farming regained a foothold around Buenos Aires. Foreign capital – mainly British – began to enter Argentina to finance the development of railroads and meat packing plants. Pedigree cattle were imported from Britain and, following the introduction of refrigerated ships in 1877, the export of fresh beef began in earnest.

In this way the cattle-based economy which Rosas had devised was transformed into a mixed rural economy by the 1880s. However, agriculture remained the basis of the Argentine economy. Argentina continued to produce and export wool, meat, hides and tallow and to import most of its consumer goods. Large land holdings remained the rule. Merchants and landowners continued to dominate Argentina's politics and economy. In the later part of the 19th century new immigrants found the land closed to them so they congregated in the towns. The towns and ports of the coast began to sprawl. Streets were paved, broad avenues and parks laid out and impressive public buildings and palatial private residences were built. Argentina became the most urbanised country in Latin America.

Emerging Nationalism

Argentina emerged from the 19th century a divided and uncertain nation. The monopoly on political power held by the conservative upper class was eroded in 1912 with the institution of the Sáenz Peña Law which provided for a secret ballot and universal male suffrage. This had been brought about by the efforts of the Radical Party, which was founded in 1891 to represent the aspiring middle-class. Subsequently the Radical leader Hipólito Irigoyen was elected president in 1916 with almost half the vote. The Radicals retained power until 1930 when a military coup deposed Irigoyen, putting Argentina back into conservative hands until the mid-1940s.

Agriculture recovered from the slump it had endured during WW I. However, Argentina was still dependent on the export of agricultural products to industrialised nations, particularly Britain. Argentina's failure to develop transport, mineral and energy resources and to introduce protectionist policies against foreign imports meant that its industry floundered for the first four decades of the century.

Industrialisation was stimulated by WW II, as Argentina had to use local products to fill the gap left by reduced imports. Industrialisation and growing population produced a large class of industrial workers, concentrated in Buenos Aires and in the strip of land north to Santa Fe and south to La Plata. By this time a whole zoo of foreign firms, including Nestlé, Philips, General Electric and Johnson & Johnson, had commercial stakes in Argentina. By the time WW II broke out, the British controlled most of the railways. The car industry was controlled by the United States. The major construction firms in Buenos Aires were German or Dutch. Foreign companies dominated the meat-packing industry. Increasing foreign economic domination coincided with a rise in Argentine nationalist sentiment, which saw Argentina suffering at the hands of foreign economic interests. Low wages and the high cost of living resulted in precarious living standards and widespread discontent.

Perón

In 1943 a group of army officers staged a successful coup. One of the leaders of this coup, though he played a minimal role, was the then Colonel Juan Perón who became vice-president. Born in 1895, Perón followed an unexceptional career in the army, yet from 1943 until his death in 1974 he dominated Argentine politics. Even today he remains a figure for many Argentines to rally around.

Perón saw, perhaps more clearly than anyone else, the need for a new type of leader who based his power on the support of the industrial workers. Following the 1943 coup, he chose for himself the then-unimportant post of head of the National Department of Labour. From that time he encouraged the development of the trade union movement and championed the cause of workers' rights.

Perón's plans were temporarily blocked when, following the end of WW II, other army officers forced him to resign. However, when presidential elections were held in 1946, which even Perón's opponents said were the most honest ever held in Argentina, he was elected president with 56% of the vote. His supporters saw his election as the beginning of a new era in which Argentina would achieve both industrial might and a secure democracy. Perón spoke of a brave new world to come:

... : Argentina's hour has arrived . . . . everyone must choose between continuing to live in a dim and shadowy manner or boldly taking the first step towards his own redemption.

Perón mixed personal charisma with appeals to national pride and the

EVA PERON

Perón also gained the support of the emerging industrial leaders who saw him as a nationalist dedicated to the development of a strong economy. In 1948 Perón spoke of creating an economically independent and self-reliant Argentina:

Without economic independence we shall get nowhere. Therefore I oppose and shall always oppose, anything which threatens it. For us it is vital: now or never. As in 1816 we said "now or never" and secured our political independence, so in 1946 we said "now or never" and we are going to gain and consolidate our economic independence. And within 15 or 20 years the persons who have made an attempt on the economic independence of the nation will be looked upon in the same way as were those who made attempts on the political independence of the Argentine Republic. Of that I am absolutely sure.

In the context of the times he was not unusual. In the years following WW II many countries, under the leadership of nationalists such as Sukarno and Ho Chi Minh, were not only throwing off the yoke of foreign imperialism but were also challenging the western domination of the world.

The rise of fascism in Germany and Italy in the 1930s, which had appeared to solve the seemingly intractable problems of floundering economies and political instability, also influenced some Argentine officers. Perón had gained some first-hand experience of European fascism while serving as military attaché at the Argentine embassy in Italy. It's likely he came away impressed by the ability of Hitler and Mussolini to mobilise their people *en masse* and that this inspired him to attempt the same in Argentina.

Although it would be unfair to call Perón a fascist in the same sense as the European dictators, he did, however, show scant regard for democracy. Many anti-Peronist politicians and labour leaders were exiled or imprisoned. Unruly provincial governors were removed from their posts and the press was gagged.

aspirations of the working class. His wife, the former film actress Eva Durate, became his chief propagandist and sought to build his image as the saviour of the nation. Despite her untimely death (of cancer in 1952, at the age of 33) Eva Perón has proved to be an even greater enigma than her husband and remains a potent symbol in Argentine politics.

Perón had, for the first time in Argentine history, given the working class a powerful voice in the government. He carried out a series of labour reforms including protection against arbitrary dismissal, establishment of a pension system, increased wages and appointment of labour leaders to government posts. He had succeeded in winning the presidency in an open and fair election, created jobs for the middle class by expanding the bureaucracy, expanded Argentina's industry, and won loyalty from a wide range of Argentines.

Secret police, political imprisonment and torture were all a part of Perón's rule, though they never reached the same degree of oppression as the military governments of the 1970s and 1980s.

Despite his brave words Perón was unable to solve the problems of the Argentine industrialisation or achieve economic independence. Towards the later part of his presidency he was openly courting foreign investment. Nor was he able to bring about the social unification of Argentina despite his position with the army and the workers.

A number of factors contributed to Perón's downfall. These included a vehement anti-clerical campaign he initiated in the last year or two of his presidency. It is said that the military feared the rise of the labour unions and the possibility that Perón might create an armed workers' militia. There were attempts by some of the military to remove Perón from power in 1951 and mid-1955. In the latter part of 1955 he was finally ousted by a military coup and went into exile.

The Intervening Years

After Perón was overthrown his party was dissolved by a decree of the new military junta. The Peronists split into conflicting factions. For years the army threatened the overthrow of any government which allowed the Peronists to re-form. Perón himself refused to concede the leadership of the party and discredited those who sought to assume his mantle.

The years between 1955 and Perón's return to Argentina in 1973 are a black hole to non-Argentines. During this time Argentine history is a series of forgotten names and faces, anonymous military juntas, shaky civilian governments, coups and counter-coups, and sometimes even open clashes between differing military factions. Although Arturo Frondizi (president from 1958 until ousted by the military in 1962), made substantial advances in industrialisation, neither he nor his successors were able to prevent the debilitating intervention of the military in politics.

By the end of the 1960s Argentina was once again suffering severe political and economic problems. Labour demonstrations, street fighting and general strikes hit the country. There were scattered instances of violence, including attacks by armed guerrilla groups on buildings occupied by foreign companies, as well as the kidnapping and execution of public figures.

The Death of Perón

In 1973 a train of events was set into motion which led to the return of Juan Perón to Argentina and the bloodiest period of military rule that Argentina has ever known. New elections were held, and won by the Peronist candidate Héctor Cámpora. He promptly resigned, paving the way for the aged Juan Perón to be elected President.

Perón's return to Argentina after 18 years in exile was a portent of things to come. Hundreds of thousands of Argentines gathered at Buenos Aires airport to welcome him home but clashes between rival Peronist factions left some 30 people dead and several hundred injured. Perón subsequently condemned the left-wing extremists of his own movement, but he did not live long enough to halt their activities or to put Argentina on a stable path. He died in mid-1974 at the age of 79. His third wife, María Estela (Isabela), succeeded him as president.

A few months after Perón's death the main guerrilla group, the left-wing *Montoneros*, resumed their fight against the government. Over the next two years the Montoneros carried out a series of kidnappings, executions and bombings. The People's Revolutionary Army (ERP), a leftist guerrilla group, committed a string of abductions and executions of businessmen, military officers and newspaper publishers.

The right-wing Argentine Anti-Communist Alliance (AAA), which was established in 1973, was responsible for the murder of trade unionists, politicians, students, priests and others it regarded as leftist. At the time of writing José López Rega, a Rasputin-like character who had been a close advisor to Juan and Isabela Perón, was awaiting trial as the alleged organiser of the AAA.

The Dirty War: 1976 to 1983
Unable to contain the violence or cope with the crumbling economy Isabela Perón was deposed by the military in 1976. As usual the military justified their actions by the need to save Argentina from 'subversion and corruption' and to restore stability to the economy.

Military men took over most key government posts. Army Commander-in-Chief General Jorge Videla was installed as President – the 10th Argentine president this century to take power through a military coup. A whole series of anti-subversive legislation was enacted including decrees which dissolved the leftist political parties and suspended the activities of all political parties, professional associations and labour unions. The right to strike was abolished (though despite severe losses, the trade union movement appeared to retain its strength and organised effective strikes involving large numbers of workers) and the death penalty for politically-related offences was introduced.

Not only were the terrorists themselves to be eliminated but so was anyone who gave them ideological or moral support. As Videla put it:

A terrorist is not just someone with a gun or bomb, but also someone who spreads ideas that are against Western and Christian civilisation.

The military coined the phrase *guerra sucia* (dirty war) to describe the battle against the terrorists. Initially it referred to the tactics of the terrorists, but soon came to be associated with the way the military fought its war against other

Argentines. By 1977 both the Montoneros and the ERP had ceased to be any real threat to national security or the status quo. Both organisations had been crushed by the military using assassination, disappearance, imprisonment, exile and sometimes pitched battles with the guerrillas.

The Disappeared
The most common tactic used against the guerrillas and other opponents of the government was to make a person 'disappear'. A person would be kidnapped by members of the security forces, and from that time the government and military would deny any knowledge of the missing person. *Nunca Mas* (Never More), a report published in 1986 following the fall of the military government, tells of 340 'detention centres' set up throughout Argentina to imprison, torture and kill the military's victims.

The majority of kidnapped people were murdered. Inexplicably, a number were released even after torture and thus lived to tell the tale. The bodies of those who were killed were disposed of in a variety of ways: some were buried in unmarked graves; some were burnt on bonfires; others were loaded on to planes and thrown into the ocean. The 'war booty' confiscated from the victim's houses would be divided up amongst the members of the security forces.

It's difficult to say how many people disappeared, though *Nunca Mas* lists almost 9000 cases of disappearances given in evidence to the Commission. The real figure is thought to be higher. The 'disappeared' came from every age group and a wide range of occupations and backgrounds. They included students, nuns and priests, journalists, trade unionists, politicians, lawyers, housewives, babies, and even police and military personnel who refused to participate in the repression.

The Falklands War

The decline of Argentina's economy was rapid during the military's rule. The monetarist (extreme free-market) economic policies introduced by the military failed to halt inflation, greatly increased unemployment and undermined local industry. Controls on prices were released while wages were held down, causing the standard of living of the middle classes to plummet. Controls on imports were released which caused local industry to close down or leave the country. By the last years of military rule Argentina had accumulated a staggering foreign debt. Inflation was once again soaring.

At the end of 1981 General Videla was replaced as president by General Roberto Viola, who was replaced a few months later by General Leopoldo Galtieri. Seeking to unite the Argentine people behind the military government, Galtieri appealed to a base form of patriotism and national pride by occupying the British-held Falkland (Malvinas) Islands, counting on British reluctance or sheer inability to defend the islands to ensure an Argentine victory.

The subsequent war, in which over a thousand British and Argentines were killed, resulted in the Argentines being defeated in June 1982. This also spelt the end of the military junta who, as one writer put it, 'surrendered to the weight of their failures'. In 1983 nationwide elections took place for the presidency, parliament and local councils. The Radical Party candidate, Raúl Alfonsín, was elected president of Argentina.

Aftermath

Alfonsín promised to bring to justice those military commanders responsible for violations of human rights during the 'Dirty War'. In 1985 nine military commanders who had previously ruled the country were brought to trial on criminal charges ranging from murder to falsification of documents. Five of the defendants were sentenced to prison terms ranging from 4½ years to life; the other four were acquitted.

Plans to prosecute all military personnel accused of human rights violations were brought to a sudden halt in 1987 by a series of revolts by the military, now referred to as the Easter Week Rebellion. Alfonsín was forced to accede to the military's demands to restrict the prosecution of officers involved in the Dirty War.

A new Law of Due Obedience was quickly rushed through Congress, granting immunity to prosecution to lower-ranking officers on the grounds that they were only following orders. Had Alfonsín pressed ahead with the prosecutions it's unlikely his government would have seen the year out, and Argentina would now be under military rule.

The memory of the Falklands War lingers on in the form of war veterans' organisations and publications, tattered posters, streets renamed 'Islas Malvinas', billboards proclaiming 'Las Malvinas son Argentinas' (The Malvinas are Argentine), and plaques commemorating the death of troops in the fighting.

The legacy of the Dirty War will also continue for many years to come. Every Thursday afternoon the mothers and grandmothers of the disappeared demonstrate in the Plaza de Mayo, outside the Casa Rosada in Buenos Aires, to remind the government that justice has not yet been done. The greying faces and sad eyes of the mothers compress all the tragedy of Argentine history into a single space. In 10 years' time they will still be walking the Plaza de Mayo every Thursday afternoon. Like so many before them they were betrayed by a country that held so much promise but failed to live up to its expectations.

GEOGRAPHY

Argentina is the eighth largest country in the world. It is four times larger than Texas and about five times larger than France. It stretches 3700 km from

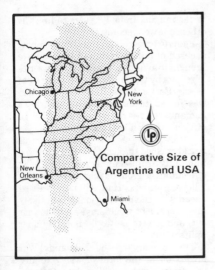

Comparative Size of Argentina and USA

northern lowlands, the pampas and Patagonia.

The Andean Regions
The Andean regions form the western frontier of Argentina and include the provinces from Mendoza in the south to Salta and Jujuy in the north. The earliest Spanish settlements in Argentina were set up here, although today it has only about 15% of Argentina's population.

The northern half of the Andean region – Jujuy, Salta and northern Catamarca and La Rioja – is actually a continuation of Bolivia with plateaus and mountains ranging in altitude from 1800 to 6000 metres. Population has always been concentrated in the valleys at the eastern edge of the northern plateau, where rainfall and streams provide an adequate water supply. Indians settled the region long before the Spanish, and even the Inca empire extended as far as Tucumán Province.

The 'Cuyo' is the southern part of the Andean region. It encompasses the provinces of Mendoza, San Juan and San Luis. These provinces are backed by the formidable Andes Mountains including Mount Aconcagua, which soars to 7500 metres. Unlike the north-western Andean provinces, the Andes of the Cuyo region are not bordered by foothills and plateaus but by arid mountains and salt flats. Streams from the snow-capped peaks disappear through evaporation or absorption by the porous soil of the salt flats.

The Northern Lowlands
The northern lowlands form the frontier to Paraguay and Uruguay. Some of the earliest Spanish settlements in Argentina were established here and nowadays the area is of great agricultural importance. The northern lowlands can be divided into two sections. The western section is known as the 'Chaco'. The eastern part lies between two rivers and is known as Argentine 'Mesopotamia'.

The western part contains the provinces

Antarctic wastelands in the south to tropical jungles in the north and is rimmed by the massive Andes mountains in the west.

It shares borders – not always happily – with Chile, Bolivia, Paraguay, Brazil and Uruguay. Argentina took several centuries to reach its present shape and size. The European settlement began with far flung Spanish settlements near the Peruvian mines in the north-west, at the foot of the Andes in the west and by the rivers in the east. In the late 18th century the Viceroyalty of the Río de la Plata was formed with its administration based at Buenos Aires. It encompassed areas of what are now modern-day Argentina, Uruguay, Paraguay and Bolivia. The revolutionary war of the 19th century split off Uruguay, Paraguay and Bolivia as independent countries. The boundaries of modern Argentina were not finalised until the late 19th century, after a number of wars and treaties with adjacent countries and extermination campaigns against the Indians.

Argentina has roughly four natural divisions: the Andean regions, the

Provinces and Territories

0   200   400 km

Islas Malvinas
(Falkland Islands)

PACIFIC OCEAN

ATLANTIC OCEAN

JUJUY
FORMOSA
SALTA
SANTIAGO DEL ESTERO
TUCUMAN
CHACO
MISIONES
CATAMARCA
CORRIENTES
LA RIOJA
SAN JUAN
CORDOBA
SANTA FE
ENTRE RIOS
SAN LUIS
MENDOZA
LA PAMPA
BUENOS AIRES
NEUQUEN
RIO NEGRO
CHUBUT
SANTA CRUZ
TIERRA DEL FUEGO

of Santiago del Estero, Chaco, Formosa and the northern parts of Córdoba and Santa Fe. These are an extension of the 'Gran Chaco', which stretches into Paraguay, Bolivia and Brazil. Argentina's part of the Gran Chaco consists of scrub forest, savannah and flood plains. However, towards Santiago del Estero the heavy rainfall decreases and irrigation is needed to support agriculture.

The eastern part lies between the Río Paraná and Río Uruguay. It includes the provinces of Entre Ríos, Corrientes and Misiones. Misiones is a continuation of the Paraná plateau of southern Brazil, a land of dense forest and heavy rainfall. At the northern boundary of the province the Río Iguazú literally tumbles over the plateau into the Río Paraná, producing the massive Iguazú Falls.

Entre Ríos and Corrientes consist mainly of grassy plains. Rainforests and swamps cover a large part of north-eastern Corrientes and there are many islands and river deltas in south-west Entre Ríos. Rainfall supports abundant agriculture.

The Pampas

The pampas is the economic centre of Argentina. This fertile plain includes the provinces of Buenos Aires, eastern La Pampa, southern Santa Fe and south-eastern Córdoba.

Erosion by wind and water has piled up a thick layer of sediment, fine clay, sand and dust to produce a huge, fertile plain on top of a granite base. In some places the granite breaks through the surface to form mountain ranges such as the Córdoba Hills.

The pampas has no major rivers. Because rainfall decreases as you approach the Andes, drought periodically threatens crops and livestock throughout large areas of La Pampa, southern Córdoba and western Buenos Aires. Nevertheless, cattle, wheat, sheep, flax and oats are important industries on the pampas.

The pampas encompasses one fifth of

Argentina's land area and is home to two thirds of its population. The country's major industries and towns, including the capital Buenos Aires, are located on the pampas.

Patagonia

Patagonia includes both the Argentine and Chilean sides of the cone of South America south of the Río Colorado. However, geographically the two sides are so different that they are impossible to consider as one.

Argentine Patagonia makes up about a quarter of that nation's area, but contains only a few percent of its population. It encompasses the provinces of Santa Cruz, Chubut, Río Negro and Neuquén. Technically, Patagonia also includes the island of Tierra del Fuego, but it is easier to consider the two separately.

In Argentine Patagonia lava flows, wind and glaciers have produced a series of plateaus which rise in regular steps towards the west on a cracked and broken granite base. The Andes rise abruptly from the western edge of the plateaus. Water and glaciers have gouged out depressions and formed a huge Lake District in Neuquén Province on the border with Chile.

The mountains in the west receive enough rainfall to support forests, but for the most part Patagonia is arid. What little precipitation there is usually falls as snow in winter. Crop farming and cattle grazing is carried out along the Río Colorado, the Río Negro and near the mouth of the Río Chubut. The Río Negro Valley is a fruit growing centre. Major industries include oil extraction at Comodoro Rivadavia and Plaza Huincal, coal mining at Río Turbio and iron ore mining at Sierra Grande. Sheep grazing is also important.

Tierra del Fuego

The Straits of Magellan separate Tierra del Fuego from the rest of South America. Tierra del Fuego is, in fact, not one island but a whole archipelago, altogether covering an area slightly smaller than Ireland. Only about 30% belongs to Argentina. The largest island is called Isla Grande de Tierra del Fuego.

The northern part of Isla Grande is a land of rolling hills and bare, windswept plains where sheep grazing and oil extraction are important. The central region includes mountains which are covered in snow in the middle of the year and are too rugged for farming or grazing. The Beagle Channel separates Isla Grande from the island of Navarino, which belongs to Chile. The channel never freezes and there are no icebergs.

Though the northern plains are bare of trees, the mountains and shores of the Beagle Channel are covered in forest and swampland. Cape Horn and the other outer islands have hardy bog plants and dwarf trees and bushes.

The Falkland (Malvinas) Islands

Argentina lays claim to the Falkland (Malvinas) Islands which have been under British control since 1833. The military government of General Galtieri went to war in 1982 in a failed attempt to wrest the islands from Britain. The islands are said to have been sighted by the English navigator John Davis in 1592, although the first authenticated sighting was made by a Dutch ship in 1600. The islands remained uninhabited until the later part of the 18th century after which there began a confusing series of attempts by the French, British and Spanish to establish and maintain claims and bases on them. Eventually a Spanish garrison occupied the large eastern island in 1774 and stayed until Argentina gained independence. In 1820 the Argentines claimed and occupied the islands as legitimate successors to the Spanish government. In 1831 the USA broke up the Argentine settlements, using the seizure of US fishing vessels (supposedly fishing in Argentine territorial waters) by the Argentines as an excuse. The British took

possession in 1833 and have controlled the islands ever since.

CLIMATE

Although most of Argentina is in the temperate zone, size and altitude produce formidable extremes of heat and cold. You bake in the north-west desert and freeze in Tierra del Fuego. There can also be rapid changes in temperature from day to night, and when you leave the plains and head up into the mountains.

If you are trying to 'do' Argentina in one stretch then the best time to visit would be September to December. This will allow you to visit the north before the height of summer and the far south after the depths of winter. You can also avoid the Argentine tourist season (January and February) which can make many places very crowded.

The North-East

The north-east, including the Chaco and Misiones provinces, has a warm, semi-tropical climate with distinct dry and wet seasons. The rainy season is during the hot, sultry summer, from October to March. The dry season is during the mild winter, from April to September. Argentine Mesopotamia, the area between the Paraná and Uruguay rivers, has a warm, subtropical climate. However, unlike the Chaco, there is no distinct dry season in the winter.

The Andes

Although the tip of north-west Argentina actually falls in the tropical zone, altitude and topography combine to produce a dry climate.

The lowland regions of Jujuy, Salta and northern Catamarca and La Rioja tend to be hot and dry, although even in the valleys summer nights can be cold. In the mountains in summer you can expect fiercely hot days alternating with bitterly cold nights. In winter, mountain areas are subject to sudden squalls and snow storms which are dangerous if you're hiking.

The region known as the Cuyo, containing the provinces of San Juan, San Luis and Mendoza, is a hot, arid land of salt-flats and dry mountain ranges. There is very little rainfall on the plains, and most of the water here flows down from the snow-covered Andes mountains. During winter the mountains passes are bitterly cold and covered in thick snow. In the mid-winter the main pass from Mendoza to Santiago is sometimes blocked.

One exception to the general picture along the Andes is Tucumán, where relatively high rainfall, mild winter temperatures and fertile, alluvial soil has made this a major agricultural area for centuries.

The Pampas

The pampas tends to be dry with rainfall decreasing as you approach the Andes. The region is subject to periodic drought. The average summer temperature on the coast is around 24°C, although days can be much hotter and nights much colder. Temperature statistics tend to be misleading for the city of Buenos Aires, which can be *very* hot and sultry during summer with temperatures climbing to 30°C and above.

Winters are mild and the temperature rarely falls below 7°C, with an average of 11°C. Snow is rare on the pampas, but during winter there may be light snowfalls in La Pampa and in the south of Buenos Aires province.

The wind is not as fierce or unceasing on the pampas as it is in Patagonia, although fierce winds from the south-east occasionally produce spectacular thunderstorms.

The Lake District

The Lake District, centred on Bariloche, has a pleasant Mediterranean climate during the summer months although cold, biting winds can sweep off the lakes and mountains. Wind-surfing, swimming and sun bathing are popular in summer.

During summer average temperatures are around 20°C. In winter the region is covered in snow and Bariloche, and several other towns, are noted for their ski resorts. During winter some of the passes between Chile and Argentina may be blocked by snow.

Patagonia & Tierra del Fuego

The best time to visit Patagonia, Tierra del Fuego and Magallanes (the southernmost province of Chilean Patagonia) is in the southern summer from December to February. Winter is June, July and August.

In these regions temperatures range from an average of 11°C in summer to an average of 4°C in winter. Heavy snows fall in the mountains in the middle of the year, and the roads to some of the major tourist sites (such as the Moreno Glacier near Calafate) will be closed to traffic. Some airports are also forced to close down because of snow. Temperatures in Tierra del Fuego can drop so low that sheep are killed. Even in summer these areas can still be afflicted with cold, gusty winds.

Rainfall in Magallanes and Tierra del Fuego is heavy and should be expected at any time of the year. Rainfall can be heavy in the mountainous fringe of Argentine Patagonia, although the plains are arid and most precipitation falls as snow during winter. Puerto Williams, the only settlement on the island of Navarino to the south of Tierra del Fuego, can have pleasant days of warm sunshine followed by days of rain and piercing cold even in summer.

Regardless of the season, rug up for crossing stretches of water in this region. The Straits of Magellan can be stormy and terrifying even on the large vehicle ferries. In Patagonia take warm clothes for boat trips on the inland lakes, since bitterly cold winds sweep off the water, glaciers and mountains.

In southern Patagonia and Tierra del Fuego there are only about seven hours of light per day in winter, and about seventeen in summer. Visitors from Canada or northern Europe will be familiar with this, but those from countries nearer the equator may find it disorienting.

GOVERNMENT

At the time of writing, Argentina has democratically elected national and provincial governments. Power is divided between the national government and two dozen provinces. The Argentine constitution, introduced in 1853 by Urquiza after the overthrow of Rosas, is the oldest in Latin America and is modelled closely on that of the USA.

The executive branch of government consists of the president, vice-president and a presidential cabinet. Under the constitution the president has extensive powers, including the ability to approve or veto Acts of Congress. The National Congress, comprising the Chamber of Deputies and the Senate, is responsible for drafting and enacting laws.

The Argentine judiciary is independent of the government. Judicial power is exercised by the Supreme Court and lower courts throughout the country. The provincial governments are headed by governors, most of whom are elected by direct suffrage.

The Political Parties

The modern party system in Argentina dates back to 1891 when the Radical Party was founded. For the next 50 years Argentine politics was more or less a conflict between the Radicals, who represented the Argentine middle class, and the conservatives who represented the old agricultural and business interests with their European connections. In the 1940s this scenario was shaken up by the emergence of the Peronist movement, with its power base in the labour organisations.

For the most part today's Peronists and the Peronist splinter groups follow the policies of their founder including the support of labour unions, social reform,

Peronist Party poster

participation of workers in the economy, and the development of an economy independent of foreign powers. Peronist supporters are usually from the urban and rural working classes and the middle class. The Radicals have generally been regarded as the representatives of established business, but nowadays their supporters are more likely to come from the middle and upper classes.

Since Argentine politics is often thrown into disarray for many years at a time, it is difficult to give an accurate picture of the political scene. Personality plays a very large role and one party can contain members with very different ideologies. The ideological stew is also confused by the posturings of the various political parties, such as the Popular Provincial Parties of the 1950s, a Peronist splinter group which campaigned with the strange slogan, 'Peronism without Perón'.

One way to get some idea of the

confusing melange of political parties in Argentina is to look at the composition of the National Congress. In 1987 the Lower House had 254 members. Of these 113 were definitely Radicals and 102 were definitely Peronists. The word 'definite' was an important distinction since the loyalties of some members were unclear. The remaining members of Congress were scattered across 16 right, centre and left-wing parties with such diverse titles as the Democratic Centre Union, Intransigent Party, Christian Democrats, Autonomist-Liberal Pact, Popular Socialists, and the Movement for Integration & Development.

The Military

The Argentine military waits like a bogey-man in the country's politics. The total strength of the armed forces is about 150,000 of which the army comprises 100,000. It is the second largest armed force in Latin America.

The military was loyal to the conservative governments which ruled Argentina from the 1860s through to 1916. The first successful military intervention in Argentine politics this century was in 1930 when the army deposed the Radical government. Since then over half of Argentina's presidents have been generals.

government corruption, immorality, inability to maintain law and order, and the threat of 'communism' as pretexts for a takeover. Anti-Peronism has contributed to at least four military takeovers, particularly after Perón's death because of the rise and apparent connection between the Montonero urban guerrillas and the Peronist movement.

As in other Latin American countries the military believes that it is not only responsible for the protection of the state from outside threats but also from internal threats. It believes it has the right to intervene in politics when and how it sees fit. Political power is not considered to be the rightful domain of civilian leaders, nor is the democratic constitution of the country considered inviolable.

For almost 60 years the active support – or at least the disgruntled acceptance – of the armed forces has been essential to the survival of Argentine governments. The Easter Week rebellion of 1987 was perhaps the most serious revolt in the armed forces since the fall of the military junta in 1983, but it was not an isolated incident. Every few months there is some revolt or 'act of disobedience' by the armed forces. If the civilian government was overthrown tomorrow by a military coup it would not surprise Argentines in the least.

Disunity & Caudilloism

Disunity is a central theme in Argentine history and, like Italy, the country often seems to be anarchic and ungovernable. An Argentine once asked me how the system of government works in Australia. Since Australia's own political conflicts pale in comparison to those of Argentina, I thought it was only fair to reply 'Quite well'.

'Quite well!' exclaimed the Argentine, 'Quite well!? If only we could say the same about this place! But here, nothing works! Nothing!'

Since 1930 there have been five major military coups and a total of 19 years of military rule. Since 1952 no elected president has managed to complete his term of office. Disunity has been the curse of Argentina since independence from Spain. In Latin America, as Jack Pizzey points out in his documentary *Sweat of the Sun, Tears of the Moon*, it is the caudillo (strongman) who holds divided nations together. During the first half of the 19th century Argentina was dominated by caudillos such as Rosas and Urquiza. Since the caudillo ruled by force, caudilloism was often coupled with terror. Domingo Sarmiento, one of Argentina's progressive presidents of the 19th century, wrote that the caudillo Rosas had a:

... butcherly instinct which led [him] to encourage cruelty and to give executions a more barbaric form which he thought would give the assassins pleasure ...

The caudillos were practical men, but men of the moment. Perón described their nature in these words:

The caudillo improvises while the statesman makes plans and carries them out. The caudillo has no initiative, the statesman is creative. The caudillo is only concerned with measures which are applicable to the reigning circumstances whereas the statesman plans for all time; the deeds of the caudillo die with him, but the statesman lives on in his handiwork. For that reason the caudillo has no guiding principles or clear-cut plan while the statesman works methodically, defeating time and perpetuating himself in his own creations. Caudilloism is a trade, but statecraft is an art.

The development of central authority based in Buenos Aires in the 1860s and 1870s ended the rule of the caudillos, but this did not mean the demise of caudilloism. Instead a new type of caudillo arose in Argentina, a politically astute leader who could muster votes, manipulate political parties and inspire huge numbers of supporters. President Juan Perón, with his charm, masculinity and common touch, embodied this new brand of caudillo. Against this background of 180 years of disunity and caudilloism it is not surprising that many Argentines are thoroughly disillusioned with politics. However, you should not underestimate the emotions which politics still fires, or the willingness of each generation to embrace it with zeal.

ECONOMY

The horizon is always making gestures of abundance ... Everyone lives as if their dreams of the future were already reality.

Ortega y Gasset

What's the quickest way to make a fortune? Buy an Argentine for what he's worth, then sell him for what he *thinks* he's worth.

South American joke

The Spanish came to Argentina in search of silver and even named the country after it; *argentum* is the Latin name for that precious metal. The estuary on which Buenos Aires now stands is called the Río de la Plata, or the River of Silver. In fact, cattle, sheep and wheat formed the basis of Argentina's economic development. They say that the soil is so rich on the Argentine pampas that if you poke your finger in the ground for a few minutes it will begin to sprout!

On paper, Argentina's abundant natural resources, relatively low population, and numerous trading contacts suggest the image of a prosperous nation. Its main crops include grain and oilseeds. Its main mineral resources include oil, coal, copper and tin. Its main industries include meat packaging, motor vehicles, consumer goods, textiles and chemicals. Its main exports are grain, meat, wool, hides, oilseeds and manufactured goods. Most exports go to the European Economic Community, Brazil and the USSR, with the balance of trade in Argentina's favour. Argentina has sufficient natural gas reserves for another 60 years' home consumption. The discovery of new oil deposits in the South Atlantic in 1981 have allowed it to become a modest oil exporter. There are important hydro-electric and nuclear energy programmes underway. Argentina built its first nuclear research plant in the 1950s.

Yet despite its formidable natural and agricultural wealth Argentina has become what some people have called the 'frustrated colossus' of Latin America. A nation which once seemed destined for great things now stumbles under the weight of soaring inflation and an enormous foreign debt which can only be repaid (if at all) by more loans and the re-scheduling of existing debts.

Argentina is a country which has always deceived its people's expectations. So much so that Argentines and other Latin Americans have tried to find the reason for this in some flaw in the Argentine character, some approach to life which has led to their downfall. The Spanish philosopher Ortega y Gasset thought it lay in their overly confident hopes for the future. To other Latin Americans the fault lies with Argentine arrogance. Some Argentines blame it on the Argentine 'mentality' or accuse their fellow citizens of an inability or unwillingness to work hard to achieve their goals.

Others lay the blame for Argentina's problems on its string of corrupt military governments, on foreign economic domination, on the concentration of power for too long in the hands of the estancieros, on the early neglect of industry and mining, and on the failure to secure strong democratic institutions and to build an honest and efficient civil service. Others fossick through Argentine history in an effort to pinpoint where things began to go wrong.

The Economic Malaise

Juan Perón spoke bravely of creating an economically independent and self-reliant Argentina. Yet Argentina has never been so beholden to foreign economic interests and so dependent on injections of hard currency as it is today. Nor has the economy ever been in such a deep recession with no apparent way out.

Argentina's balance of trade is in her favour to the tune of a billion American dollars a year. However this has to be viewed against a foreign debt of about US$60 billion. Any hope of immediate benefit from the trade surplus is wiped out by the need to use it to repay the debt and the interest on it. The debt continues to grow as the country keeps on borrowing money in order to stay afloat. In Argentina they call this 'the bicycle' – they always have to keep on pedalling.

One way to get some idea of how fast an Argentine has to pedal is to look at events over a two or three month period.

In the month before I arrived in Argentina to research this book the Austral had been devalued *eleven* times. The black market exchange rate (such an integral part of the Argentine economy that it is reported in the daily newspapers) was about 3.5 Australs to one US dollar. Within two months the rate had risen to 4.5 Australs to the dollar and was expected to double within a year.

Interest rates were hovering around 15% *per month* on savings accounts and around 18% *per month* on bank loans. In my first week in Argentina six banks in Buenos Aires collapsed. Employees' placards outside one of the crumpled banks protested that 550 families had been left without work and more or less damned Alfonsín for not keeping promises to increase employment.

Government figures put the rise in the cost of living at around 13% per month. Unofficial estimates placed it somewhere between 12% to 17% per month. The price of many products, such as *yerba mate*, sugar, eggs and milk, rose at a greater rate. Inflation was running at just over 100% per year. The rising cost of living provoked a series of strikes including workers in the banks, post offices, railways, retail and health services.

To get this into perspective you have to look at Argentine wages. Argentine office workers make US$100 per month. A teacher makes about US$125 to US$150 per month. The General Confederation of Labour put the minimum monthly needs of a working family with two children at around US$330 per month, well above what even better-paid workers earn. The great mystery to the casual observer is how Argentines manage to survive on their paltry wages. Even when you ask the Argentines about this, you often get no more illuminating a reply than: "Well, we do . . ." Many Argentines hold down two, sometimes three poorly-paid jobs, but even this doesn't really explain how they keep going.

These are not, of course, problems which affect everybody. The upper classes and upper middle classes still maintain an affluent lifestyle. They dress in the most fashionable clothing they can afford; they talk and flirt ceaselessly in the confiterias; consume such gigantic slabs of red meat in the parrilladas (grill houses) that Australian or North American cooking seems mean by comparison; and they still find the stamina to drive their social lives into the small hours of the morning. You come across them skiing in the mountains above Bariloche in winter and sunbathing on the beaches of Mar del Plata in summer.

Contrasting their lifestyle with that of the slum dwellers in the formidable *villa miserias* that have risen on the outskirts of virtually every Argentine city, you start to think of Argentina not so much as one country but two. The first is a modern, developed nation akin to Australia or northern Europe. The other is a poor, third-world country akin to Peru or Bolivia.

The frustration of living a poor life in a country which is liberally endowed with natural wealth weighs heavily on the Argentines. Not only do you find frustration, but sometimes embarrassment when meetings with comparatively wealthy foreigners force them to discuss the country's economic straits and their own declining standards of living. If the Argentines are gradually losing everything else, they refuse to let their pride slip away from them. Those who can, still try to keep up appearances. No one likes to be thought of as poor, or to be treated as such.

POPULATION & PEOPLE

There are well over 30 million Argentines. Over 80% are urban dwellers. Some 10 million live in Buenos Aires, the third largest city in Latin America. The rest are spread across Patagonia, the mountain valleys of the north-west, the lowlands of the north-east and the fertile plains of the pampas.

Unlike most other Latin American countries, which have large Indian populations, about 85% of Argentines are of direct European descent. As Bruce Chatwin points out in his book *In Patagonia*, the history of Argentina is written in its phone directories. Throw open the Buenos Aires phone directory and you are confronted with such an array of Kachanoskis, Schlesingers and Watsons that they're almost pushing the Morenos, Ibañezs and Santiagos off the pages.

There are Italians, Basques, Poles, Ukrainians, Lombards, Bavarians, Swiss, Welsh and English. The Welsh and Anglo-Argentines in particular have tended to maintain a sense of their own, distinctive identity. Chilean immigrants can be found in large numbers in Patagonia, where they work on the estancias and in the mines and industry.

One of the anomalies of Argentina which surprises foreigners is that the majority of Argentines are of Italian, not Spanish, descent. In the large immigrations of the 1880s Italian immigrants outnumbered Spanish immigrants three to one. By virtue of similar culture, religion and language the Italians blended easily with the original Spanish settlers. For the most part Argentina developed as a predominantly Italianised Spanish country.

In the later part of the 19th century and the first half of the 20th century government policies, which respected foreign customs, helped encourage mass European immigration. Freedom of religion was first granted to Protestant British settlers in 1825 and was extended to all foreigners by the constitution of 1853. By the turn of the century only two years' residence was required in order to assume Argentine nationality, and resident foreigners were exempt from military service.

By a policy of exclusion, Argentina has remained a predominantly white, European society. Asian immigration to Argentina has never been encouraged, although there have been some Palestinian, Syrian, Chinese and Japanese immigrants. The blacks, descendants of slaves imported from Africa by the Spanish, dwindled in number long ago and their fate is something of a mystery. The Indian problem was solved in the 19th century by the extermination campaigns, although there are still some 'pure-blood' Indians and many people of predominantly Indian descent.

LANGUAGE

Spanish is the national language of Argentina, as it is of most Latin American countries. The main exception is Portuguese-speaking Brazil. There are also many Indian languages spoken all over Latin America, but none of them is the primary language of any country. There are variations, however, between the Spanish spoken in different countries, caused by variations in the original imported Spanish dialects and the influence of indigenous languages.

In written Spanish, question marks (?) and exclamation marks (!) appear not only at the end of the sentence, but also before the first word, upside down. You'll soon get used to this in Latin America, though it's not done in the examples below.

Highland & Lowland Spanish

There are two important variations in the way Spanish is spoken in Latin America. These are 'highland' and 'lowland' Spanish.

Highland Spanish is spoken in the Mexican mountains and the plateaus of the Andes. It tends to sound clipped. Some of its consonants are pronounced more strongly than lowland Spanish.

Criollos and Españoles, from a 16th century drawing

Top: Mothers of the Plaza de Mayo
Bottom: Tango Trio

Vowels often disappear. Confusions between *e* and *i* and between *o* and *u* crop up. There are many other peculiarities.

Lowland Spanish is distinguished by its relaxed pronunciation of consonants – so much so that they almost disappear. In Argentine and Chilean Spanish the *s* often becomes 'h'. For example, *los hombres* is pronounced 'loh hombreh'. Argentines and Chileans tend to speak fast and rather lazily, so many phrases are hard to understand unless you're a native speaker.

There are also important differences between the Spanish spoken in Spain and the Spanish spoken in South America. Usually *z* and *c* before *e* are pronounced as 'th' in Spain, but as 's' in Latin America.

In Latin America personal pronouns (I, you, he, she, we, they) are rarely used but are implied by the verb. In Argentina people often substitute the word *vos* for *tu* ('you'). *Vos* is a shortening of the word *vosotros*. *Vosotros* is the plural form of *tu* but is now used only in Spain.

Another common feature of American Spanish is the *ll* sound which is usually pronounced as a 'y' rather than 'ly'. The main exception to this is Argentina where the 'll' sound is pronounced like a soft 'j' or like 'sh'. So Río Gallegos is pronounced something like 'Rio Ga-shay-goh'. In Chile it is pronounced 'Rio Ga-yay-go'.

Vocabulary

You should be aware of some of the differences in vocabulary between the Spanish spoken in Spain and the Spanish spoken in Latin America, as well as differences between individual Latin American countries and subtle distinctions between certain words.

In Central America the word for 'matches' is *cerillos*, but in South America it's the old Spanish word *fósforos*. People will ask you if you have *fuego* (fire), which is the same as an English-speaker asking for a 'light' for a cigarette. The gender of a noun can also vary, for example *la radio* (fem.) in Spain is *el radio* (masc.) in Latin America.

Phrase Books & Dictionaries

If you don't speak Spanish in Latin America your conversations are going to consist of a few clichés and stock phrases. This is almost heartbreaking in Argentina because, once you overcome the language barrier, meeting people is extraordinarily easy! English is quite commonly spoken in Argentina, especially in Buenos Aires. All the same it is essential to know at least enough Spanish to cope with everyday problems. Fortunately, Spanish is a relatively straightforward language and the basics are picked up quickly.

The Berlitz phrasebook, *Latin-American Spanish for Travellers* is a good one to bring with you; it's oriented to Mexico but is clear, concise, easy to use and works very well in Argentina.

A dictionary is also worth bringing. One which is commonly recommended is the paperback *University of Chicago Spanish-English, English-Spanish Dictionary*, which has many more entries than most pocket-sized dictionaries. It also contains words used in Latin America but not in Spain.

Worth getting is *Teach Yourself Essential Spanish Grammar* (Teach Yourself Books, Hodder & Stoughton, UK) by Seymour Resnick. This is a very clearly set out pocket-size book. It also contains a very useful list of 2400 Spanish/English cognates – words which have the same meaning and are either identical or very close in spelling.

When you get to Latin America don't worry about making mistakes. Spanish-speaking Latin Americans don't look down on people who mangle the language. Another advantage is that many Spanish words are similar to English or French – you can often figure out what they mean.

Pronunciation

In order to pronounce a Spanish word correctly you need to be aware of three things: pronunciation of the individual letters; pronunciation of diphthongs; and stress rules.

Letters The letters *f, k, l, m, n, p, t, y* and *ch* are pronounced as they are in English. Other pronunciations are described below, but remember that there are variations from country to country. *Ch* is a separate letter in the Spanish alphabet and words beginning with it are listed in the dictionary after *c*. *Ll* and *ñ* are also separate letters and words beginning with them are listed after *l* and *n* respectively.

a is like 'a' in 'dart'

e is like 'a' in 'gate'

i is like 'ee' in 'meet'

o is like 'o' in 'hot'

u is like 'oo' in 'boot'

y is considered to be a vowel when it's by itself or when it's at the end of the word. At these times it is pronounced like 'ee' in 'meet'. Elsewhere it is much the same as English 'y'.

b is usually pronounced as it is in English. When it's between vowels it has a sound half-way between 'b' and 'v'

c is pronounced like 's' in 'sit' when it's before e and i. Otherwise it is like 'k' in 'kitten'

d is usually pronounced like 'd' in 'dog' though less distinctly

g is pronounced like the 'ch' in the Scottish word 'loch' before *e* and *i*. Otherwise it's like 'g' in 'got'

h is always silent. For example, the word *habitación* (room) is pronounced 'abitación'

j is like the slightly guttural 'ch' in the Scottish word 'loch'. For example, the word *bajo* would be pronounced something like 'ba-ko' with a slurred 'k'

ll In Chile this letter is pronounced 'y' like in 'yacht'. In Argentina it sounds like a soft 'j' or 'sh'.

ñ is like the 'ny' sound in 'canyon'

qu is like 'k' in 'kitten'

r is usually rolled, particularly at the start of a word

rr is very strongly rolled

s is generally like 's' in 'sock'. In Argentina and Chile it usually becomes a breathy sound something like the English 'h' when it comes at the end of a word. So *las ciudades* would be pronounced 'lah ciudadeh'.

v is like 'b' in 'bad' but not as distinct. When it's between vowels it sounds half-way between 'b' and 'v'

x is usually like 'x' in 'taxi'. It's like 's' in 'sock' when it's before a consonant

z is like 's' in 'sock'

Diphthong A diphthong occurs when there are two vowels together in a word but only one syllable is formed. In Spanish there are 'weak' and 'strong' vowels. The vowels 'i' and 'u' are weak. The vowels 'a', 'e' and 'o' are strong.

When two weak vowels are together in a word only one syllable is formed. When there is one strong and one weak vowel together only one syllable is formed. When there are two strong vowels together then two syllables are formed. Remember that accent marks on vowels override these rules.

For example, the word *caoba* (mahogany) has two strong vowels together and is pronounced with two syllables in the middle. The word *despacio* (slow) has only one syllable at the end since 'i' is a weak vowel and 'o' is strong.

Stress It is important to put the em*pha*sis on the right syl*la*ble so you need to get stress under control. This is important in Spanish since the meaning of the word is sometimes changed by the stress. For example, *papá* is the colloquial word for 'father', whereas *papa* (without the stress on the final letter) means 'potato'. The rules for stress are:

If a word ends in a vowel, or in the consonants *n* or *s* then the stress falls on the second last syllable. If the word ends in a consonant other than 'n' or 's' then the stress falls on the last syllable. Exceptions to both these rules are indicated by an accent mark on the word.

For example, the word *rápido* (fast) has an accent mark on the 'a' so you stress this letter. In the word *despacio* (slow) you stress the second last syllable -*pa*- since the word ends in a vowel. When Spanish words are written in capital letters the accent marks (if there are any) may be left off, although this does not change the position of the stress.

Useful Phrases

Listed below are a number of phrases in both Spanish and English which I have found useful while in Argentina.

At the Hotel

hotel
  hotel, pensión, residencial,
room
  habitación
I'd like a ....
  Quisiera una ....
Is there ....? Are there ....?
  Hay ....?

Do you have a ....?	*Tiene una ....?*
single room	*habitación sencilla*
double room	*habitación doble*

What is the price ....?	*Que es el precio ....?*
per night	*por noche*
for full board	*por pensión completa*

That's too expensive.
  Es demasiado caro.
Is there anything cheaper?
  Hay algo más barato?
May I see the room?
  Puedo ver la habitación?
No, I don't like it.
  No, no me gusta.
the bill
  la cuenta

Toilets

In Argentina the word for 'toilet' is generally *servicio* or *baño*. They are often marked *hombres* or *caballeros* and *señoras* or *damas*. In some Latin American countries the toilet is called the *urinario, sanitario, retrete* or *excusado* (literally 'the excused') depending on which country you're in.

General

Where?	*Dónde?*
Where is ....?	*Dónde está ....?*
Where are ....?	*Dónde están ....?*
When?	*Cuándo?*
What?	*Qué?/Como?*
How?	*Cómo?*
I'll have	*Tomaré ....*
a coffee.	*un café.*
a beer.	*una cerveza.*
How much?	*Cuánto?*
How many?	*Cuántos?*

Useful Words

and	*y*
to/at	*á*
for	*para/por*
of/from	*de*
in	*en/dentro de*
with	*con*
without	*sin*
before	*antes de*
after	*después de*

soon	*pronto*
already	*ya*
now	*ahora*
immediately	*imediatamente*
here	*aquí*

Civilities

yes	*sí*
no	*no*
please	*por favor*
thank you	*gracias*
it's nothing/ you're welcome	*de nada*
hello	*holá*
good morning	*buenos días*
good afternoon	*buenas tardes*
good evening	*buenas tardes*
good night	*buenas noches*
goodbye	*hasta luego*
I don't speak much Spanish	*no hablo mucho español*
I understand	*entiendo*
I don't understand	*no entiendo*
Write it down for me please.	*Escríbamelo, por favor.*

Argentine Spanish is influenced by the massive Italian immigration. You often hear people use the Italian greeting *buongiorno!* rather than the Spanish *buenos dias*. *Chau*, which you use on parting with someone, is the Spanish spelling of the Italian *ciao*.

Transport

bus	*bus*
ship	*barco, buque*
train	*tren*
plane	*avión*
car	*carro*
taxi	*taxi*
bicycle	*bicicleta*
motorcycle	*motocicleta*

I want a ticket to ....
  Quiero un boleto para ....
What's the fare to ....?
  Que es el precio á ....?
What time does the next plane/train/ bus leave for ....?

  A que hora sale el próximo avión/tren/bus para ....?
first/last/next
  primero, último, próximo
first/second class
  primera/segunda clase
single/return (round-trip)
  ida/ida y vuelta
sleeper coach (train)
  coche cama

Left Luggage

Most bus stations and train stations have left-luggage rooms. These may have various names including *custodia*, *guadería*, *equipaje* and *depósito de equipajes*.

Around Town

tourist information centre	*centro de información turística*
airport	*el aeropuerto*
(railway) station	*estación (de ferrocarril)*
bus station	*central de autobuses*

Post & Communications

post office	*(oficina de) correos*
letter	*carta*
parcel	*paquete*
postcard	*postal*
air mail	*correo aéreo*
registered mail	*certificado*
stamps	*estampillas*
person to person call	*llamada personal*
reverse charges call	*llamada por cobrar*

Countries

Australia	*Australia*
Argentina	*Argentina*
Bolivia	*Bolivia*
Canada	*Canadá*
France	*Francia*
Great Britain	*Gran Bretaña*
Japan	*Japón*
New Zealand	*Nueva Zelanda*
Peru	*Perú*
Sweden	*Suecia*

United States	*Estados Unidos*	500	*quinientos*
West Germany	*Alemania*	600	*seiscientos*
	Occidental	700	*setecientos*
		800	*ochocientos*
Numbers		900	*novecientos*
1	*uno*	1000	*mil*
2	*dos*	1100	*mil cien*
3	*tres*	1200	*mil doscientos*
4	*cuatro*	2000	*dos mil*
5	*cinco*	5000	*cinco mil*
6	*seis*	10,000	*diez mil*
7	*siete*	50,000	*cincuenta mil*
8	*ocho*	100,000	*cien mil*
9	*nueve*	1,000,000	*un millón*
10	*diez*		

11	*once*
12	*doce*
13	*trece*
14	*catorce*
15	*quince*
16	*dieciséis*
17	*diecisiete*
18	*dieciocho*
19	*diecinueve*
20	*veinte*
21	*veintiuno*
22	*veintidós*
23	*veintitrés*
24	*veinticuatro*
30	*treinta*
31	*treinta y uno*
32	*treinta y dos*
33	*treinta y tres*
40	*cuarenta*
41	*cuarenta y uno*
42	*cuarenta y dos*
50	*cincuenta*
60	*sesenta*
70	*setenta*
80	*ochenta*
90	*noventa*
100	*cien*
101	*ciento uno*
102	*ciento dos*
110	*ciento diez*
120	*ciento veinte*
130	*ciento treinta*
200	*doscientos*
300	*trescientos*
400	*cuatrocientos*

Days of the Week

Monday	*lunes*
Tuesday	*martes*
Wednesday	*miércoles*
Thursday	*jueves*
Friday	*viernes*
Saturday	*sábado*
Sunday	*domingo*

Time

Telling time follows a logical pattern. For example, 9 o'clock is *las nueve*. 10 o'clock is *las diez*. 10.05 is *las diez y cinco* or literally '10 and 5'. Some useful terms to know are:

in the morning	*por la mañana*
during the day	*durante el día*
in the afternoon	*por la tarde*
in the evening	*por la tarde*
at night	*por la noche*
yesterday	*ayer*
today	*hoy*
tomorrow	*mañana*
the day after tomorrow	*pasado mañana*
next week	*la semana próxima*

There is no 'am' or 'pm' when telling time in Spanish. Instead, a Spanish-speaker would say *a las dos de la tarde* (at two in the afternoon), or *a la una de la mañana* (at one in the morning).

There are many variations in telling time in Spanish just as there are in

English. Some common terms are *la una y cuarto* (quarter past one). You can also say *las tres y media* (half past three) or *las tres y treinta* (three-thirty).

When approaching the hour you can say *a la una menos diez* which literally means 'one minus 10' or '10 to one'. *A las dos menos cinco* is 'five to two'.

In railway stations, bus stations and airports the Argentines have habit of using the 24-hour clock. So *a las ocho* is 8:00 and *a las catorce* is 14:00.

Geographical Expressions

There are a number of Spanish geographical expressions, used in this book as well as in Spanish language maps and books, which you should be familiar with. These are:

estate (ranch, station)	*estancia*
bridge	*puente*
glacier	*ventisquero, glaciar*
lake	*lago*
mountain	*cerro*
mountain range	*cordillera*
national park	*parque nacional*
pass	*paso*
river	*río*
small farm	*rancho*
waterfall or rapids	*cascada, catarata, salto*

Facts for the Visitor

VISAS

Visas for Argentina are required by everyone except citizens of most West European countries, Canada, Japan and a number of Latin American countries. US, British, Australian and New Zealand citizens *do* require visas.

Visas can be obtained from the Argentine embassies in neighbouring countries and from Argentine consulates, which are quite widely scattered. In Chile, for example, there is an Argentine embassy in Santiago and consulates in Punta Arenas, Puerto Montt, Arica and Antofagasta.

US citizens can obtain, free of charge, a multiple entry tourist visa good for four years. Holders of British, Australian and New Zealand passports pay about US$20 for a multiple entry tourist visa, valid for 12 months from the date of issue and 90 days from first entry into Argentina.

You can usually hop across to the border towns of neighbouring countries without problems. For example, if you want to see the Brazilian side of the Iguazú Falls, you can cross from Argentina to the Brazilian border town of Foz do Iguaçu in the morning, take a local bus to the falls and return to Argentina in the afternoon. You don't need a Brazilian visa, only your passport. The same applies to the La Quiaca/Villazón crossing between Argentina and Bolivia.

British passport-holders had problems getting visas for Argentina following the Falklands War, but at the time of writing Britons weren't being discriminated against. Those who were born in Argentina, or who have had Argentine national status, are required to travel with their Argentine documents, regardless of their current citizenship. It is always wise to check the latest visa requirements before departure.

Visa Extensions

Most people are given an entry stamp on arrival which allows them to stay for up to 90 days, and this can be renewed for an

Four year multiple entry visa for a U.S. passport

39

additional 90 days. If you want to stay longer than six months it's probably best to make a short trip to an adjoining country, then return and start your six months all over again.

CUSTOMS

Customs looks for different things depending on what country you're entering Argentina from. If you're coming from Chile or Brazil they check for fruit, as it's absolutely forbidden to carry fruit into Argentina or to take it into Chile or Brazil. If you're coming from Bolivia they check for drugs.

Although there may be no checks at the actual border itself, the customs check-post may be several km down the road from the border town. This means that your car or bus gets stopped and a very thorough search is made of everyone on board – including foreigners.

Customs also check foreign passports for visas. Although you can move back and forth as you like between some border towns, you could have real problems if you head any further into Argentina without a visa.

MONEY

The unit of currency is the Austral (A) which replaced the peso in mid-1985 as part of an economic package designed to stabilise the economy and get inflation under control.

When the new currency was first introduced the old notes continued to be used, some stamped with their new denominations. These were being phased out at the time of writing and it's unlikely you'll see any.

The new notes are in denominations of A100, A50, A10, A5 and A1. Coins are in denominations of 5, 10 and 50 *centavos*. One Austral is equal to 100 centavos.

Changing Money

Cash and travellers' cheques can be changed at some banks, and at some money-changers (*casa de cambio*), hotels and travel agents. US dollar cash can be changed just about anywhere. The black market for US dollars is such an integral part of the Argentine economy that the black market (or 'parallel dollar') rate is listed daily in the Argentine newspapers.

Exchange Rates

It's pointless to quote exchange rates for the Argentine Austral because the exchange rate is always steadily increasing.

When I first went to Argentina to research this book the black market exchange rate was about 3.5 Australs to one US dollar; within three months it had risen to 4.5 Australs and now it is 12 Australs to the dollar.

All prices in this book are given in US dollars but, with the rapidly increasing exchange rate and inflation running at 100% per year, even that doesn't really indicate what you'll be paying once you get to Argentina.

Credit Cards

Useful credit cards include American Express, Diners Club, Visa, Mastercard and Carta Franca, all of which can be used quite widely in Argentina.

TOURIST INFORMATION
Foreign Embassies/Consulates
Australia
    Santa Fe 846 (tel 3126841)
Bolivia
    25 de Mayo 611 (tel 3117365)
Brazil
    Pellegrini 1363 (tel 3945260)
Canada
    Suipacha 1111 (tel 3129081)
Chile
    San Martín 439 (tel 3946582)
France
    Santa Fe 846 (tel 31224425)
Ireland
    Santa Fe 1391 (tel 449987)
Netherlands
    Maipú 66 (tel 336066)
Peru
    Tucumán 637 (tel 3921344)
Paraguay
    Maipú 464 (tel 3926536)

West Germany
    Villanueva 1055 (tel 7715054)
Switzerland
    Santa Fe 846
UK
    Dr Luis Agote 2412 (tel 8037070)
USA
    Colombia 4300 (tel 7747611)

GENERAL INFORMATION
Post & Communications
There are post offices in all towns. International airmail rates for letters and postcards are very cheap. However, it is moderately expensive to airmail small packets and parcels. For example, to airmail a one kg packet to Australia will cost about US$13.

Telephones
The state-owned telephone company is called *ENTEL*, which has offices in all major towns where you make international phone calls. By ringing off-peak you can sometimes get a 50% reduction in the rate to some countries.

Discount rates for international calls are: US$2 per minute to Australia; US$1.60 per minute to West Germany, Europe and Canada; and US$2.30 per minute to the USA, regardless of when you call. You can make reverse-charge calls to certain countries such as the United States but not to others (such as Australia).

Public telephones use tokens called *cospeles* which you buy from newspaper and cigarette kiosks, and from the cashier's desk in restaurants and bars.

Telegrams
International telegrams can be sent through the state-owned *ENCOTEL* company. International telegram charges are: to Australia US$1 per word; to USA US$0.40 per word; to Europe US$0.50 per word.

Business Hours
Banks are open Monday to Friday from 10am to 4pm. Office hours generally are from 9am to 12 noon, then 2 to 7pm. Shops tend to close for the midday siesta, except in Buenos Aires where they usually remain open.

HEALTH
Vaccinations
No vaccinations are required to enter Argentina from any country. There is a malaria risk from October to May in a tiny strip of Argentine territory bordering Bolivia.

Travel Insurance
You may never need health insurance, but if you do it's worth a million, so get some! There are lots of travel insurance policies available and any travel agent will be able

to recommend one. Get one which will pay for your flight home if you are really sick. Make sure it will cover the money you lose for forfeiting air tickets, and that it will cover the cost of flying your travelling companion home with you. Get your teeth checked and treated before you set out.

Medical Kit

Medical supplies and drugs are available from pharmacies so there's no need to bring a supply with you unless it's something you're definitely going to be using.

Health Precautions

Generally speaking, as far as health is concerned, Argentina harbours only two real problems: altitude and extremes of climate.

Altitude Sickness Although you are more likely to be affected by altitude on the high plateau of Ecuador, Peru and Bolivia (where the average height is 3000 to 4000 metres) you can get altitude sickness – also known as *soroche* or mountain sickness – crossing some of the high mountain passes between Chile and Argentina, or if you visit high mountain settlements like San Antonio de los Cobres in the Argentine Andes.

Unfortunately there is no way of predicting who will suffer from altitude sickness. It afflicts healthy, physically fit people as much as people who are in poor health or in poor physical shape. Even people who have never had problems at high altitudes before can suddenly be afflicted by it.

Basically, what happens is this: at high altitudes (3000 metres and above) your body has to make more red blood cells in order to absorb more oxygen from the thin air. In most people this process takes a few days. In that time you should avoid any strenuous activity, stop smoking, and drink no alcohol.

Until your body has adjusted to the higher altitude your lungs and heart have to work harder to make up for the reduced supply of oxygen. You can also expect general physical weakness, headaches, loss of appetite, insomnia, shortness of breath, nausea, dry cough, some loss of coordination, and a puffy face or hands in the morning.

Symptoms of severe altitude sickness include severe loss of coordination, dizziness, walking as if you were drunk, severe headaches, serious shortness of breath even after only mild physical activity, severe nausea and vomiting, acute weariness, loss of appetite, loss of interest in personal survival, abnormal speech and behaviour (which can turn into delirium and coma), reduced urination, bubbly breath, and coughing spasms that produce watery or coloured saliva.

For most people, symptoms of altitude sickness are usually mild and pass after a few days. If they do not – or if they get worse – then you must descend to a lower altitude immediately. The only *cure* for altitude sickness is to get to a lower altitude. Extreme cases can kill you!

Oxygen can provide temporary relief. A pain-killer for headaches and an anti-emetic for vomiting will help relieve the symptoms. Keeping up your fluid intake will help. Carbohydrates might help.

In South America the traditional relief for altitude sickness is *mate de coca* which is tea made from coca leaves. You can get this in most cafés and markets in Peru and Bolivia. The leaves also find their way down into Chile, though I haven't seen them in Argentina. If you chew the leaves you have to add some ash or bicarbonate of soda so that the cocaine is leached out of the leaves.

However, these leaves will only *relieve* the symptoms of mild altitude sickness; they will not cure it.

Heat Exhaustion & Sunburn In hot climates – like the north-west desert of Argentina – you sweat a great deal and lose both water and salt. Make sure you drink sufficient liquid and have enough salt in your food to make good the losses (a teaspoon of salt a day is sufficient). If you don't, you run the risk of suffering from heat exhaustion and cramps. Heat can also make you impatient and irritable, so try to take things slowly. Good sunglasses are essential. Sunburn is a *real* problem in these places and you need a powerful sunblock, some headgear which shades your whole face and neck, and a light long-sleeved shirt to cover your arms.

Hypothermia At the other end of the temperature scale, hypothermia is a simple, effective killer – usually referred to as 'exposure'. Basically, the body loses heat faster than it can produce it and the core temperature of the body falls. It's deceptively easy to fall victim to it through a combination of wind, wet clothing, fatigue and hunger, even if the air temperature is well above freezing. Hypothermia's symptoms include a loss of rationality – so people can fail to recognise their own condition and the seriousness of their predicament.

Symptoms of hypothermia are exhaustion, numb skin (particularly toes and fingers), shivering, slurred speech, irrational or violent behaviour, lethargy, stumbling, dizzy spells, muscle cramps, and violent bursts of energy. This can progress to collapse, unconsciousness and death.

Anticipate the problem if you're cold and tired, and recognise the symptoms early. Immediate care is important, since hypothermia can kill its victims in two hours.

The first response should be to find shelter from wind and rain, remove wet clothing and replace with warm dry clothing, drink hot liquids (not alcohol) and eat some high calorie, easily digestible food. These measures will usually correct the problem if symptoms have been recognised early. In more severe cases it may be necessary to place the patient in a sleeping bag insulated from the ground,

with another person if possible, while they are fed warm food and drinks.

There are a few things you should *not* do with a person suffering from hypothermia. Do not rub the patient. Do not place the patient near a fire. Do not give food or drink to an unconscious patient. Do not remove the patient's wet clothes in the wind. Do not give the patient alcohol.

You could face this problem if you're trekking, day-walking or hitching anywhere in southern Argentina and Chile or anywhere in the mountains. Be prepared for cold, wet and windy conditions.

Get under cover before you get soaked, and keep your sleeping bag dry. If you're day-walking and don't have the proper gear (*not* a good idea), turn back if the weather looks threatening. Warm, waterproof clothes are essential. These should retain their insulating qualities even when wet (use wool and various synthetics, *not* cotton) and protect all parts of the body, including hands, feet, neck and head. Solid shoes are also essential. Thermal underwear, or at least a thermal underwear top, is a good investment.

Books
A useful book to browse through is *The Traveller's Health Guide* (Roger Lascelles, London, 1979) by Dr A C Turner. For a run-down on problems faced by trekkers and campers in Argentina and Chile see Hilary Bradt and John Pilkington's *Backpacking in Chile & Argentina* (Bradt Enterprises, 1980).

ACCOMMODATION
In Argentina you can get a roof over your head for anywhere between a few dollars to several hundred dollars a night. A great deal depends on where you are, what you're satisfied with in terms of comfort and cleanliness, how much searching you're prepared to do after a long journey, and whether you're in a city or a small town. In general, however, most accommodation in Argentina is good value by Australian,

North American or Northern European standards and prices.

In practice, although the bottom-end hotels tend to vary quite a bit in standard, the mid-range hotels are nondescript. Apart from location or number of floors there is really nothing much to distinguish them. You get a rectangular room, a bed and a bathroom, and that's pretty much it. Some of the older ones are in great sprawling buildings, often with big, bright rooms at the front and dim, dark rooms at the rear. What you get often depends on when you travel. If you're in Argentina in the tourist season, when hotels are busy, you may have to take a lower standard of accommodation.

Accommodation can be divided into *hospedajes*, *residenciales*, *hotels* and *pensiones*.

Hospedajes & Residenciales
The cheapest places go under the title of *hospedaje* or *residencial*. Distinctions are somewhat academic, but a hospedaje is usually a family house with a room or two for rent. These are often excellent value; they have hot water and you share the lounge with the family. Hospedajes are sometimes permanent affairs but are often only in business temporarily. Some of these places are mentioned in this book; others can be found by asking at the tourist offices.

A residencial is a small permanent hotel with a number of rooms to rent, often run by a family who also lives in the same building. They're usually fairly basic, providing only a bed, table and chair in an otherwise bare room. Usually clean sheets and blankets are provided. Some of them have heating units in the room. Some have rooms with attached bathrooms, but usually there are shared toilets and showers. Most have hot water, particularly those in the south.

The price of rooms in residenciales and hospedajes will often include breakfast. The quality and quantity of this will vary. In the very cheapest hotels and residenciales

it's often just a cup of coffee, and maybe a piece of bread with butter or jam. If you pay more, your breakfast may well be a whole buffet of fruit juice, bread, butter, jam, biscuits, eggs, and a pot of coffee. It's worth paying extra for a place which offers a good breakfast because you'll rarely be able to buy one for the same price in a restaurant.

Hotels & Pensiones
Pensiones are generally somewhat more expensive than residenciales and hospedajes, though the distinction is often obscure. Most pensiones tend to have slightly better facilities, and services of a higher standard. For anything from one to a few dollars more than you pay in an hospedaje you will probably have a private shower and toilet. Quite a few have their own restaurant, but so do some residenciales.

The term hotel, though often used by some very cheap and basic places, is usually applied to mid-range and up-market accommodation. At the bottom end of this price bracket are hotels which provide you with a small room, attached bathroom and toilet, hot water, private telephone and television. These usually have a moderately-priced restaurant.

Beyond this there's not much difference until you get to some of the magnificent hotels in Buenos Aires with international standard, five-star rooms, swimming pool, room service, shopping arcades and so on. You can always find excellent mid-range hotels in the larger towns right through Argentina, though real international and luxury standard hotels are largely restricted to the main cities.

Youth Hostels
The Youth Hostel Association (tel 451001) is at Office 6, 2nd floor, Talcahuano 214, Buenos Aires.

There are Youth Hostels in Buenos Aires, Mar del Plata, Córdoba, Puerto Iguazú, Mendoza and Humahuaca. There are several in the vicinity of San

Carlos de Bariloche, although these are just *refugios* built to shelter hikers and can be used by anyone whether or not they're members of the YHA.

The YHA network in Argentina is very limited. The cheapness of Argentine hotels makes the youth hostels less important than they are in Europe and Australia.

Camping & Refugios

Argentina's national parks offer marvellous opportunities for camping, sometimes for a small charge and sometimes for nothing. You can find official camping sites on the outskirts of many towns, but often you'll need your own car to make it practical to stay there. Some campsites are very tacky affairs and not particularly pleasant places to stay.

Refugios are huts set up in the national parks to provide shelter for walkers and trekkers. The refugios are only open in summer (usually November through to April).

FOOD

Latin American food has been influenced by the original Indian settlers, the Spanish invaders and colonisers, and later European and African immigrants. Each Latin American country has developed a distinctive cuisine. Corn-based food like *tortillas*, and soups and beans are the backbone of the Mexican diet. In Peru it's potato with corn. Chile is noted for its seafood.

In Argentina the going thing is meat, from a simple slab of grilled beef dished up with a truckload of chips (french fries) to elaborate meat stews. Argentine cuisine is also strongly Italian-influenced; macaroni, spaghetti and other pastas (sometimes with a heavy use of garlic and onions) make quick, cheap meals.

Places to Eat

One of the striking features of Argentina is the homogeneity of its restaurants. From the cheapest hash house to the most

expensive restaurant the style is almost always the same, with small, square tables, jacketed waiters and a menu which features grilled meat. Rustic bars and vegetarian restaurant smorgasbords dent the pattern, but for the most part Argentine restaurants base themselves on (or at least aspire to) the *porteño* model.

You can eat cheaply from many small restaurants in the towns and cities. Another good hunting ground for cheap eats is city markets – particularly good for buying fresh fruit. Some visitors cut costs by buying food at shops, supermarkets and local city markets.

Bars serve snacks and both alcoholic and non-alcoholic drinks. *Cafeterías* and *hosterías* are straightforward restaurants. *Snack bars* sell fast food. Fully fledged *restaurantes* are distinguished by their quality and service but the name is applied to both the simplest and the most illustrious establishments. They all serve alcoholic and non-alcoholic drinks.

In Argentina the standard snack joint is called a *confiteria*, which is a cross between a café and a snack bar. These range from humble holes in the wall with half a dozen tables and a dozen bar stools, to extravagant affairs like the famous *Café Tortoini* in Buenos Aires.

Ordering so much as a coffee and a sandwich in a slightly up-market confiteria can involve an awe-inspiring technique of waitering that makes Australian and North American coffee shops seem primitive by comparison. Napkins, tissue paper, a cash register receipt, no less than three packets of sugar, complimentary sweets and a sandwich impaled with toothpicks all rain down on your table. Somewhere amidst this, you also get your cup of coffee.

Unlike, say, Australia, where eating out tends to be done both for the social occasion and for the food itself, eating out in Argentina seems to be mainly a social occasion.

Except at the top-end restaurants in a few major cities, restaurant food tends to be fairly ordinary and pretty standard throughout the whole country. While most restaurants are OK, few are outstanding or memorable. However, it's never difficult to find a cheap place to eat anywhere in Argentina; the city centres abound with them.

Eating low-budget in Argentina tends to be unremarkable but consistent. For something different you need to move a bit up-market. Many places put on a cheap set meal (*comida corrida*) both for lunch (*almuerzo*) and dinner (*comida* or *cena*). Breakfast (*desayuno*) is rarely a set meal and you generally order whatever you like. Following European custom, you usually get exactly what you ask for. If you ask for chicken and rice you get chicken and rice. If you want trimmings you must ask for them. Salad is *ensalada*. Vegetables are *verduras*.

Some common dishes are listed below but since it's impossible to mention all the possibilities, you really need a dictionary and a phrasebook with a good food section. The Berlitz *Latin American Spanish for Travellers* is very good.

Tipping

Except in places run and worked by families it is customary – and expected – that you tip waiters 10% of the bill. The menu is *la carta*. The bill is *la cuenta*.

Snacks

Empanadas are similar to Cornish pasties. They're stuffed with vegetables, or combinations of vegetables, meats and cheese. Two or three of these with a coffee will get you going for the day. Empanadas can be fried (*fritas*) or baked (*al horno*). In some South American countries empanadas are known as *saltenas*.

Humita is better known in western cookbooks as seasoned pureed corn, which is corn kernel and milk mashed into a thick pulp. This is found in one form or another in every Latin American country. It's frequently wrapped in corn husks and steamed. When served this way it is known as *humitas en chala* and makes a tasty change from empanadas.

Breakfast

For breakfast the usual eggs and bread rolls are the main alternatives to empanadas. *Huevos fritos* are fried eggs, *revueltos* are scrambled, and *pasados* or *a la copa* are boiled or poached. As far as the last two are concerned, *bien cocidos* means well-cooked and *duros* means hard.

Tostadas is toast, and *pan* is bread. Eat these with *manteca* which is butter, *mermelada* which is jam, *jamón* which is ham, and *queso* which is cheese. In some Latin American countries butter is called *mantequilla*, but in Argentina it's just *manteca*.

Main Dishes

In Argentina, lunch and dinner are the biggest meals of the day, and the main course in the restaurants is usually meat. A *parrillada* is a grill house which cooks steak, sausages and other types of meat over charcoal fires.

Bife is a steak which is prepared from any of the usual cuts used for roasting. *Churrasco* is brisket or shank steak. *Bife de chorizo* is a steak cut off the rib. *Bife de lomo* is sirloin steak. *Bife de costilla* is much the same as T-bone steak. *Tira de asado* is a strip of roast rib.

Vacio is the bottom part of what North Americans and Australians refer to as sirloin, porterhouse and the flank.

Matambre arrollado is another popular dish. It's served cold and the meat comes rolled up like a Swiss Roll with a spinach, onion, carrot and egg filling. Sometimes this is served hot off the grill, in which case it comes without the filling.

If you want your beef cooked rare than ask for *jugoso*. Medium is *a punto*. Well-done is *bien hecho*.

Some variations on meat dishes include *bife a caballo*, which is not horse meat but a slab of beef with an egg or two on top ('on the horse'). A *carbonada* is a mix of minced meat, onions and tomatoes. *Morchilla* is 'blood pudding'. Some parrilladas serve cattle testicles.

A popular dish is *puchero*. Variations include *puchero de gallina* which is a mixture of chicken, sausage, maize, potatoes and squash. *Milanesa* is wiener schnitzel. *Locro* is a thick corn or maize stew which includes sausages, pumpkin, white beans, beef and herbs. *Ñoquis* are potato dumplings served in meat and tomato sauce.

Common chicken dishes include *pollo con papas fritas* which is chicken with fried potatoes. *Pollo con arroz* is chicken with rice. *Pollo a la cubana* is Cuban chicken, which is chicken with rice and a banana.

Dessert

Dessert (*postre*) is commonly ice cream (*helado*). *Helado de fresa* is strawberry flavoured and *helado de chocolate* and *helado de vainilla* require no further explanation.

Rice pudding is *arroz con leche*. Cakes are *tortas*. A sadistically sweet desert is

dulce de leche which is a pale ooze made of milk and sugar. *Dulce de batata* is a variation on the *dulce* theme and is made from sweet potato.

Almendrado is ice-cream rolled in crushed almonds. *Alfajores* are maize-flour biscuits which are filled with jam or *dulce de leche*.

DRINKS

If one drink distinguishes Argentina from any other country it's the distinctive herbal tea known as *yerba mate*. *Yerba* is the name of the herb, *mate* is the cup from which it is drunk and *bombilla* is the pipe with which the tea is sucked from the cup. The herb is a greenish colour, ground to about the size of ordinary tea leaves. It is mixed with hot water and drunk through the *bombilla* which has a filter at the end to prevent the leaves being sucked up.

A proper *mate* is roughly spherical with a small hole in the top. When the liquid is finished more hot water is poured in. This drink is consumed all over Argentina and in some parts of Chile. If you can't find it in the restaurants then buy it in small packets from the shops and supermarkets.

Argentines have a habit of drinking it like some people chain-smoke cigarettes – which seems appropriate, since the taste of this foul drink is not unlike moist tobacco. Unfortunately, Argentines have a habit of inflicting it on guests.

Tea & Coffee

Tea is served black, usually with sugar and a slice of lemon. If you want milk in your tea ask for *té con leche* which gets you something akin to muddy water.

Café con leche means 'coffee with milk' but is literally milk with coffee; a teaspoon of coffee is scooped into your cup which is then filled with hot milk. If you don't want milk you ask for *café solo* (coffee only).

Restaurants and confiterias will usually give you a cup of coffee or a cappuccino with three or four small paper-packets of sugar. You see a lot of bad teeth in Argentina.

Wine

Many fine wines are produced in Argentina. Some are world class and they're certainly amongst the best and cheapest in South America. In fact, Argentina is the fourth biggest producer of wines in the world, behind France, Italy and Spain. Not much, however, is exported. About two-thirds of Argentine wines are produced in Mendoza province.

Vino tinto is red wine. *Vino blanco* is white wine. *Seco* is dry. *Dulce* is sweet. When ordering wines remember that terminology differs. For example, Argentine Chablis has no resemblance to a French Chablis.

Fruit Juices & Soft Drinks

Other drinks available include *jugos* or fruit juices. *Naranja* is orange. *Toronja* is grapefruit. *Piña* is pineapple. *Mora* is blackberry. *Maracuya* is passion fruit. *Sandía* is watermelon. *Limón* is lemon.

All your favourite multinational soft drinks like Sprite, Coca Cola and Fanta are sold in Argentina. 'Sprite' is pronounced 'esprite' for some reason.

BOOKS & BOOKSHOPS

Before you read about Argentina it's worth reading about Latin America. It's impossible to understand modern Argentina without some understanding of the early Indian settlement and of the Spanish and Portuguese conquest of the continent.

General History

A good starting point is the *History Of Latin America* by George Pendle (Penguin, 1973) a pocket-sized account of the period from the Spanish conquest to the mid-1970s.

Sweat of the Sun, Tears of the Moon by Jack Pizzey is a fine, journalistic overview of modern South America. The documentary, and book of the same name, takes its title from the Inca expressions for gold (the sweat of the sun) and silver (the tears of the moon).

The most bitter account of the social and political struggles of South America since independence from Spain is Eduardo Galeano's *Open Veins of Latin America: Five Centuries of the Pillage of a Continent* (Monthly Review Press, 1973).

A detailed account of the South American independence wars against Spain is given in *The Spanish-American Revolutions 1808-1826* (WW Norton & Company, New York, 1973) by John Lynch.

A very readable account of Argentine history from the time of the Spanish conquest until 1970 is *Argentina – A City & a Nation* (Oxford University Press, 1971) by James Scobie. He gives a comprehensive account of the country's social, political, economic and cultural development.

In an attempt to explain Argentina's economic decline in the 20th century, a number of books have compared Argentina with Australia and Canada – all of which were recently settled by Europeans and developed on the basis of the export of primary products. Probably the most readable of these is *Australia & Argentina – On Parallel Paths* (Melbourne University Press, 1984), by Tim Duncan and John Fogarty. Also interesting is *Argentina, Australia and Canada – Studies in Comparative Development, 1970-1985* (MacMillan Press, London, 1985) edited by D C Platt and Guido di Tella.

The Rosas Dictatorship

An interesting account of the post-independence period is given in *Argentine Dictator – Juan Manuel de Rosas* (Clarendon Press, Oxford, 1981) by John Lynch.

Life in the Argentina Republic in the Days of the Tyrants (Hafner Press, New York, 1974) by one-time Argentine president Domingo Sarmiento, is a classic account of the country under the rule of Rosas. It was first published in 1868.

Far Away and Long Ago (Dent, London, 1918) by William Henry Hudson, who grew up in Argentina during Rosas' rule, includes a vivid, personal account of that time.

The Perón Era

Perhaps the most comprehensive and readable book on the late President Juan Perón is *Perón - a biography* (Random House, New York, 1983) by Joseph Page.

Also interesting is *Juan Perón and the Reshaping of Argentina* (University of Pittsburgh Press, 1983) edited by Frederick Turner and José Enrique Miguens.

The story of the Montonero guerrillas is told in *Soldiers of Perón - Argentina's Montoneros* (Clarendon Press, Oxford, 1982) by Richard Gillespie.

The Return of Eva Perón (Alfred A Knopf Inc, New York, 1980) by the Trinidad writer V S Naipaul, is a scathing essay on Perón, Argentina and the Argentines. Naipaul's strongly expressive style provokes images of Argentina which are as relevant today as when the essay was written some 15 years ago.

La Razón de Mi Vida (The Reason for My Life) is Eva Perón's ghost-written autobiography.

The Dirty War

The 'dirty war' under the last military junta is documented in *Nunca Mas* (Never More), the report compiled by Argentina's National Commission on Disappeared People and published by Editorial Universitaria de Buenos Aires. An English language translation has been published by Faber & Faber.

Portrait of an Exile (Junction Books, London) by the Anglo-Argentine journalist Andrew Graham-Yooll, gives a personal and sometimes bizarre account of life in Argentina during the first years of the Dirty War.

A disturbing portrayal of the same period is *Imagining Argentina* (Bloomsbury Publishing, 1987), a novel by Lawrence Thornton.

With Friends Like These (Pantheon Books, New York, 1985) compiled by the Americas Watch, describes United States policy towards Argentina during the Carter and Reagan presidencies.

Movies *The Official Story*, a film by the Argentine director Luis Puenzo, is set in 1983 on the brink of the fall of the military junta. The film challenges middle and upper class Argentines who are content to accept the 'official story'. *The Night of the Pencils*, by Argentine director Hector Olivera, portrays the true story of the kidnapping and torture of six high school students during the early years of the Dirty War. *Las Madres of the Plaza de Mayo*, produced by Susane Muñoz and Lourdes Portillo, is a documentary about the mothers and grandmothers of the disappeared.

Travellers' Tales

Although there is a wealth of academic works on Argentina, it's probably fair to say that it was accounts by travellers which opened Argentina to the outside world. The 19th century travel writers, many of them British, were concerned not only with recording detail but also with conveying a generous amount of personal impression and opinion. Read in chronological order, their books tell a great deal about Argentina's development through the centuries.

One of the first accounts of European contact with Argentina is provided by the Italian Antonio Pigafetta, who sailed with Magellan and lived to tell the tale. A translation of his account of the round-the-world voyage was made and published by the Hakluyt Society under the title *First Voyage Round the World by Magellan*.

The first account of the exploration of the Río de la Plata was by a Bavarian, Ulrich Schmidt, who sailed with Pedro de Mendoza's expedition. Another early account was a narrative of Alvar Nuñez Cabeza de Vaca's expedition across central South America. A translation of these works into English was made by the

Hakluyt Society under the title *The Conquest of the River Plata*.

A Description of Patagonia (Armann & Armann, Chicago, 1935) by Thomas Falkner, was first published in 1774. Despite the title it actually gives a first-hand description of the region north of the Río Negro and otherwise relies mainly on second-hand accounts for the country south of the Río Negro. Falkner was born in England in 1707 to Irish parents, went to sea as a ship's surgeon, and because of illness was forced to convalesce in Buenos Aires.

There he converted to Catholicism, joined the Jesuit order, and worked as a missionary until the Jesuits were expelled from South America in 1768.

An early 19th century description of Argentina and Chile is provided by *Travels in Chile & La Plata* (Baldwin, Cradock & Joy, London, 1826) by John Miers. Miers spent several years in the region, having been contracted by the Buenos Aires government to set up the machinery for a mint.

The Voyage of the Beagle (first published in 1839) by Charles Darwin includes an interesting first-hand account of Argentina in the days of Rosas.

Among the many books which wax lyrically on the wonders of Argentina in the first half of the 20th century are: *The Amazing Argentina: a new land of enterprise* (Cassel, UK, 1914) by the British writer John Foster Fraser; *Argentina, Past & Present* (Kegan Paul, Trench, Trübner & Co, London, 1910) by K H Koebel; and *Argentine Tango* (Hodder & Stoughton, London, 1932) by the British writer Phillip Guedalla.

Southern Cross to Pole Star (Century, UK, 1982) is by A F Tschiffely, a Swiss author, traveller and one-time school-master. The book was first published in 1932 and is a record of his extraordinary 16,000 km, 2½ year journey from Argentina to Washington on horseback.

Patagonia & Tierra del Fuego

Although the majority of Argentines seem to have little interest in their own outback, Patagonia and Tierra del Fuego have attracted both the attention and the fascination of foreigners for the past century.

The classic account of Patagonia is the naturalist William Henry Hudson's *Idle Days in Patagonia* (first published in 1893 and now reprinted under the Everyman label). Hudson went to Patagonia to track down the migratory birds which roosted near his home in La Plata.

Through the Heart of Patagonia (Thomas Nelson & Sons, London, 1911) by H Hesketh Prichard describes a journey to the fringe of the Patagonian Andes in search of the giant ground sloth or Mylodon. The remains of such a sloth had been found in a cave near Puerto Natales (in the Chilean province of Magallanes) in such a good state of preservation that it was thought living specimens might still be roaming Patagonia.

The Uttermost Part of the Earth (first published in 1948) by E Lucas Bridges is about his life among the Indians of Tierra del Fuego.

Bruce Chatwin's *In Patagonia* (Pan Books, 1979), pieces together the often bloody history of Latin America's 'wild south' before the days of oil towns and tourists. He retraces the steps of Butch Cassidy and the Sundance Kid, searches for records of the mythical unicorn and describes his audience with His Royal Highness Prince Philippe of Araucania & Patagonia – amongst many other intriguing tales.

Paul Theroux's *The Old Patagonian Express* (Penguin, 1980) surveys Latin American life from the vantage point of a train window. This is very much a book of impressions and conversations, a record of one man's thoughts as he moves across America until the train line ends deep in Argentine Patagonia.

Other Guides

In a guidebook of this size and scope it's not possible to cover every conceivable aspect of travel in Argentina. Hopefully it will give you some starting points and make the routine aspects of travelling easier and cheaper. The following books can help you with a few other alternatives.

Lonely Planet's *South America on a Shoestring* by Geoff Crowther is a concise overview of the entire continent designed for low budget travellers. If you intend visiting other Latin American countries Lonely Planet also has individual guides to Ecuador & the Galapagos Islands, Peru, Colombia, Bolivia, Brazil, Mexico, and Chile & Easter Island. Also look for Lonely Planet's forthcoming phrasebook, *Latin American Spanish*.

The South American Handbook edited by John Brooks (Trade and Travel Publications, UK) is generally regarded as the standard guide to the continent and tells you about everything from saunas in Potosi to manzanilla trees in Willemstad (Bolivia and Netherlands Antilles respectively). It's an impressive collection of information which caters to people on low, medium and high budgets.

The most comprehensive guide to Tierra del Fuego is *Tierra del Fuego* (Ediciones Shanamaiim, Buenos Aires, 1978) by Rae Natalie Prosser Goodall. The book is in both Spanish and English and can be bought in Argentina.

Good, local guides to Argentina include the *Guías Regionales Argentinas* series, which are in Spanish. The *Guías Almar* series is in both Spanish and English.

Trekking Guides

For trekkers, there's a series of guidebooks on South America published by the British-based Bradt Enterprises, including the very amusing and informative *Backpacking in Chile & Argentina plus the Falkland Islands* (Bradt Enterprises, UK) by Hilary Bradt and John Pilkington.

If you're trekking in the Argentine lake district, around Bariloche, then get a copy of *Las Montañas de Bariloche* (Guías Regionales Argentinas) by Tonçvek Arko and Irina Izaguirre.

MAPS

The best maps of Argentina are available from the headquarters of the Automóvil Club Argentino at Avenida del Libertador 1850, Buenos Aires. Outside Argentina specialist map and travel shops may stock their maps.

The best overall map of the country is probably the road map called *República Argentina* produced by the Automóvil Club Argentino, which shows the principal roads, cities and towns, and provincial boundaries. They also produce a series of maps of individual Argentine provinces which are extremely detailed, with all sorts of natural landmarks and places of tourist interest marked. They're very clear and easy to use. If you intend doing some fairly extensive travel in the country then you really need these maps.

Tourist offices in Buenos Aires and the provinces always have city maps and maps of the local area, either free or for a small charge. The quality varies from place to place, although they're usually detailed and accurate.

Outside Argentina the best map of the country you're likely to get is by an independent cartographer, Kevin Healey, of Melbourne, Australia. His map is called *A Contemporary Reference Map of South America* and the scale shows Argentina quite well. If you can't get Healey's map then Bartholomew's *America, South* is the next best.

WHAT TO BRING

Travel light! An overweight pack or carry bag will quickly become a disaster, particularly if it's hot. The main thing to remember is that if you need something – from skis and trekking gear to everyday necessities – you can buy it in Argentina.

Personal preference largely determines the best way to carry your stuff. A large zip-up bag with a wide shoulder strap is easy to get on buses and easy to put down and pick up, but it's hard to carry for long distances and throws you off balance if it's heavy. A backpack is most convenient if you have a lot of walking to do. There is no prejudice about backpacks and their owners – Argentines of all ages travel with backpacks, so you just blend into the crowd. A very useful type is one with an internal frame and a cover which zips over and protects the straps so they don't get snagged when the bag is stowed in the bowels of buses or planes.

After that, what you take largely depends on what you want to do and where you want to go. If you intend to camp or trek keep the extremes and difficulties of Argentina's climate in mind. In the far south of Argentina the wind blows almost unceasingly and a stove will be useless unless it has a wind-shield. Likewise you have to have a tent whose flaps can be secured so that they don't keep you awake flapping in the wind.

I generally found that even the cheapest hotels in Argentina provided sufficient blankets and gave me more if I asked for them, so sleeping bags are not essential. Camping gear will, however, give you extra freedom of movement and may cut down on accommodation costs. Some of the best parts of Argentina, particularly the mountain fringe of Patagonia, can only be experienced properly if you trek and camp.

If you're travelling right through Central and South America you can keep the weight of your pack down by initially taking clothes for hot and temperate climates and buying things like sweaters and ponchos when you need them in places like Chile and Argentina. You'll find these to be relatively cheap compared with the prices at home and the quality is very good.

In northern Argentina you generally won't need any heavy-duty clothing, unless you're going up into the mountains where it can be freezing at any time of

the year. Even if you're staying on the plains you still need warm clothing as it gets quite cold travelling on the trains and buses across the pampas. The northern deserts can, of course, be freezing at night. In southern Argentina warm jackets, socks, solid footwear, gloves, scarves and headgear are essential. Thermal underwear, or at least a thermal underwear top, is a good investment. Your clothing must be wind-proof and water-proof.

Don't forget small essentials like a combination pocket knife or Swiss Army knife; needle and cotton and small pair of scissors; contraceptives; sunglasses; swimming gear and so on. All the usual stuff like toothbrushes, etc, can be bought in Argentina. The only places you may have difficulty getting things are villages and small towns.

VISITING CHILE

This book also includes information on the Chilean Patagonia and Tierra del Fuego. For the most part travel in Chile is similar to travel in Argentina. Much the same information in this chapter can be applied to Chile. For the full story see *Chile & Easter Island – a travel survival kit* by the same author. Some useful information on travelling to Chile is given below.

Visas

Most West Europeans as well as British, Australian, Canadian and United States passport-holders do not require visas. New Zealand passport-holders *do* require visas. Check on the current situation before you depart for Chile.

If you don't require a visa you'll be given an entry stamp on arrival which allows you to stay for up to 90 days, and this can be renewed for an additional 90 days. If you want to stay longer than six months it's probably easiest just to take a trip to neighbouring Argentina or Peru and then return to Chile and start your six months all over again.

If you don't require a visa for Chile your

three-month tourist pass starts all over again each time you re-enter the country. In this case you can hop back and forth between Chile and Argentina as often as you like, within the time and entry restrictions of your Argentine visa.

If you need a Chilean visa you should check that it's good for multiple entry, otherwise you'll have to pick up another Chilean visa in one of the Chilean consulates in Argentina. Whatever you do, don't turn up at the border without a visa or you may find yourself tramping back to the nearest consulate.

Customs

Officially you're allowed to import 400 cigarettes and 50 cigars, two litres of alcoholic beverages, and gifts and souvenirs. It is absolutely prohibited to bring fruit into Chile from anywhere. If you're entering from Argentina your bags are likely to be checked for fruit.

Money

The unit of currency is the Chilean peso (Ch$). Notes come in denominations of 100, 500, 1000 and 5000 pesos, though the 100 peso note was being phased out and you're not likely to see any.

The new set of copper-coloured coins come in denominations of one, five, 10, 50 and 100 pesos. There is an old set of silver-coloured coins which were also being phased out and you may not come across any by the time you're using this book.

The peso has been floating against the US dollar and is falling in value. Although the rate of devaluation is mild by South American standards, it's still only worth quoting prices in this book in US dollars.

Health

No vaccinations are required to enter Chile, and the country is free of malaria and yellow fever. Generally speaking, the same health problems which apply to Argentina also apply to Chile. See the section on 'Health' in this chapter.

Transport

Except for the occasional winter journey in a 2nd-class railway carriage (if the heating fails to work), travel in Chile is comfortable, with generally good roads, fast and punctual bus services, reasonably cheap flights and a number of useful passenger shipping services.

There are two national airlines: LAN-Chile and Ladeco. Both have domestic and international services. There are also some smaller airlines, such as DAP, which connects Punta Arenas with Chilean Tierra del Fuego.

All the main roads are surfaced and only in the rural areas do you come across dirt and gravel roads. All the buses on the main roads are comfortable (some of the them are luxurious), well-maintained, fast and punctual. For the most part the buses in Chile operate in much the same way and are of similar standard to Argentine buses.

The trains of greatest interest to travellers are those from Santiago to Valparaíso, and Santiago to Puerto Montt via Concepción and Osorno. There are no railways south of Puerto Montt. From Osorno and Puerto Montt you can take buses and boats through the Lake District into Argentina.

The same pros and cons of driving in Argentina apply to Chile. A number of international and local car rental firms operate in Chile, including Hertz, Avis, National, Dollar, and Budget. The *Automóvil Club de Chile* also rents cars.

Getting There

If you're overlanding through Latin America then Argentina is just one more border to cross. The major connections between Argentina and neighbouring Latin American countries are listed below, although there are many more possibilities.

You can fly direct to Argentina from the USA, Australia, New Zealand, Britain and Europe. You might also consider flying to another Latin American country or to the USA, and then overlanding or taking a connecting flight to Argentina.

One interesting possibility is a 'Round the World' air ticket with Aerolíneas Argentinas and Qantas, which connects Argentina with New Zealand, Australia, South-East Asia and Europe. For details, see the section below on Round the World (RTW) tickets.

AIR

Discount air tickets can considerably cut the cost of getting to South America. The amount saved depends on a number of factors: whether you can buy your ticket in advance, how flexible you are about your travelling arrangements, and whether you have a student card. The main types of cheap air tickets are:

Advance Purchase Advance Purchase Excursion tickets must be bought weeks or months prior to departure. These tickets have minimum and maximum stay requirements, strict and heavy ammendment and cancellation charges, and often don't allow stopovers.

IT Independent Inclusive Tour Excursion tickets are tickets to popular holiday destinations. Officially they're only available as holiday package deals which include hotel accommodation. Many agents will sell you one of these and issue you with phoney hotel vouchers in the very rare event that you're challenged at the airport.

Economy Class This is a full economy fare ticket. These tickets are valid for 12 months.

MCO Miscellaneous Charges Order is a voucher which can be exchanged with any IATA airline for a flight of your choice. You use it as a flexible alternative to a specific onward ticket. Panama, Colombia, Venezuela, Guyana, and Trinidad require visitors to have an onward ticket or an MCO.

Standby This can be one of the cheapest ways of flying. You turn up at the airport and if there are spare seats available on a flight you can buy a ticket at a considerable discount. If you intend flying from Europe to Latin America via the USA this can be a very cheap way of getting to the USA.

RTW Round the World tickets can be a cheap way of travelling. There are some excellent deals available and you can sometimes get RTW tickets for less than the cost of a return excursion fare.

You must travel around the world in one direction and you cannot back-track. The number of stop-overs you're allowed often depends on the price paid. Tickets are valid for six months to a year although in some cases you can extend this by paying more. RTW tickets offer a combination of airlines, with each airline carrying you on one leg of the journey. Many travel agents will put together RTW tickets using discounted fares on a variety of airlines. These are often excellent value.

If you do intend doing a round the world trip then you should seriously consider buying the RTW ticket offered by the Australian airline Qantas and the Argentine airline Aerolíneas Argentinas. This extraordinary ticket allows you to circle the world via Australia, New Zealand, Argentina, Europe and South East Asia in either an eastbound or a westbound direction.

For example, if you start in Australia you can fly out of any one of nine Australian cities. Heading east you fly to either Christchurch, Wellington or Auckland in New Zealand. From Auckland you fly to Buenos Aires. A side-trip to either Santiago (in Chile) or Montevideo (in Uruguay) is included in the ticket. From Buenos Aires you can fly direct to a number of European cities including Madrid, Paris, Frankfurt and Athens, or via Río de Janeiro and Sao Paulo in Brazil. From Europe you can fly back to Australia via a number of Asian cities, including Bombay, Singapore and Bangkok. There are many other possible stop-overs. The ticket is valid for one year. The economy fare is A$3199 but should be available at a discount from travel agents.

With a few exceptions, a return ticket is nearly always cheaper than two one-way tickets. It's generally cheaper to add stops to a long-haul ticket rather than buy a series of short hops. Buying airline tickets in most Latin American countries is expensive because of high sales tax and because there is rarely, if any, ticket discounting.

Bucket Shops
In addition to the official fare structure there are discount tickets available from many travel agents – in Britain these are known as 'bucket shops'. Bucket shop tickets are generally cheaper than normal Advance Purchase fares and often don't have advance purchase requirements or penalties for cancellation.

Most bucket shops are well-established and reliable but it's not unknown for fly-by-night operators to set up office, take the money and disappear before they give you a ticket. Most bucket shops insist on a deposit for a ticket but only hand over the full amount when you have the ticket in your hands.

If you're travelling on a student-discount ticket make sure you have a student card or you may be required to repay the discount at the airport. Tickets, regardless of where they are bought, are non-transferable and airlines usually check that the name on the ticket and the name on your passport match when you check in.

In Europe two of the best places for buying cheap tickets are London and Amsterdam. There are numerous bucket shops in both places and their services and prices are well advertised. In Canada and Australia there are several outlets for discount air tickets. Airline deregulation in the US has made it much easier to find cheap air tickets.

Buying International Air Tickets in Argentina
If you buy an international flight ticket in Argentina you *must* pay in US dollars. You cannot pay in local currency. This includes tickets for flights to adjoining Latin American countries.

FROM THE USA & CANADA
By some quirk one of the best deals from the USA to South America is to Lima in Peru, but via Canada. Tickets are available on Canadian Pacific Airlines from Vancouver and Toronto to Lima, and include a connecting flight from San Francisco or Los Angeles to Vancouver. The economy fare to Lima starts from C$700 return.

You can fly direct from the USA and Canada to Argentina. Aerolíneas Argentinas has flights from Montreal, New York, Los Angeles and Miami direct to Buenos Aires. The regular economy fare from New York to Buenos Aires is US$1130 and US$1100 from Los Angeles. An advanced purchase ticket with a maximum stay of 90 days costs US$903 from New York, US$853 from Miami and US$1050 from Los Angeles.

Cheap Tickets

To find cheap tickets peruse the travel sections of the Sunday papers for likely looking agents. The *New York Times*, *San Francisco Chronicle-Examiner* and the *Los Angeles Times* are particularly good. Tickets go for about US$800 from LA and US$700 from NY.

In the USA the American Student Council Travel (SCT) and the Student Travel Network know a lot about cheap tickets and interesting routes. You don't have to be a student to use their services. In Canada the equivalent organisation is Travel Cuts.

Student Travel Network

Los Angeles – Suite 507, 2500 Wilshire Boulevard (tel (213) 380 2184)

San Diego – 6447 El Cajon Boulevard (tel (619) 286 1322)

San Francisco – Suite 702, 166 Geary St (tel (415) 391 8407)

Honolulu – Suite 202, 1831 South King St (tel (808) 942 7455)

Dallas – 6609 Hillcrest Avenue (tel (214) 360 0097)

Student Council Travel

New York – 205 East 42nd St (tel (212) 661 1450); and 356 West 34th St (tel (212) 239 4257)

Los Angeles – 1093 Broxton Avenue (tel (213) 208 3551)

San Diego – 5500 Atherton, Long Beach (tel (213) 598 3338); UCSD Student Center, B-023, La Jolla (tel (619) 452 0630); and 4429 Cass St (tel (619) 270 6401)

San Francisco – 312 Sutter St, San Francisco (tel (415) 421 3473); 2511 Channing Way, Berkeley (tel (415) 848 8604);

Boston – 729 Boylston St, Suite 201 (tel (617) 266 1926)

Seattle – 1314 North-east 43rd St (tel (206) 632 2448)

Travel Cuts

Travel Cuts is Canada's national student travel agency and has offices in Vancouver, Victoria, Edmonton, Saskatoon, Toronto, Ottawa, Montreal and Halifax. You don't have to be a student to use their services.

FROM AUSTRALIA & NEW ZEALAND

If you're coming from Australia or New Zealand and want to travel overland from the USA to Latin America then the cheapest option is to fly to San Francisco or Los Angeles and make your way south to Mexico.

If you want to go direct to South America from Australia or New Zealand you can fly either to Santiago in Chile or to Buenos Aires in Argentina.

Australian travel agents offer discounts on direct flights to Argentina, Chile and the USA and on Round the World tickets. One of the best places to buy discount tickets in Australia is STA Travel. For other discount tickets check the travel agents' advertisements in newspapers like Saturday's *Age* or the *Sydney Morning Herald*.

STA Travel

STA Travel has some of the cheapest discount air tickets. You don't have to be a student to use their services. STA offices are located at:

Melbourne – 220 Faraday St, Carlton (tel (03) 347 6911)

Hobart – Union Building, University of Tasmania, (tel (002) 233 825)

Sydney – 1A Lee St, Railway Square, (tel (02) 212 1255)

Adelaide – Level 4, The Arcade, Union House, Adelaide University (tel (08) 223 6620)

Perth – Hackett Hall, University of WA, (tel (09) 380 2302)

Canberra – Arts Centre, Australian National University, (tel (062) 470 800)

Brisbane – Northern Security Building, 40 Creek St (tel (07) 221 9629)

To Argentina

You can fly direct to Argentina from Australia and New Zealand. This involves a flight from Australia to New Zealand, and an Aerolíneas Argentinas flight from New Zealand to Buenos Aires. The one-way economy fare from the east coast of Australia to Buenos Aires is A$2028 via Auckland, or A$2433 via the USA. The return economy fare via Auckland is A$2616, and A$3125 via the USA.

One of the best tickets available is the RTW ticket offered by Qantas/Air New Zealand and Aerolíneas Argentinas. For details, see the section above on RTW tickets.

To Chile

You can fly direct from Australia to Chile and then enter Argentina by land or air. This allows you to stop off in Tahiti and Easter Island on your way to South America.

Your first option is to fly to Santiago via Tahiti and Easter Island. Qantas or UTA take you from Australia to Tahiti where you catch the LAN-Chile flight to Easter Island and Santiago. From New Zealand there are flights to Tahiti with Air New Zealand and UTA. Cheapest one-way economy fares from Sydney to Santiago are A$1960 via Auckland, and A$2351 via the USA; return fares are A$2496 via Auckland and A$2984 via the USA.

To the USA

From Australia the cheapest way to get to the USA is to fly to Los Angeles or San Francisco from Sydney or Melbourne. An Advance Purchase one-way ticket from Australia to Los Angeles or San Francisco is A$1127. A return ticket fare varies from A$1725 in the low season to A$2025 in the shoulder season, and A$2169 in the high season.

FROM THE UK

In Britain there are a number of magazines which have good information about flights and agents. One of the best sources of information about cheap air fares is the monthly magazine *Business Traveller*, which is distributed internationally and is available direct from 60/61 Fleet St, London EC4.

Others include *Trailfinder* which is free from the Trailfinders Travel Centre, 48 Earls Court Road, London W8 6EJ. *Time Out* is the London weekly entertainment guide which is widely available in London or from Tower House, Southampton Street, London WC2E 7HD. *LAM* is a free weekly magazine for entertainment, travel and jobs and is available from 15 Abingdon Road, London, W8 6AF. *The News & Travel Magazine (TNT)* is another free weekly magazine.

Bucket Shops

Two reliable London bucket shops are: Trailfinders at 46 Earls Court Rd, London W8; and STA Travel at 74 Old Brompton Rd, London SW7 or 117 Euston Rd, London NW1.

To the USA

Many bucket shops offer cheap tickets on the Britain to USA route. Fares from London to New York can be as low as £125 one-way and £200 return. Fares from London to San Francisco start from £180 one-way and £289 return.

To South America

If you want to fly direct from Britain to South America the bucket shops offer lots of possibilities.

From London, the cheapest places to fly to are generally Bogotá in Colombia and Caracas in Venezuela. London to Caracas is about £450 return. London/Caracas/Santiago ticket will cost about £600 return.

Other fares from London include Lima for £640 return, Santiago for £680 return, Buenos Aires and Montevideo for £640 return, and Río de Janeiro for £580 return.

Flying to Río de Janeiro in Brazil is an interesting way of getting to Argentina because you can enter via the Iguazú Falls on the Argentine/Brazilian border.

FROM EUROPE

From Europe it is usually cheaper to get to Latin America by first flying to the USA, though sometimes direct flights to Mexico cost only slightly more than flights to the USA.

If you don't want to go through Central America then the cheapest places to fly to are Colombia and Venezuela. One route which has become quite popular is from East Berlin to Lima via Cuba using cheap Aeroflot or Interflug flights.

You can also fly direct to Argentina from a number of European cities. For example, Aerolíneas Argentinas has direct flights between Buenos Aires and Madrid, Paris, Rome, Zürich, Frankfurt and Amsterdam.

If you only want to fly from Europe to the USA one-way there's no point in going to a bucket shop since a one-way standby ticket is the cheapest ticket you can get. Almost all the airlines operating between major European cities and the USA offer stand-by fares.

Similar fares to those from London are available from other European cities direct to Latin America.

In Paris try Nouvelles Frontières at 74 Rue de la Fédération, Paris (tel 273 25 25); and Uniclam-Voyages at 63 Rue Monsieur le Prince.

The Netherlands, Brussels and Antwerp are other good places for buying discount air tickets. Some agencies to try include WATS in Antwerp, SOF Travel and Sindbad in Zürich, and Stohl Travel in Geneva.

FROM CHILE

The only way to get between Chile and Argentina is by road or air. The main overland crossings are Santiago to Mendoza, several connections through the Lake District, and several connections between Chilean and Argentine Patagonia and Tierra del Fuego.

Flights

The Chilean airline LAN-Chile has daily flights from Santiago to Buenos Aires; the fare is US$187. The Chilean airline Ladeco flies from Santiago to Mendoza two days a week; the fare is US$70. Aerolíneas Argentinas has flights six days a week between Santiago and Buenos Aires.

Antofagasta to Salta

There are buses at least once a week during summer between Antofagasta and Salta. These are operated by Buses Gemini which has offices in Antofagasta and Calama in Chile, and in Salta in Argentina. Take warm clothing with you as it gets *very* cold going over the mountain passes at any time of year!

Santiago to Buenos Aires & Mendoza

There are several companies which cover this route. You can book at either the Terminal de Buses Norte on Calle General MacKenna, or at the Terminal de Buses Sur at Alameda Bernardo O'Higgins 3800, both in Santiago. Try bus companies like Tas Choapa, Chile Bus, Igi Llama, Fenix Pullman Norte, and TAC. Fares from Santiago are: to Mendoza US$18; and to Buenos Aires US$51. This route can be blocked by snow in mid-winter. Coitram, at Huerfanos 1359 in Santiago, has *taxi colectivos* to Mendoza.

Through the Lake District

There are four main routes through the Lake District from Chile to Argentina. Three of them terminate at Bariloche and the others at Zapala or Nuequén. The most popular route is from Puerto Montt to Bariloche via Lago Todos los Santos, since it has the most spectacular scenery. The gist of the story is given below and details can be found in the relevant sections of this book.

Puerto Montt to Bariloche, via Lago Todos los Santos There are two ways of doing this trip from Chile. One is to go straight through with one of the bus companies operating out of Puerto Montt or Puerto Varas. However the best way is to take the trip in stages with overnight stops at Ensenada, Petrohué and Peulla. In winter the roads are sometimes blocked by snow.

The first stage takes you from either Puerto Montt or Puerto Varas on the daily bus to Ensenada and Petrohué. At Petrohué you catch a ferry to Peulla at the other end of the lake. From Peulla a bus takes you over the border to Puerto Frías in Argentina.

The next step is Puerto Frías, Puerto Allegre, Puerto Blest, Puerto Pañuelo, to Bariloche. The first part of the trip involves crossing Lago Frías on a small launch. This is followed by a short bus ride to Puerto Blest. From there you board a ferry for Puerto Pañuelo. Finally there is another short bus hop from Puerto Pañuelo to Bariloche.

Osorno to Bariloche via Lago Puyehue & the Puyehue Pass This journey is entirely by road and passes by four lakes. Snow may occasionally cause delays in winter. There are daily buses from Osorno to Bariloche. There are several buses a week from Osorno to Zapala, Mendoza, Rosario and Buenos Aires. There are also direct buses from Puerto Montt to Bariloche. All of these go via Osorno and the Puyehue Pass.

Valdivia to Bariloche via Lago Panguipulli, Lago Pirehueico, Lago Lacar & San Martín de los Andes The first step of the journey is by bus from Valdivia to Panguipulli, and then by bus from Panguipulli to Choshuenco and Puerto Fry (sometimes spelt Puerto Fuy or Puerto Fui). From Puerto Fry you take a ferry across Lago Pirehueico to Pirehueico.

From Pirehueico you take a local bus to Puerto Huahun where you clear Argentine customs. The next step is Puerto Huahun to San Martín de los Andes via Lago Lacar. There is a ferry across the lake between the two towns which connects with the buses from Pirehueico and Puerto Huahun. From San Martín de los Andes there are daily buses to Bariloche.

From Panguipulli there is an alternative route into Argentina via Lago Calafquén and the Carrirrine Pass. There are also bus companies in Valdivia which allow you to do the Valdivia-Bariloche trip in one hop.

Valdivia/Temuco to Junín de los Andes via Villarrica & Puesco This road route between Chile and Argentina goes across the Tromen Pass, which can be blocked by snow for four months of the year. The first step is to go by bus from Valdivia or Temuco to either Villarrica or Pucón. From Villarrica you take a bus to Curarrehue. Between Curarrehue and Junín de los Andes there is no public transport so you'll have to walk or hitch.

The Southern Routes
South of Puerto Montt there are a number of crossings between Argentine and Chilean Patagonia and Tierra del Fuego. The main routes are listed below though there are several others. Details of each route are in the relevant sections of this book.

Coyhaique to Comodoro Rivadavia There are direct buses between Comodoro Rivadavia and Coyhaique.

Chile Chico to Los Antígos – Bus & Ferry The first step is to take a bus or taxi colectivo to Puerto Ibáñez on the shores of Lago Carrera. Next you take the ferry across the lake to Chile Chico. From Chile Chico you either hire a jeep or ford an unbridged river to the Argentine township of Los Antígos. From Los Antígos there are two buses a week to Caleta Olivia on the coast via Perito Moreno.

Punta Arenas & Puerto Natales to Río Gallegos There are daily buses from Río Gallegos to Río Turbio. From Río Turbio you catch one of the frequent workers' buses over the mountains to Puerto Natales in Chile. There are buses daily from Río Gallegos direct to Punta Arenas in Chile.

Punta Arenas to Tierra del Fuego & Navarino
There's a daily ferry from Punta Arenas to Porvenir on the Chilean side of Tierra del Fuego. If the weather is too rough for the ferry you have to take one of the daily flights from Punta Arenas to Porvenir. From Porvenir there are buses twice a week to Río Grande in Argentina. From Río Grande there are daily buses to Ushuaia. There used to be a weekly ferry from Ushuaia to Puerto Williams on the island of Navarino but this service appears to have been discontinued.

FROM BOLIVIA
The main road and rail route to Bolivia passes through the northern Argentine towns of Salta and Jujuy and crosses the border at La Quiaca/Villazón. There are also two minor routes further east. The first is Salta, Orán, Aguas Blancas/Bermejo, Tarija. The second is Salta, Embarcación, Yacuiba, Santa Cruz.

Via La Quiaca/Villazón
There are daily buses between Jujuy and Salta and the Argentine border town of La Quiaca. The trains from Jujuy and Salta are cheaper than the buses but they take much longer and can be very crowded. Trains do not cross the border so you have to get off at La Quiaca and either take a taxi to Villazón or walk the two km between the two stations.

Via Aguas Blancas/Bermejo
There are daily buses in either direction between Salta and Orán. From there you need to take another bus to Aguas Blancas on the border. Alternatively there's usually one bus per day direct from Salta to Aguas Blancas. From Aguas Blancas you have to take a ferry across the river to Bermejo on the Bolivian side and then a bus from there to Tarija.

Via Yacuiba
This is the route to take if you're heading to or from Santa Cruz. There are buses and trains from Salta to Aguaray. From there you must take a taxi across the border to Yacuiba. From Yacuiba you can pick up the *tren rapido* to Santa Cruz.

Flights
The Bolivian airline, Lloyd Aerolíneas Boliviano SA, has flights three days a week from Buenos Aires to La Paz. The economy one-way fare is about US$305. Aerolíneas Argentinas has flights once a week between Buenos Aires and La Paz.

FROM PARAGUAY
There are three main ways of getting between Argentina and Paraguay.

The first is to take one of the daily buses to Asunción from a northern Argentine town like Formosa.

The second is to take a launch across the Río Paraná between Posadas and Encarnación and then take a bus or train from Encarnación to Asunción. At the time of writing a bridge was under construction between Posadas and Encarnación.

The third route is by bus from the Argentine town of Puerto Iguazú to Puerto Stroessner via the Brazilian town of Foz do Iguaçu near the Iguazú Falls.

The Paraguayan airline, Líneas Aéreas Paraguayas, has flights five days a week between Asunción and Buenos Aires. The one-way economy fare is US$178. Aerolíneas Argentinas has flights two days a week between Buenos Aires and Asunción.

FROM BRAZIL
Almost everyone makes the crossing between Argentina and Brazil via the Iguazú Falls, one of South America's most spectacular sights. There are regular buses between Puerto Iguazú on the Argentine side and Foz do Iguaçu on the Brazilian side. For details see the section on the Iguazú Falls.

There are also direct buses between Río de Janeiro, São Paulo and Buenos Aires.

There are daily flights between Buenos Aires and Río de Janeiro with Aerolíneas Argentinas and the Brazilian airline Varig.

FROM URUGUAY

There are a bewildering number of routes between Argentina and Uruguay. The main companies operating buses and ferries between the two countries are Ferrytur, Buquebus and ONDA.

In Buenos Aires the Ferrytur office is at Florida 780. In Montevideo the office is at Río Branco 1368.

In Buenos Aires the ONDA office is at the corner of Florida and Lavalle. Tickets for their buses can also be bought at the ONDA office at the Estación Terminal del Omnibus near Retiro Train Station. In Montevideo the ONDA office is at San José 1145.

In Buenos Aires the Buquebus office is at Suipacha 776.

Bus/Ferry via Colonia

Ferrytur and ONDA operate ferries from Buenos Aires to Colonia. From Colonia you catch a connecting bus to Montevideo. Ferries depart Buenos Aires for Colonia at 8 am daily. The fare to Colonia is US$14. The bus from Colonia to Montevideo costs US$4. Night ferries depart Buenos Aires for Colonia at 9 pm. The fare to Colonia is US$14 for a seat and US$18 for a sleeping berth.

Direct Bus

ONDA and Buquebus operate direct buses between Buenos Aires and Montevideo. ONDA has three buses a day to Montevideo; the fare is US$14. Buquebus has two or three departures per day.

Bus/Ferry via Carmelo & Tigre

ONDA operates ferries from the Argentine port of Tigre to Carmelo in Uruguay. Tigre is north of Buenos Aires and you can get there on the direct train from Retiro Station in about 50 minutes. There are ferries from Tigre to Carmelo departing Tigre at 8 am daily from the Estación Fluvial, Local 13. The fare is US$5. From Carmelo you take a connecting bus to Montevideo for US$4.

Across the Río Uruguay

All of the above are ways of getting between Montevideo/Colonia and Buenos Aires. If you don't want to end up in Buenos Aires you can take one of the routes which crosses the Río Uruguay. This river forms one border between the two countries. There are international bridges across the river between Fray Bentos and Gualeguaychú and between Paysandú and Concepcíon. About 20 km north of Salto is the Salto Grande dam which crosses the river; the dam has a road across the top connecting Uruguay to Argentina. The third possibility is Salto to Concordia.

Flights

PLUNA, the airline of Uruguay, has daily flights from Buenos Aires to Montevideo. The one-way fare is US$84. Aerolíneas Argentinas has daily flights from Buenos Aires to Montevideo.

TOURS

A mind-boggling assortment of companies run tours to Argentina and other Latin American countries. The travel sections and classified advertisements of daily newspapers will tell you what's available. Some of the more off-beat possibilities are mentioned below.

In Britain *Journey Latin America* (tel (01) 747 3108) 16 Devonshire Road, Chiswick, London W4 2HD, specialises exclusively in small group tours to Latin America using local transport and mid-range hotels. It gives you instant travelling companions and someone else to handle the donkey work, which could make it fun.

The Australian-based *Peregrine Bird Tours* has taken bird-watching enthusiasts to destinations as far afield as Kenya, Central Soviet Asia and Argentine Antarctica. For more details contact Peregrine Bird Tours, 2 Drysdale Place, Mooroolbark, Victoria, 3138, Australia (tel (03) 726 8471).

The ubiquitous *World Expeditions*

(formerly *Australian Himalayan Expeditions*) (tel (02) 261 1974), 3rd floor, 377 Sussex Street, Sydney, 2000, has trekked out of Nepal and now offers everything from bicycle rides in China to dog-sledge expeditions in Greenland. Their South America excursions include a 28-day assault on Cape Horn in a 15 metre ocean-going yacht, starting from the southern Chilean city of Punta Arenas. To qualify for this trip you need to have at least two years' serious ocean sailing experience and to have completed at least one long ocean voyage. The cost per person is around US$5600. They also have one month excursions to Argentina which include two weeks of trekking in the Mount Aconcagua and Fitzroy Mountain areas.

LEAVING ARGENTINA

Aerolíneas Argentinas
  Peru 2 on the corner with Rivadavia (tel 3625008). There's also a branch office at the corner of Santa Fe and Esmeralda.
Aeroflot
  Santa Fe 822 (tel 3125573)
Aero Peru
  Santa Fe 840 (tel 3116431)
Air France
  Santa Fe 800 (tel 3119863)
American Airlines
  Córdoba 657 (tel 3928849)
Austral
  corner of San Martín and Corrientes (tel 499011)
British Airways
  Córdoba 657 (tel 3926037)
Canadian Pacific
  Córdoba 656 (tel 3939090)
Eastern
  corner Santa Fe & Suipacha (tel 340031)
KLM
  Suipacha 1109 (tel 3118921)

LAN Chile
  Córdoba 879 (tel 3115334)
LADE
  Perú 710 (tel 3610853)
Líneas Aéreas Paraguayas
  Cerrito 1026/30 (tel 3931000)
Lloyd Aerolíneas Boliviano SA
  Pellegrini 141 (tel 353505)
Lufthansa
  Alvear 636 (tel 3128171)
Pan American
  Peña 832 (tel 450111)
PLUNA
  Lavalle 528 (tel 3946210)
Swissair
  Santa Fe 846 (tel 3120669)
TWA
  Córdoba 699 (tel 3120399)
United Airlines
  Alvear 590 (tel 3120664)
Varig
  Florida 630 (tel 353014)

Warning This chapter is particularly vulnerable to change – prices for international travel are volatile, routes are introduced and cancelled, schedules change, rules are amended, special deals come and go, borders open and close. Airlines and governments seem to take a peverse pleasure in making price structures and regulations as complicated as possible and you should check directly with the airline or a travel agent to make sure you understand how a fare (and a ticket you may buy) works. In addition, the travel industry is highly competitive and there are many lurks and perks. The upshot of this is that you should get opinions, quotes and advice from as many airlines and travel agents as possible before you part with your hard-earned cash. The details given in this chapter should be regarded as pointers and are not a substitute for your own careful, up-to-the-minute research.

Getting Around

AIR

The main Argentine airlines, Aerolíneas Argentina, Líneas Aéreas de Estado (LADE) and Austral Líneas all have extensive internal networks.

Given the enormous distances to be covered in Argentina it's definitely worth flying occasionally. In the far south of the country, in Patagonia and Tierra del Fuego, the airfare will sometimes work out cheaper than a combination of bus fares. The only problem is that there can be a heavy demand for air tickets. During the tourist season planes can be booked up weeks in advance. If so, get yourself on the waiting list.

Fares

The airfare chart on page 64 shows one-way airfares (in US dollars) around Argentina.

It's sometimes thought that flights with Austral are cheaper than with Aerolíneas but they are actually the same price. LADE fares tend to be cheaper because they fly smaller planes, but their routes are much less extensive than the larger airlines.

Night flights are considerably cheaper than day flights. For example a one-way daytime fare from Posadas to Buenos Aires is US$67. The night fare is half that. The only catch is that there might only be one or two night flights a week, and they're likely to be heavily booked.

Air Passes

Aerolíneas Argentinas has a 'Visit Argentina' fare which costs US$290 for 30 days. This ticket entitles you to fly anywhere in Argentina but only allows one stop in each city (except if you're catching a connecting flight). The ticket can only be bought outside Argentina. There is also a 14 day airpass for US$199, but this only allows you three stop-overs.

Departure Tax

Airport departure tax is US$9 for international flights and US$2 for domestic flights.

Timetables

If you go to Buenos Aires, get hold of a copy of the airline schedules and fares. The head offices of the airlines are listed in the Buenos Aires chapter of this book. The tourist office in Buenos Aires has timetables and fare lists for each airline.

TRAIN

There is an extensive network of railways in northern Argentina with frequent services between towns. There is no railway network in Patagonia. The most southern train station is Esquel which is south of Bariloche. From there on you have to use road and air transport.

Journey times are generally longer on trains than they are by bus, but on long rides they're much more pleasant because you can move around or visit the dining car. Trains are worth taking if you're doing a long haul, but for short trips you'll generally find the buses much more frequent and convenient.

Timetables

Altogether there are six different rail networks, three of which share the same terminus at Retiro Station in Buenos Aires while the remainder have their terminals at Constitución and Lacroze Stations. In Buenos Aires you can get train timetables, information and buy tickets for all lines at the Galerias Pacífico, Florida 729 (tel 3116411).

Classes & Fares

There are four classes on the Argentine trains. In descending order of price these are: *coche cama*, *pullman*, *primera* and *turista*.

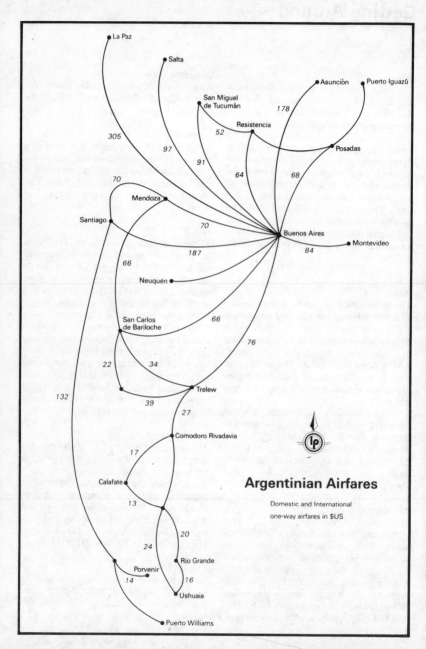

Argentinian Airfares

Domestic and International
one-way airfares in \$US

EL MEJOR HOMENAJE:
EL VOTO DE SU PUEBLO

1895 · 8 de Octubre · 1987
Aniversario del nacimiento
del Gral. Perón

equipos de difusión

BATIÓ
JUSTA"

AHORA
LOS
LTIMOS
IAS DE
FONSIN

¡ ESTÁ
DER?

APARECIO

ARGENTINO
y PERONISTA

PROPUESTAS
DE ACCION

MUNICIPALES
A UN AÑO DE GESTION

U.C.R

Top: Peronist poster
Left: Political posters
Right: Radical Party symbol

Top: 'Che lives!', Communist Party poster
Bottom: Political graffiti

Coche cama or *coche dormitorio* is the most expensive. These carriages are divided into compartments with bunkbeds for two people. During the day the lower bunk can be used as a bench seat. The compartments are air-conditioned and have their own wash basin and coat lockers. This is a very insular way to travel but on long overnight journeys it really is worth taking a sleeper.

Pullman is the next most expensive class. Pullman carriages have reclining vinyl-covered seats and air-conditioning. Carriages tend to be cleaner and better maintained than *primera* carriages, but apart from that and the air-conditioning there's not much between them.

Primera (first) class carriages have reclining vinyl seats and overhead fans (no air-conditioning).

Turista is the cheapest class. Carriages have upright bench seats and though these are OK for short trips they're not recommended for long journeys and definitely not for overnight trips. If you're trying to travel cheaply I would recommend at least taking *primera* for overnight trips.

Your train ticket shows coach number (*coche*), seat number (*asiento*), date of travel (*fecha viaje*) and departure time (*sale*). Conductors come around quite often to check tickets and they may collect them before the final stop.

Costs

As a foreign tourist you'll find Argentine train fares quite inexpensive in comparison to what you'd pay in Western Europe or Australia. For example, fares from Buenos Aires to Bariloche (on average a 24 hour trip, depending on the train) are: US$58 *coche cama*; US$46 *pullman*; US$30 *primera*; US$23 *turista*.

Rail Passes

There is a rail pass known as the 'Argenpass' which you can buy in Argentina. In Buenos Aires it's available from the Railway Booking Office at Florida 729. The pass allows you unlimited *primera* class travel on Argentine trains. A 30 day pass costs US$82; a 60 day pass is US$138; and a 90 day pass is US$190.

BUS

Most of the buses in Argentina are modern, comfortable and fast. On the main routes they're usually large Mercedes or Brazilian-made coaches, similar to large Greyhound coaches in the USA. Argentine buses are not particularly cheap in comparison to those in other Latin American countries, but on the main roads they are fast and punctual. The large coaches usually have a toilet and sometimes provide coffee and tea on board.

Theft is not a great worry. You can fall asleep, or get off a bus for a snack, and your bags will stay where you left them. You can't be so nonchalant at the bus terminals themselves – although they're not nearly as bad as the terminals in the Andean countries to the north.

Most Argentine cities have a central bus terminal where all the bus companies are gathered, although in some cities the bus companies have their own separate terminals. At the central bus terminals the individual bus companies have their own offices. The bus terminals are well organised and even if your Spanish isn't very good it's easy finding the right ticket office since schedules and fares are usually prominently displayed. You rarely need to book a ticket more than a few hours in advance. On really long trips or on routes served by a single company it's sometimes wise to book seats as soon as possible. Seats on buses are numbered.

There are ordinary buses and sleeper buses. Sleeper buses (*bus cama*) have reclining seats and footrests similar to those in 1st class on planes, and cost about twice the price of ordinary buses. The sleeper buses go on long hauls and usually depart at night. Although the ordinary buses on these long routes are comfortable the sleeper buses are worth considering.

Things are a bit different on the back roads. Although the main roads and many of the minor roads are surfaced, that still leaves plenty of gravel or dirt. Transport on these back roads is slower, the buses are less frequent, older, and stripped down to basics. You might get one or two buses a day between some small rural towns; sometimes only one or two a week.

On weekends, public holidays and during the Argentine holiday season (January and February) buses can be packed out everywhere. Sometimes the bus company will let you stand in the aisle if there are no seats available, but this seems to apply only to short trips.

TAXI

It's possible to hire a taxi and driver for the day. Rates to hire a taxi are, of course, entirely negotiable.

BOAT

There are not that many opportunities for travel by water in Argentina. There used to be a weekly ferry (on Sundays) between Puerto Williams on the Chilean island of Navarino and Ushuaia in Argentine Tierra del Fuego. At the time of writing this service had been suspended. During the tourist season there may be boats for tour groups run by private operators. Shipping out of Buenos Aires is listed in the English-language *Buenos Aires Herald*.

DRIVING

The advantages of a car include freedom from timetables, the ability to stay wherever you like (particularly if you bring camping equipment), the opportunity to get off the beaten track, and the chance to stop when you see something interesting.

Although you can get to all the major tourist destinations by public transport my general impression is that, like the United States and Australia, you really need your own car to enjoy Argentina to the full. Travelling on buses and trains I have zoomed past a formidable number of places I would have liked to have stopped at!

The chief disadvantages include expense, the difficulty of arranging safe garaging (particularly if you go trekking) and to some extent isolation because you don't have the opportunity to meet people on public transport. However, the advantages outweigh the disadvantages in much the same way as they do in Australia and the United States.

There's no need to bring your own car with you. Many international car rental companies as well as local companies operate in Argentina. Sharing the cost with a few other people can make car hire quite cheap.

International car-rental firms operating in Argentina include Avis, with offices in most major cities, and Hertz, with offices in Buenos Aires and Bariloche.

The cheapest cars available from Avis, for example, are Fiat 147 Spazios. These cost US$24 per day plus US$0.25 per km. The weekly rate is US$140 and US$0.25 per km. You can also rent cars with unlimited km for US$280 per week, US$505 for 15 days, and US$940 for 30 days.

Note that there may also be insurance charges for all cars. You have to be at least 25 years of age to rent a car. Larger cars, such as Ford Sierras, cost considerably more to rent: around US$45 per day plus US$0.45 per km.

Local companies often have cheaper rates. For example, Lan-Car, which operates in nine or ten cities, has Renault 4Ss for US$13 per day plus US$0.15 per km. However, it would pay to shop around if you intend renting a car for any length of time. Find out if there are any additional charges (such as insurance) and how much they will cost.

One of the problems with driving yourself is the dare-devil nature of the Argentines when they're behind the wheel – and this seems to apply equally to men and women. Argentine traffic is fast and ruthless, particularly in the cities. By the end of your stay you may conclude that there are *no* road laws.

BICYCLE

If you are contemplating cycling across Argentina then you're not the first. While researching this book I came across quite a few people tackling the country this way. Multi-speed bikes and mountain bikes can be bought in Argentina. A mountain bike could be a wise choice for the gravel roads of Patagonia and other remote areas of the country.

HITCHING

Hitch hiking is fairly easy in Argentina. It's unlikely you'll ever be asked to pay for a lift – unlike some Latin American countries where it is a recognised form of public transport. This applies as much in Patagonia and Tierra del Fuego as in the more developed northern part of the country.

In Patagonia you may have to wait *much* longer for a lift as fewer people live there and there is less traffic. I met one person who had taken three days to hitch the 300 km from Ushuaia to the Argentine/ Chilean border at San Sebastián in Tierra

del Fuego. On one six-hour bus ride from Rio Gallegos to Calafate I saw no more than half a dozen cars and three trucks. The moral of the story is that hitching in the off-season, even to a major tourist destination, can be a very time consuming task!

If you do intend hitching then make sure you have warm, *wind-proof* clothes in the south and something to cover your head from the hot sun in the north.

LOCAL TRANSPORT
Airport Transport

Depending on where you are there may be a special airport bus (as in Buenos Aires) or a local bus which will go by or close to the airport. In some small towns the airport is close enough to walk to. In some places the airline may have its own bus to take passengers to the airport or it may have an arrangement with a local travel agency which provides a bus for airport transport. Sometimes you have to take a private taxi. The best thing to do is to enquire about the arrangements when you buy your air ticket.

Buenos Aires

Introduction

Just before the outbreak of WW I, the British author John Foster Fraser visited Argentina and noted that the proud Argentines referred to Buenos Aires as the 'Paris' of the southern hemisphere. Today, Buenos Aires is a megalopolis of 10 million people. A third of Argentina's population lives there. It dwarfs other Argentine cities in much the same way as Paris and London dwarf French and British cities. Yet this prominence was only gained after a shaky start and decades of civil war and struggles with the *caudillos* of the interior.

The first attempt to colonise the banks of the Río de la Plata in 1536 failed, and it was not until 1580 that an expedition from Asunción managed to establish a permanent colony. For the next two centuries Buenos Aires led a precarious existence as a backwater town on the fringe of the Spanish empire.

The city's name – which means 'good air' – is said to have been provided by Spanish sailors who found the fresh air of the Río de la Plata invigorating. More likely the city was named after an Italian saint who was popular with sailors in the Mediterranean: *Nuestra Señora Santa María del Buen Aire* or Our Lady Saint Mary of the Good Air.

The city was founded on the edge of the Argentine pampas, an Indian word which means 'flat land'. When the Spanish arrived the pampas was a wilderness inhabited by nomadic Indians, rheas (flightless birds resembling ostriches) and guanacos (animals related to the llama).

When horses and cattle were released onto the pampas by the early Spanish settlers they bred in great numbers on the fertile grasslands. Before long the Indians had tamed the horses and put them to good use hunting down flocks of rhea as well as raiding Spanish outposts.

Buenos Aires

Apart from the Indians, marauding British and Portuguese warships also threatened the survival of Buenos Aires. A lively smuggling trade supported by foreign ships grew up along the Argentine coast. The unofficial trade attracted many fortune-seekers and by 1750 the population of Buenos Aires reached 12,000. When trade restrictions were abolished at the end of the 18th century, Buenos Aires expanded rapidly. By 1810 the population had quadrupled. By 1852 it had doubled again to 90,000.

It was not until the 1880s, after half a century of struggle, that Buenos Aires finally asserted itself as leader of the Argentine confederation. Until then the unruly caudillos of the interior had governed their domains very much as they pleased. Their power was based on the command of *gaucho* cavalries. The *gauchos*, or Argentine cowboys, were of mixed Spanish and Indian descent whose hardiness and sense of independence was moulded by the endless expanse and hard life of the pampas. They owed their allegiance to local caudillos, and for decades resisted both the Spanish and the criollos of Buenos Aires, both of whom sought to bring the interior under centralised control.

Buenos Aires grew rapidly in the later half of the 19th century as the government embarked on European-style modernisation, developing industry, agriculture, railways and docks, and encouraging immigration to expand the labour force. The Patagonian Indians were finally subdued by military expeditions. The *gaucho* began to fade into history.

As wealth was scooped up from the fields it was just as quickly either sent overseas or shovelled into architectural extravaganzas that make other Latin American cities, and sometimes even European cities, pale by comparison. The monumental scale of these buildings provides an inkling of their creator's aspirations. Buenos Aires was destined to become one of the great cities of the world, and Argentina a world power.

Wealth created demand for consumer goods and by the end of last century foreign visitors to Buenos Aires waxed lyrically about the 'Parisian splendour' of its shopping centres where goods of every description could be bought.

In 1938 the North American poet Archibald MacLeish wrote a dazzling description of the colour and gaiety of Buenos Aires, characterising it as a 'great city as the ancients measured great cities'. MacLeish's words hardly seem out of place today. Even current plans to move the capital from Buenos Aires to Viedma, a town 1000 km to the south on the edge of Patagonia, would not really change the character or the pre-eminence of Buenos Aires.

Yet a closer look at the megalopolis suggests that the city is in a steady state of decline. If there is a severe downpour then the storm-water drains, which were last expanded over 60 years ago, cannot control the deluge. The streets flood and electricity, gas and telephone services are cut off for days.

Above the streets downtown you can see giant cobwebs of wires strung from one building to another. These are telephone lines, most of them illegal, designed to side-step the slow and inefficient state-owned telephone company. Ridiculous as it may sound it can often be quicker to walk to someone's house than try to telephone them. For a city which prides itself on being a modern capital, as many as a third of its houses have no running water and almost half have no sewerage system.

The Anglo-Argentine journalist Andrew Graham-Yool, in his book *Portrait of an Exile*, describes Buenos Aires' Florida shopping mall as a 'lane leading to a dream country of rich possessions'. Such descriptions conjure up an image of a city which thrives on future hopes, while the magnificent public buildings of downtown suggest that it lives off past glories.

If there really is a quality to Buenos Aires which makes spending your life there worthwhile, then it is a difficult one for a foreigner to grasp in a short visit. Buenos Aires leaves you with a curious gut feeling that its *belle epoque* passed by 50 years ago and that so far nothing much of any significance has replaced it. The chances are you will leave Buenos Aires scratching your head, trying to figure out why the pieces of the jigsaw don't slot together quite so neatly as you would expect.

Information & Orientation

Back in the 1880s, when Buenos Aires was officially merged with the towns of Flores and Belgrano (now suburbs) a member of the National Congress warned that Buenos Aires would become 'a monster, with more than a million inhabitants'. A hundred years and nine million more people later Buenos Aires is often thought of as an unwieldy leviathan rather like Los Angeles.

Trying to get a grasp on the entire city is a bewildering job for the first-time visitor. However, the downtown area, in which most of the main tourist sights are contained, is surprisingly compact.

The Plaza de Mayo is the focus of downtown Buenos Aires. Heading due west is the Avenida de Mayo which ends in front of the Congress Building. The main shopping and commercial district is on the northern side of Avenida de Mayo, and includes streets such as Corrientes, Lavalle and Florida. A bit further north is the main railway station, Retiro.

To the south of Avenida de Mayo is the San Telmo district which is noted for its restaurants and markets. Further south is a district known as La Boca. Both San Telmo and La Boca are of considerable historical significance.

The other streets of interest to visitors are Avenida 9 de Julio and Avenida Libertad. The famous Cólon Theatre is on Libertad. If you keep heading north and then veer north-west along Avenida del Libertador, you'll come to the prestigious Recoleta, Palermo and Belgrano districts.

Tourist Office The main tourist office is at Santa Fe 883 (tel 312300). There is also an information kiosk on Florida on the block between Paraguay and Córdoba. The main office is open Monday to Friday from 9 am to 5 pm. The staff are very friendly and helpful and they have some free maps and leaflets. Pick up a copy of their free booklet *Where in Buenos Aires* which has lists of sights, restaurants, entertainment venues and other useful information. The English-language tourist newspaper *The Buenos Aires Times* is worth looking through. The English-language *Buenos Aires Herald* is a mine of useful information for both residents and visitors.

Casas de Turismo In addition to the national tourist information office, most of the provinces also maintain their own information offices in Buenos Aires. They are known as *Casas de Turismo* and are listed below. The Bariloche branch is a good source of general information and

sells excellent maps of all parts of Argentina.

Buenos Aires, Callao 235
Bariloche, Florida 755
Catamarca, Córdoba 2080
Chaco, Callao 322
Córdoba, Callao 332
Corrientes, San Martín 333
Entre Ríos, Cangallo 451
Formosa, Irigoyen 1429
Jujuy, Santa Fe 967
La Pampa, Suipacha 346
La Rioja, Callao 745
Mendoza, Callao 445
Misiones, Santa Fe 989
Nuequén, Cangallo 687
Río Negro, Tucumán 1916
Salta, Diagonal Norte 933
Santa Cruz, Córdoba 1345
Santa Fe, 25 de Mayo 358
San Juan, Maipú 331
San Luis, Azcuénaga 1083
Santiago del Estero, Florida 274
Tierra del Fuego, Santa Fe 790
Tucumán, Mitre 836

Post The Correo Central (Central Post Office) is at the corner of Sarmiento and Alem. It's open Monday to Friday from 8 am to 8 pm. International phone calls and telegrams can be sent from this building.

The Correo Postal Internacional (International Post Office) is on Antartida Argentina, near the main bus terminal. It's open Monday to Friday from 11 am to 5 pm. Although you can post international mail from the Correo Central, packets over one kg have to be sent from the International Post Office.

Telephones The state-owned telephone company is called ENTEL. The main international telephone office is the República branch at the corner of Corrientes and Maipú. The Catedral branch at the corner of Rivadavia and Maipú is also convenient.

International phone calls out of Argentina are very expensive. However, if you ring Monday to Friday from 6 to 10 pm, or

Saturday and Sunday from 7 am to 10 pm you get a 50% reduction in the rate to some countries. This only applies to calls made from the República, Catedral, Culpina, Ezeiza and Agüero branches.

Argentines take great advantage of the night-time discount rates and the telephone offices are jammed with people in the evening. You may have to wait well over an hour to get your call through. If you're prepared to pay more then make your call during the day when there will be few people in the telephone office.

Making a local telephone call in Buenos Aires can be a frustrating experience. The system is hopelessly overloaded. There are two types of public telephones; the small, counter-top phones that you find in public buildings, and the larger street-phones which are housed in a sort of half-dome. Both types use tokens called *cospeles* which you buy from newspaper and cigarette kiosks, and from the cashier's desk in restaurants and bars.

If you ring between 8 am and 8 pm on a workday or between 8 am and 1 pm on a Saturday then one cospele will allow you to make a two-minute call. At any other time it will allow you six minutes.

Telegrams International telegrams can be sent through the state-owned ENCOTEL company. The most convenient branch is at Corrientes 711.

Bank Travellers' cheques and foreign cash can be changed into local currency at some banks and at the *casas de cambio* (exchange houses). Banks tend to give better rates than the money changers but you may find it more convenient to change money at the latter.

To change foreign cash or Thomas Cook and American Express travellers' cheques go to the Puente Hnos Casa de Cambio at the corner of Corrientes and San Martín, or to Forexcambio at Alvear 566. These will change cheques for both Argentine Australs and US dollars. There are more money-changers along San Martín in the block between Corrientes and Sarmiento, and along Florida.

Thomas Cook (tel 302730) is on 8th floor, 25 Avenida de Mayo 140. Although you can get lost and stolen cheques replaced here they no longer cash cheques.

The agent for American Express is the City Service Travel Agency (tel 3128416) on 4th floor, Florida 890. They do not change cheques for cash.

You can change Argentine currency back into foreign exchange at the casa de cambio in the international departure terminal of Ezeiza Airport. You must have bank receipts of the initial transaction to cover the amount of Argentine currency you want to change back into hard currency.

Bookshops El Ateneo at Florida 340 has a good collection of Spanish and English books including fiction and non-fiction. For more books in English try Lottes Corner at Córdoba 785. Possibly the best range is available from Librerias ABC at Córdoba 685 which has a fine collection of books in Spanish, English and German.

Film There are many film processors in the downtown area, with processing machines which develop prints in an hour or two. Try Le Lab at Viamonte 612, and Laboclick at Esmeralda 444.

Maps The tourist office has a free map of Buenos Aires called *Plan de Buenos Aires* which shows the downtown area and the San Telmo and La Boca districts. This is the most practical map of the main tourist area.

Possibly the best map of the city is *Carta Vial de Buenos Aires y Alrededores* published by the Automóvil Club Argentino. It's very detailed and has an index of street names. The Automóvil Club Argentino (tel 8026061) is at Libertador 1850.

The best map of the Buenos Aires subway is on the reverse side of a city map which is sold with a booklet called *Guia*

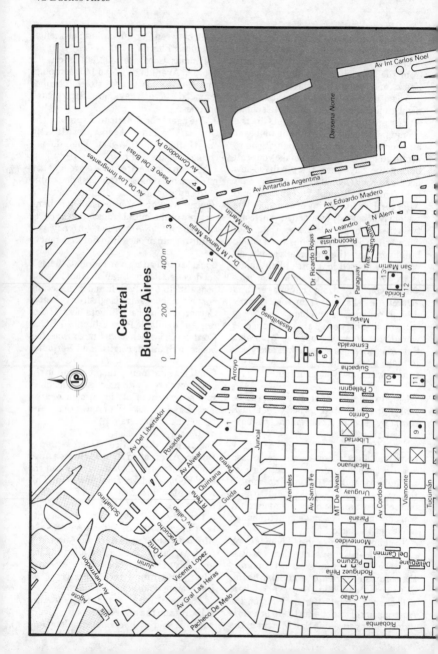

Central Buenos Aires

1 Playoleta Pellegrini
2 Retiro Train Station
3 Long Distance Bus Station
4 International Post Office
5 Tourist Office
6 Aerolíneas Argentines
7 National Parks Office
8 Hotel Central Córdoba
9 Colón Theatre
10 Petit Hotel Goya
11 Hotel Apolo
12 Railways Information &
   Booking Office
13 Phoenix Hotel
14 Hotel O'Rei
15 Florida House
16 Acapulco Hotel
17 Austral
18 General Post Office
19 National Congress
20 Hotel Turista
21 Airport Bus (to Ezeiza Airport)
22 Hotel Avenida
23 Cabildo (Town Hall)
24 Metropolitan Cathedral
25 Plaza de Mayo
26 Casa Rosada
27 LADE
28 Plaza Dorego

Peuser – La Guia de Buenos Aires. You can buy it at many magazine kiosks in the city. This is the only subway map which clearly shows the connections between different lines. The booklet lists bus routes and the addresses of public buildings.

If you intend living in Buenos Aires or spending a lot of time there you might get the *Buenos Aires* map published by Auto Mapa at Bulnes 2094. It covers the entire city but is too big to be of practical use on a day-to-day basis.

Extremely detailed road maps of Argentina can be bought at the Automóvil Club de Argentina. Even if you're not driving these are some of the best maps of the country you'll find.

National Parks The National Parks Information Service is at Santa Fe 690. They have some free maps of major national parks like those around the Iguazú Falls, Calafate and Bariloche.

Emergency Emergency telephone numbers in Buenos Aires are: City Medical Attention, 34 4001; Coronary Mobile Unit, 107; Police, 101.

Things to See

If you arrive in Buenos Aires by train at Retiro Station, one of the first things you see is a replica of London's Big Ben standing opposite in the Plaza Británica. The monument, known as the **English Tower**, was presented to Argentina in 1910 by the city's grateful British community.

The close ties between Britain and Argentina impressed one English author, Philip Guedalla, so much that after his visit to Argentina in 1930 he wrote that an Englishman was 'honoured and esteemed' there 'on the simple ground of being English'. The British had good reason to be appreciative of their host country. If India was the jewel of the British empire then Argentina was the corner-stone of its economy. Argentina, though not under direct British control, had been a

Spanish-speaking outpost of the British empire since the middle of the 19th century.

The British were not the only ones to contribute to the misfit architecture of Buenos Aires. Across the plaza from the English Tower and a short walk down Avenida San Martín or Florida, you can find many reminders of past eras. The North American essayist Waldo Frank, in an article in 1931, wrote of the 'chaos and confusion' of the city's buildings where the visitor could find examples of every type of architecture – from Neo-Classical edifices to southern Californian bungalows and London East End tenement blocks.

Depending on how you look at it, Buenos Aires is either an architect's nightmare in which an array of mismatching buildings nudge each other on the streets, or a historian's dream in which every event for almost 200 years has been recorded in stone. By working your way through this giant open-air museum, from building to building and district to district, it's possible to piece together the story of the city's development.

Foundation

Buenos Aires began with a stutter in 1536. In that year a fleet under the command of the Spanish nobleman Pedro de Mendoza, sailed from Spain. Mendoza commanded 14 ships and 1500 men, a far greater force than Pizarro and Cortés had used to topple the Inca and Aztec empires.

The first foundation of Buenos Aires occurred at what is now **Lezama Park** on the edge of the San Telmo district. A large statue of Mendoza in the park commemorates the event. However, starvation set in when supply ships failed to arrive from Spain. Indian attacks further depleted the colony.

In 1537 part of the colony moved up the Paraná River to settle Paraguay, followed four years later by the other survivors. Mendoza himself died on the return voyage to Spain.

It was not until 1580 that another

Buenos Aires in 1794

attempt was made to settle the Río de la Plata. This time an expedition under the command of Juan Garay set out from Asunción and established a settlement just north of Mendoza's failed colony.

Garay pegged out a grid system of streets centred around what is now the **Plaza de Mayo** (May Square). A fort was built on the east side of the square, guarding the river approach when the shoreline came much further inland than it does now. A town hall (cabildo) was built on the west side, on the site of the present building. On the north side stood the church, now the site of the **Metropolitan Cathedral**.

The British Invasion

One of Buenos Aires' most interesting residential districts is the **Southern Quarter**, situated to the south of the Plaza de Mayo. Today this area is centred on three streets: Defensa, Balcarce and Bolívar.

Further south is the **San Telmo** district,

bounded in the north by Chile, in the east by Paseo Colón, in the west by Bernardo de Irigoyen and by the Parque Lezama in the south. San Telmo is centred on Plaza Dorrego which was once a parking area for ox carts and lined with bars patronised by gauchos.

It is strange to think that, in 1807, fierce battles were fought along these streets against invading British troops. As fighting continued along Defensa the local citizens poured boiling oil and water from the roofs of their homes onto the British troops in the street below.

As the British battled towards the 17th century building at **Defensa 372**, now used as an art market, they were fired on by cannons installed on its balconies. This was originally the home of a wealthy merchant, a city councillor and a monarchist to boot, Francisco Tellechea. Because of his unfailing loyalty to the Spanish king, he was eventually executed by firing squad in 1813.

Other historic buildings along Defensa

are either in disrepair or have disappeared altogether.

From the end of the 18th century both San Telmo and the Southern Quarter became favoured for the residences of the well-to-do. Large brick homes replaced mud and thatch cottages. When the upper classes eventually moved north in the 19th century their original houses were turned into tenement houses to accommodate the immigrants who entered Argentina. From then on San Telmo and the Southern Quarter remained poor districts until the 1960s when cheap rents and proximity to the central city began to attract the middle class.

Nowadays the district has been turned over to antique dealers, restaurants, cafés and bars.

Independence

The successful defence of Buenos Aires against the British gave the porteños confidence in their ability to defend their colony without help from Spain, and led directly to a fully-fledged independence movement.

The name of Buenos Aires' main square, the **Plaza de Mayo**, commemorates Argentine independence. It has been variously known as the Plaza del Fuerte (Fort Square), the Plaza del Mercado (Market Square) when it served as the city's main trading area, and the Plaza del Victoria (Victory Square) to celebrate the ousting of the British. The square was finally named the Plaza de Mayo in honour of the 25 May 1810 when Argentina's link with Spain was broken.

Nevertheless, the image of masses of porteños rushing to the plaza to assert their independence is more a work of journalistic licence than fact. Leaving aside women and children and the indifferent black, Indian and *mestizo* working class, the city's population (then only 45,000) would have been too small to have gathered up much of a 'revolutionary mass'.

Had you been able to sit in on the

proceedings you would have stood ankle-deep in mud on a cold winter's day. You would have strained to hear the aspiring nation-builders shout themselves hoarse with speeches, the wind sweeping their words away to the Río de la Plata. The fishmongers, butchers and grocers would have stared out from their shops, housed under an archway built across the plaza a few years before, while Indian and *mestizo* peasants huddled in the background wondering what all the fuss was about.

The real scene on 25 May 1810 would probably have been something in the mould of a hearty Argentine demonstration, with rowdy enthusiasts stoking up a rabble of excited porteños. The leaders had, however, gained the support of the city's criollo militia and had gathered them in the plaza in a show of force before the Cabildo.

Faced by such an overwhelming display of armed strength and with nothing to oppose it, the viceroy and town council surrendered their powers to a criollo junta. Although the junta was to rule in the name of the Spanish crown it soon became apparent that they intended transforming Argentina into an independent nation.

Argentina's economy developed rapidly after independence from Spain was attained and controls on international trade released. Paintings in the various museums and galleries of Buenos Aires depict the growth of the city in these early years. In 1833, on the voyage of the *HMS Beagle*, Charles Darwin visited Buenos Aires and found it to be an agreeable city of 60,000 inhabitants. He wrote:

The city of Buenos Ayres is large; and I should think one of the most regular in the world. Every street is at right angles to the one it crosses, and the parallel ones being equidistant, the houses are collected into solid square[s] of equal dimensions, which are called quadras. On the other hand the houses themselves are hollow squares; all the rooms opening into a neat little courtyard. They are generally only one story high, with flat roofs, which are fitted with seats, and are much frequented by the inhabitants in summer. In the centre of the town is the Plaza, where the public offices, fortress, cathedral, &c., stand. Here also, the old viceroys, before the revolution, had their palaces. The general assemblage of buildings possesses considerable architectural beauty, although none individually can boast of any.

Although the Plaza de Mayo was still a muddy courtyard at the time of Darwin's visit it already boasted one of the city's most impressive buildings. This was the **Metropolitan Cathedral**, a monumental building with a neo-classical facade. The first church in Buenos Aires stood at this site, built in 1585 and consecrated as a cathedral in 1622. Work on the present building began in the late 18th century but was not completed until 1827.

Today the cathedral houses the regimental flags and banners captured in various wars and battles by Argentine troops. General San Martín, the patron saint of Argentina's independence wars, is entombed in the Cathedral. Guards in the uniforms of the *Granaderos a Caballo* (mounted grenadiers), a regiment created by San Martín in 1813, stand watch over his resting place.

La Belle Epoque

Downtown Buenos Aires started to take on its present appearance in the 1880s. Until then it had been a flat city with few buildings over two storeys high. In 1883 plans were laid to open a wide avenue leading towards the west. By 1894 the **Avenida de Mayo** was finished and within 15 years was lined with most of the impressive facades you see today.

Beginning at the Plaza de Mayo, the first building of interest is the **Casa Rosada**, on the east side of the plaza. The palace was once an annexe to the old fort, long since removed. The Casa Rosada dates from 1894 when the offices of the president were merged with the adjoining Customs and Post Buildings. The palace contains the offices of the president and takes its name from its distinctive reddish-orange colour.

Anti-clockwise from the Casa Rosada is the Banco de la Nación Argentina. Across the Diagonal Norte from the Metropolitan Cathedral is the Municipal Executive Building which was built in 1902 and houses the mayor's office and city council offices.

The next building of historic importance is the distinctive **Cabildo** on the west side of the plaza. This was the town hall during the Spanish rule, and when independence was attained the first Argentine government was set up here. Today it houses the City Museum. The present building dates from 1751 and originally had five arches on either side. When redevelopment of the city was begun in the 1880s three archways on either side were demolished to allow the construction of the diagonal roads leading from the plaza towards the south-west and north-west.

The Avenida de Mayo starts at the Plaza de Mayo and ends at the Plaza de los Dos Congresos (Plaza of the Two Congresses). The construction boom along Avenida de Mayo had, by the first few years of the century, produced buildings with the then unheard of height of five storeys. In a few years this street housed Buenos Aires' most respected hotels, theatres, newspapers, shops and cafeterías.

It is an era remembered as the 'belle epoque' of Buenos Aires. This was a few decades of prosperity for the middle and upper classes from which it was optimistically, and perhaps not unrealistically, presumed Argentina would reach even greater heights. The British author, John Foster Fraser, was so impressed that he wrote that any visitor familiar with the other countries of Latin America, would have to to blink and rub their eyes with wonder on seeing the civilised appearance of Buenos Aires.

A walk up the Avenida de Mayo begins at the Municipal Executive Building on the Plaza de Mayo. Next door is a French-style edifice which was once the home of *La Prensa*, which is still one of the city's major daily newspapers. A few blocks up is the famous **Cafe Tortoni** at Avenida de Mayo 829. The imposing facade of the Castelar Hotel is at 1522. The Chile Hotel is at the corner of Avenida de Mayo and Santiago del Estero.

Across Santiago del Estero is a building which was once one of Buenos Aire's finest hotels and which now houses part of the Internal Revenue Service. On the other side of the Avenida is the monumental 19-storey **Palacio Barolo** (Barolo Palace), built in 1923. The first subway line was built under the avenue, from Plaza de Mayo to Primera Junta, and was opened in 1913.

At the end of the Avenida de Mayo is a series of small plazas known as the **Plaza de los Dos Congresos**. The name of the plaza refers to the two assemblies (one in Buenos Aires in 1810 and the other in Tucumán in 1816) which led to Argentina's independence. Each has a monument or statue, but the most bizarre is the Monument of the Two Congresses, a cacophony of architectural extravagance featuring dancing cherubs and winged horses, built to commemorate the 150th anniversary of the Tucumán Congress.

Political graffiti of all persuasions is daubed across the monument. Drunks slumber on the granite steps which symbolise the Andes Mountains. Spouting streams of water represent the main rivers of the plains. Equally bizarre is the Congress Building itself, which was completed in 1906 and features Corinthian columns and some of the finest ornamental Italian pastry work in the city.

Had you visited Buenos Aires between 1869 and 1962 your main means of transport would have been the **tramway**. The first line, with horse-drawn carriages, ran from the Plaza de Mayo to the Congress Building. In the 19th century, when the city had few paved roads and barely any public transport, the tram business boomed. Several companies were set up to exploit the trade and by 1870 the city had 12 km of line and about 40 carriages.

By 1900 both had increased ten-fold, and electrification allowed further expansion. The trams improved transport so much that they allowed several new suburbs to develop between Buenos Aires and what were then independent towns of La Boca, Flores, Chacarita and Belgrano. Today, the only reminders of this era are a few tram tracks embedded in the pavement. A tourist tram runs on weekends from the corner of Emilio Mitre and Directorio, in Caballito (the A and E subway line will get you there).

1955 Rebellion

Lolling around the Congress Building or lounging on the bench seats of the Plaza de Mayo, it's hard to imagine that Buenos Aires has been anything but tranquil and prosperous. It is especially hard to imagine that, within living memory, bombs have been dropped on the Casa Rosada and hundreds of people slain in the streets. The bloodiest military coup in Argentine history was acted out in 1955, using downtown Buenos Aires as a stage.

On 16 June 1955 a navy rebellion erupted which intended to kill President Juan Perón and overthrow his government. Light bombers and Catalina flying-boats swooped down over Avenida Alem and dropped their bombs on the Casa Rosada. Marines attacked the War Ministry and planes strafed the Avenida de Mayo and the Congress Building.

By late afternoon the army had crushed the uprising, but over 300 civilians had been killed and over 600 wounded. By early evening, inspired by revenge and Perón's anti-clerical campaign, people had began ransacking and setting fire to a dozen churches in the downtown area. The Communists, the Freemasons, the police, the unions, government employees, the Peronists and even the Catholics themselves were variously blamed for sacking the churches.

For a different sort of spectacle, make your way from the Congress Building back to Libertad, turn left and walk to the junction with Tucumán. Overlooking the Plaza Lavalle is the **Colón Theatre**, the most grandiose Italian-style building in the city.

The original Colón Theatre was built in 1857 and stood by the Casa Rosada in the Plaza de Mayo, on what is now the site of the Banco de la Nación. In 1888 plans were laid for the present building, although it was not completed until 1908. Three architects supervised the work, the first of whom did not survive to see the finished masterpiece.

The focus of Buenos Aires eventually shifted away from Avenida de Mayo to Corrientes, Córdoba, Santa Fe, Florida and Lavalle. Today this is the 'downtown' area of Buenos Aires, where the main offices and shopping areas, such as the Florida and Lavalle malls, are located. Buskers provide some of the best entertainment in Buenos Aires – just take a night-time stroll up the Florida and Lavalle pedestrian malls.

La Boca

By the turn of the century the area to the south of San Telmo, La Boca, developed as a strongly Italian area, as did the Barracas district. The English and Germans took to Hurlingham and Belgrano. The Jews congregated north and west of Corrientes and Callao avenues. In the ports north of the Plaza de Mayo there were large numbers of Syrians. However, these districts were never as distinct as, for example, New York's Puerto Rican or black districts. Today La Boca, centred on the **Plaza de Solís**, is a sharp contrast to the wealthy Recoleta and Palermo districts northwest of downtown.

Until the middle of last century La Boca was mainly farm land. Small ships used to shelter on the **Riachuelo**, a small waterway that flows into the Río de la Plata. As the port of Buenos Aires expanded, warehouses and meat-salting plants were built along the Riachuelo. Genoese sailors and their families settled there, some in their own houses and others in tenement blocks. The tattered houses you see today, made of corrugated iron and supported by piles, are the originals.

The monotony is broken by the gaudily-coloured *cantinas* of **Necochea**, where these days you can scratch your head at the peculiar sight of middle-class porteños and tourists dancing to bad cabaret tunes pumped out by Hammond organs and toy drums.

Nearby, the **Caminito** (little street) has an artist's market and brightly painted timber and corrugated iron pop-art houses. The paintings depict local architecture and that distinctly Argentine dance, the tango. The tango is supposed to have originated in the bars which once stood around Caminito.

La Recoleta

La Recoleta takes its name from the monastic order which founded the Basilica of Our Lady of Pilar, and the adjoining convent which now houses the Buenos Aires Cultural Centre. Next door is the Cementerio del Norte which contains the tomb of Eva Perón. The Recoleta developed as an upper-class suburb after 1870 when the Southern Quarter and the San Telmo districts, the original home of the elite, were deemed unhealthy because of malaria. The upper classes gradually moved to the higher ground of the Recoleta and the surrounding area, now called the Barrio Norte.

A good place to start is the **Plaza Pellegrini**. The plaza is flanked by ostentatious buildings which now house the French and Brazilian embassies. These were built at the turn of the century and were originally private homes. The streets called Alvear (which begins at the Plaza Pellegrini) and Quintana cut through the oldest quarter of the Recoleta.

From the Plaza Pellegrini you can walk down Alvear to the Cultural Centre and the Basílica del Pilar. Today this is an area of large public buildings, like the

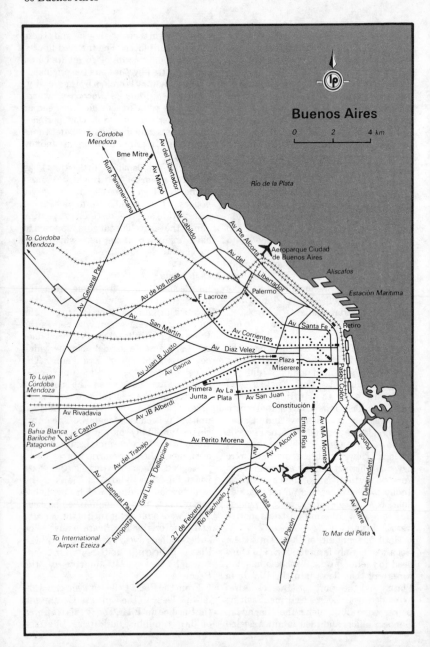

Buenos Aires

0   2   4 km

Río de la Plata

To Córdoba
Mendoza

Bme Mitre

Av del Libertador

Av Maipú

Ruta Panamericana

Av Cabildo

Av Pte Alcorta

To Córdoba
Mendoza

Av General Paz

Av del
Libertador

Aeroparque Ciudad
de Buenos Aires

Aliscafos

Estación Marítima

Av de los Incas

F Lacroze

Palermo

Av San Martín

Av
Santa Fe

Retiro

Av Corrientes

Av Díaz Velez

Av Juan B Justo

Av Gaona

Plaza
Miserere

Paseo Colón

Primera
Junta

Av La
Plata

Av San Juan

Constitución

To Lujan
Córdoba
Mendoza

Av Rivadavia

Av JB Alberdi

Entre Ríos

To Bahía Blanca
Bariloche
Patagonia

Av E Castro

Av Perito Morena

Av

Av A Alcorta

Av MA Montes

A Debenedetti

Av del Trabajo

Av General Paz

Gral Luis T Dellepiane

Autopista

27 de Febrero

Río Riachuelo

La Plata

Av Pavón

Av Mitre

Ponce

To International
Airport Ezeiza

To Mar del Plata

colonnaded University of Buenos Aires Law School and the National Fine Arts Museum, expensive shops and apartment buildings, and the exclusive **Jockey Club**.

More interesting is the neighbouring park where an arts and crafts market – with a hippie feel to it which seems curiously out of time and place – is set up on Saturdays and Sundays.

Palermo & Palermo Chico

Near the Recoleta is 'Palermo Chico' (Little Palermo), with its ostentatious buildings, many of which are now used as embassies and consulates. On the edge of Palermo Chico is the **San Martín Museum**, a replica of the house in which he lived out his exile in France.

Palermo proper is a large northern suburb of Buenos Aires, a great green patch on the map which includes the City Zoo, the Botanical Gardens, the Argentine Horsetrack and National Polo Fields.

Until 1836 Palermo was uninhabited marshland, but in that year the dictator Rosas built a house there and had the marsh drained to make way for a park and orchards. The house stood on the site of the 'Spanish Monument', a statue outside the gates of the City Zoo on Libertador. Work was abandoned on the park after Rosas was deposed in 1852. Two decades later the area was made into a public park.

The Botanical Gardens and the Zoo were added in the 1890s, and the area became a playground for the wealthy. Just before WW I, John Foster Fraser gasped at the thousands of expensive cars in Palermo, and concluded that Argentine life was one of ostentation where 'appearances count for everything'. Not a great deal has changed since.

Museo Histórico Nacional

The San Telmo district offers an opportunity to piece together the Buenos Aires jigsaw. This is the Museo Histórico Nacional at Defensa 1600. Room by room,

the museum unfolds the story of Argentina and Buenos Aires since the coming of the Europeans. It's open Tuesdays to Fridays and on Sundays from 3 to 7 pm.

The first room of the museum is called the 'Conquest' room. Paintings depict scenes in the Spanish conquest of the Americas, including the murder of the conquistador Pizarro, and the arrival of Columbus at the royal court of Spain after returning from his first voyage across the Atlantic. An interesting piece is a map of the original settlement of Buenos Aires drawn by Juan de Garay, the second founder of the city.

Also interesting are the rooms devoted to the main characters of the independence movement. The slender, almost anorexic, figure of the Venezuelan-born Simon Bolívar peers down from the wall as if he finds his full ceremonial uniform a touch claustrophobic. The obese Sarmiento makes a startling contrast to the iron-headed Rosas. The sturdy face of San Martín in his prime contrasts sharply with his feeble appearance in later life.

Early paintings and illustrations depict life in Buenos Aires during the 19th century, including satirical cartoons on the comic possibilities of the enormous bone hair-pieces fashionable among women at the time. Other pictures ridicule the British invasion of 1807.

Other Museums

The **City Museum** on the 1st floor at Alsina 412, San Telmo, has exhibitions on life in Buenos Aires. It's open daily from 11 am to 7 pm, except on Saturdays when it's open 2 to 8 pm.

The **Colón Theatre** at Tucumán 1161 has a museum displaying costumes, musical instruments, photos and other para-phenalia related to the performers who have trod its boards. It's open Monday to Friday from 10 am to 6 pm.

The **Creole Museum 'de los Corrales'** at Avenida de los Corrales 6476, has an exhibition of artefacts from daily life on the estancias of the pampas.

The **National Historical Museum of the Cabildo & May Revolution** is at Bolivar 65 and is housed in the old Cabildo (Town Hall) which faces the Plaza de Mayo. Artefacts and pictures relating to the independence movement are displayed here. It's open Thursday to Sunday from 2 to 6 pm.

The **Historical Museum of Dress & Uniforms** at Chile 832 is a museum of military and civilian dress from colonial days until the present. It's open on Sunday afternoons.

The **Historical Museum of Buenos Aires** is at Republiquetas 6309, in Saavedra, and has an exhibition on life during the colonial period and in the first decades after independence. It's open Tuesday to Sunday from 2 to 6 pm.

The **Sarmiento Historical Museum** is at Cuba 2079, in Belgrano. The National Congress and the offices of the Argentine president were once in this building. The museum contains documents and personal belongings of Domingo Sarmiento, one of Argentina's progressive presidents of the 19th century. It's open Wednesday to Friday from 2.30 to 7 pm, and on Saturdays, Sundays and holidays from 3 to 7 pm.

The **Museum of the National San Martín Institute** is at the junction of Mariscal Ramón Castilla and Aguado, in the Palermo Chico district. The museum is a replica of the house in which San Martín lived while in exile in Boulogne-sur-Mer in France. It's open Monday to Friday from 9 am to 12 noon and 2 to 5 pm, and on Saturday and Sunday 2 to 5 pm.

The **Mitre Museum** at San Martín 336 is in the house of the 19th century Argentine president and soldier, Bartolomé Mitre. It's open Tuesday to Friday from 1 to 6 pm.

The **Government House Museum**, at Balcarce 24, is housed in what once used to be the Buenos Aires Customs House. Sections of the fort which once stood there are included in the building's construction. The museum houses documents and personal effects of past Argentine presidents. At the time of writing this museum was closed.

Art Galleries

The **Enrique Larreta Municipal Museum of Spanish Art** at Juramento 22291, Belgrano, houses the private collection of the Argentine writer Enrique Larreta. It's open daily from 3 to 7.45 pm, except Thursdays when it's closed.

The **Isaac Fernández Blanco Museum of Spanish-American Art** at Suipacha 1422, has one of the largest collections of colonial art in Buenos Aires. It's open Tuesdays to Sundays from 3 to 8 pm.

The **Museum of Modern Art** is on the 9th floor, Corrientes 1530. Its collection includes works by Renoir, Dali and Picasso. It's open Tuesday to Sunday from 4 to 8 pm.

The **Eduardo Sívori Art Museum** at Junin 1930 (in the Buenos Aires Cultural Centre in La Recoleta district) houses works by Argentine artists, including contemporary and 19th century works. It's open daily.

The **José Hernández Museum of Popular Motifs** at Libertador 2373, has a large collection of Argentine folk art, including Indian, gaucho and colonial artefacts. It's open Monday Friday from 10 am to 8 pm, and Saturday and Sunday from 4 to 8 pm.

The **Museum of Oriental & Decorative Art** at Libertador 1902 is in the same building as the **Decorative Art Museum**. The first houses collections of paintings, porcelain, furniture and other bric-a-brac. It's open Wednesday to Monday from 3 to 7 pm.

The **Boca Museum of Fine Arts** at Pedro de Mendoza 1935, in La Boca, has a collection of contemporary Argentine painting. It's open Wednesday to Friday from 8 am to 6 pm, Saturday from 8 am to 12 noon and 2 to 6 pm, and Sunday from 10 am to 6 pm.

The **National Museum of Fine Arts**, at Libertador 1473, is mainly devoted to Argentine painters of the 19th and 20th centuries, though it also has a number of works by foreign painters. The collection includes works by Van Gogh, Monet,

Renoir, Picasso and Rodin. It's open Tuesday to Sunday from 9 am to 12.45 pm and 3 to 7 pm.

Religious Art

The **San Roque Museum of the Basilica of Saint Francis** at Alsina 340, in the Southern Quarter, has a small museum of old and new religious art from Argentina, Brazil and Peru.

The **Basilica of the Rosary Museum** at Defensa 422, in San Telmo, is housed in the Santo Domingo church. British and Spanish regimental flags, captured during the independence wars, are on display. It's open daily from 9 am to 1 pm and from 4.30 to 8.30 pm.

Places to Stay

Buenos Aires has a considerable range of accommodation. Even some of the bottom-end places can be great sprawling affairs, with spacious rooms, wide stairways and decorated ceilings which provide a faint reminder of a more glamorous past. There are many fine mid-range hotels, and a selection of up-market hotels which are the equal of anything you'll find in Europe or North America. Some hotels have an additional service charge (*laudo*) and tax. Hotels with red-green lights or marked *Albergue Transitorio* are hotels for couples where you pay by the hour.

Places to Stay - bottom end

Although there is still a fair selection of lower-budget hotels to choose from, real shoestring accommodation is hard to come by in Buenos Aires. Cheap hotel rooms start at around US$5 per person per night. There are a number of hotels in the central city area which are cheap and conveniently located:

The *Hotel O'Rei* at Lavalle 733 has rooms without private bathroom from about US$3 per person. More expensive rooms have private bathrooms. It's clean and centrally located but it's often full.

The *Acapulco Hotel* (tel 3931381) at Lavalle 472 has some spacious rooms with large double beds, as well as dark, dingy, windowless rooms. Whether or not you like this place will largely depend on which room you get. Although it was fairly run-down and the rooms quite bare and sterile, it was being renovated at the time of writing. Rooms without private bathroom are US$4 a single and US$6 a double. Doubles with private bathroom are US$10.

One of the best is the centrally-located *Florida House* at Florida 527, on the Florida pedestrian mall. Although still a respectable place it was obviously a very fine hotel in its early days. Singles and doubles without private bathroom start from US$8. These tend to be quite small, but there are more spacious double and triple rooms with private bathrooms. Try to avoid the front rooms as these get a *lot* of noise from the Florida mall. There are some hobbit-holes available in an upstairs annexe for US$6 per person.

The *Phoenix Hotel* (tel 3124845) at San Martín 780 is a rambling building of several storeys built around two courtyards. Rooms without private bathroom are US$4 a single and US$6 a double. Rooms with private bathroom are US$5 a single and US$7 a double. Larger rooms are very spacious with ceiling fans. Some of the smaller rooms tend to be a bit gloomy. Nevertheless, it's clean, centrally-located and good value.

The *Hotel Central Córdoba* (tel 3111175) at San Martín 1021/23 is only four or five blocks from the bus terminal and one block from Florida. It's a good, clean place and there are laundry facilities on the roof. Rooms are moderately priced. Spartan singles are US$7. Rooms with private bathroom are US$10 a single and US$14 a double.

The *Hotel Apolo* (tel 3936970) is at Tucumán 951 near the corner with Pellegrini. It's rather run-down and mouldy, although rooms at the rear should be quiet. Some people might find it rather dark and gloomy, but if you can find nothing else then give it a try. Rooms without private bathroom are US$6 a single and US$7 a double. Rooms with private bathroom are US$8 a single and US$10 a double.

Also try the *Petit Hotel Goya* on Suipacha, between Viamonte and Córdoba. Rooms without private bathroom are US$3 a single and US$4 a double. Rooms with private bathroom are slightly more expensive.

The *Avenida* (tel 345664) at Avenida de Mayo 623, near the corner with Florida, is *very* spartan but clean. Rooms at the rear should be quiet. Rooms without private bathroom are US$5 a single and US$7 a double. Rooms with private bathroom are a dollar or two more.

Nearby, the one-star *Hotel Turista*, (tel 3312281) at Avenida de Mayo 686, has singles for US$9 and doubles for US$12, both with private bathroom.

Places to Stay - middle

Buenos Aires offers plenty of mid-range accommodation.

Basic mid-range hotels include the *King's Hotel* (tel 3928161) at Corrientes 623 near the corner with Florida. Doubles with private bathroom are US$16.

Worth trying is the *Hotel Waldorf* (tel 3122071) at Paraguay 450, near the corner with Reconquista, which has singles from US$12 and doubles from US$15.

The *Plaza Roma* (tel 3111679) at Lavalle 110, just down from Alem, has singles from US$17 and doubles from US$21, both with private bathroom.

The *Regis* (tel 3935131) at Lavalle 813, near the corner with Esmeralda, has rooms with private bathrooms, air-conditioning and television.

The *Diplomat* at San Martín 918 has rooms with private bathroom for US$15 a single and US$17 a double.

The *Tucumán Palace Hotel* (tel 3112298) at Tucumán 384 has singles for US$17 and doubles for US$21.

Moving slightly up-market there are a number of hotels with single rooms for US$22 and US$27 and doubles for US$27

to US$39. These include the *San Antonio* at Paraguay 372; the *Liberty* (tel 460261) at Corrientes 628; the *Italia Romanelli* (tel 3126361) at Reconquista 647; the *Gran Hotel Argentino* (tel 353071) at Pellegrini 37; the *Orly* at Paraguay 474; the *Camino Real* at Maipú 572; and the *Gran Dora* (tel 3127391) at Maipú 963.

Places to Stay - top end

Top end hotels start with single rooms from US$40 to US$50 and doubles from around US$50 to US$60. These include the *Colón* at Pellegrini 507; the *Regidor* at Tucumán 451; the *Lancaster* (tel 3124161) at Córdoba 405; the *Gran Buenos Aires* at Alvear 767; and the *Principado* at Paraguay 481.

There are a number of up-market hotels with single rooms for US$60 and doubles for around US$70. These include *El Conquistador* (tel 3133152) at Suipacha 948; the *Regente Palace* (tel 3136628) at Suipacha 964; the *Elevage* (tel 3132082) at Maipú 960; and the *Grand Hotel* (tel 353071) at Tucumán 570.

For some architectural elegance try the *Alvear Palace Hotel* (tel 8044031) at Alvear 1891. If the rooms match the sumptuousness of the foyer and ground floor shopping arcades and dining halls, then this is definitely the place to sample something of the wealth and splendour of up-market Buenos Aires. Singles start from US$90 and doubles from US$120. All rooms have private bathroom, air conditioning, colour television and telephone.

Other up-market hotels include the *Libertador* (tel 3922095) at the corner of Córdoba and Maipú which has doubles from US$115. The *Sheraton* (tel 3116330) at San Martín 1225, opposite Retiro Station, has singles from US$136 and doubles from US$160. The *Plaza* (tel 3115011) at Florida 1005 has singles from US$105 and doubles from US$120. The *Claridge* at Tucumán 535 has singles from US$97 and doubles from US$109.

You can rent serviced apartments and short-term lease flats in Buenos Aires.

A number of agencies which handle these are listed in the guide called *Where in Buenos Aires*, available free from the tourist office.

Places to Eat

It goes without saying that there are a formidable number of restaurants in Buenos Aires, from dingy hash-houses and greasy-spoons to huge grill-houses dishing up giant slabs of beef. The following is a gastronomic pot-pourri of restaurants in Buenos Aires, though it barely scratches the surface.

For more possibilities peruse the advertisements in the pages of the English-language *Buenos Aires Herald* and its regular four-page 'Good Living' supplement. The English/Spanish tourist newspaper the *Buenos Aires Times* is also worth looking through. The free guide booklet from the national Tourist Office, *Where in Buenos Aires*, lists restaurants of many different cuisines and price brackets.

For cheap eats it's not really worth singling out any particular place. The streets around Retiro Station and around Avenida San Martín downtown have many small restaurants, as do the San Telmo and La Boca districts.

At up-market restaurants American Express, Diners Club, London Card, Mastercard and Visa credit cards are useful.

Parrillada The place to start is, of course, with meat. An Australian bumper-sticker would apply equally well to Argentina: 'This is cattle country, so eat beef you bastards!' There are over 50 million head of cattle in Argentina and about eight million are slaughtered annually for human consumption. The common practice is to grill the carcass over coals then carve it up into thick, juicy slabs. It is said that the finest Argentine steak needs no knife and can be carved with a fork.

Visitor and cow usually confront each other in a *parrillada* or grill house, from the word *parrilla* which means 'grill'. In Buenos Aires these are such extravagant affairs, some seating hundreds of people at a time, that it's easy to think of yourself being processed through in much the same way as the meat.

La Cabaña at Entre Ríos 436 tends to be recommended by gourmets, and is favoured for the steak of young calves.

Las Nazarenas at Reconquista 1132 is a stone's throw from the Sheraton Hotel and popular with foreign visitors. It's a genial place although relatively expensive.

La Estancia at Lavalle 941 is a lively place and is popular with both locals and foreigners. The servings are huge, the waiters are amiable and it's a relaxed place to eat if you're on your own. I'd particularly recommend it for lunch.

La Chacra at Córdoba 941 is a huge place with a very extensive menu in Spanish, English and German. Despite the stylish surroundings two people can stuff themselves here for about US$10, and the gluttonous can feast on 12 mm thick slabs of beef which threaten to crack the plate under their weight.

La Rural at Suipacha 453 is probably more pleasant than *La Chacra* if you're on your own and the atmosphere is less *en masse* than at *La Estancia*. The food is, however, rather more expensive.

La Posta del Gaucho at Pellegrini 625 is surprisingly plain, but it's a lively place for lunch.

Apart from these established names there are lots of cheaper grill houses where you can get a hunk of meat with side-servings for a few dollars. They're really just eat-and-run places, not for lingering in. Typical of these would be the oddly named *La Jirafe Azul* (The Blue Giraffe) at Tucumán 732 which definitely does not serve up exotic African animals. Similar is the *Parrilla La Posada de Lavalle* at Lavalle 889, which is probably the better of the two.

Typical bottom-end places include the *Restaurant Parrilla Salmon* which is a hole-in-the-wall at Reconquista 968 serving meat and seafood dishes. It's easy to find similar places. They're worth investigating, not only because they're conducive to lingering but the staff are often quite chatty when they're not run off their feet.

Café Society The corner-stone of Argentine gastronomy is not so much the restaurants but the cafés. In Argentina you get the impression that eating is done less for its own sake than for the social occasion it entails. The dry, hot climate of the north allows the restaurants and cafés to spill out onto the footpaths, where the fine art of conversation is developed over the evening meal and washed down with endless glasses of wine and cups of coffee.

It sounds clichéd but to label Argentina, or at least that part of the Argentine population which can afford to indulge itself, a 'café society' does tally up with personal observation. In his book *Portrait of an Exile*, the Anglo-Argentine journalist Andrew Graham-Yooll speaks of café culture in Buenos Aires as not only a social inevitability, but an essential part of political and commercial enterprise.

The *Café Tortoni* at Avenida de Mayo 829, still has something of that character. Founded in 1858, this is one of the few to have preserved the outward appearance of grace and charm, if only in terms of architecture and decor. You can still shoot pool and dice, and there are jazz shows on weekends. Like Buenos Aires it tends to live on past glories as a place where the famous and even the infamous passed their free time. Tourist leaflets allude to the 'odd conspirator or two' concocting plans and fermenting revolution over cups of coffee. Such images are not entirely untrue.

Amongst the former clientele of the Tortoni was Mario Roberto Santucho who came here to indulge in games of chess. He was chief of the leftist People's Revolutionary Army until he was killed in a gun battle in 1976.

Other cafés of a similar vein include the 80 year-old *Del Molino* on the corner of Rivadavia Ave and Callao Ave, across the road from the Congress Building. The name comes from the windmill-like ornamentation on the exterior.

Other cafés and tea rooms of note include: the *Florida Garden* at Florida 899; *La Paz* at Corrientes 1599; *Bar Baro* at Tres Sargentos 451; the *Bidou Bar* at Perú 271, which is a reconstruction of a turn of the century café; *Five O'Clock* at Alvear 1719, which is an afternoon tea-room; and *La Giralda* at Corrientes 1457, and *Los Angelitos* at the corner of Rincón and Rivadavia, both of which retain their old-style appearance. Those in the Recoleta district include: the *Café de la Paix* at Quintana 595; *La Biela* at Quintana 600, and one of the most popular in La Recoleta; and *La Rambla* at Posadas 1602. *Los 36 Billares* at Avenida de Maho 1271 is a billiards hall, as is the nearby *Park Lane Club* at Quintana 570.

Confiterias In downtown Buenos Aires the *confiterias*, a cross between a café and a snack bar, also cater to the Argentine propensity for talk. They can be found on almost every street corner though there's virtually nothing to distinguish one from the other except the name. The *London City Cafe* at the corner of Avenida de Mayo and Perú, just up from the Plaza de Mayo, is typical of the larger places. Others include the *Confiteria Young Men's* at Cordoba 800 and the *Confiteria La Estrella* at the corner of Maipú and Lavalle.

Thinking of the Café Tortoni I can't help but finish this section with a minor gastronomic treasure hunt. Two restaurants which may or may not reward a visit are the *Plaza Grill Room* at the Plaza Hotel at Florida 1005, and the newly reopened restaurant in *Harrod's Department Store* on the Florida mall. Like the Cafe Tortoni both are said to preserve something of the distinctive *belle epoque* of turn-of-the-century Buenos Aires, an appearance and style which has largely been lost under the rash of redevelopment and modern decor.

French European immigration to Argentina has left its mark on the restaurant scene in much the same way it has in the United States and Australia. French and Italian cuisine is the most visible European influence in Argentina, but Swiss, Swedish and English fare are also available.

The *Au Bec Fin* at Vicente López 1825 is commonly regarded as one of the best, if not the best up-market French restaurant in Buenos Aires. Although it's not a vegetarian restaurant its menu is reputed to include some of the best non-meat dishes in Buenos Aires, including *camembert en croute* which is a sort of brioche pastry filled with cheese, and *champignons farcis* which are mushroom heads filled with chopped mushroom stalks, cheese and cream.

Other French restaurants include *Catalinas* at Reconquista 875, which is rated by the gourmets as one of the top French restaurants in Buenos Aires.

There's also *Chez Moi* at San Juan 1223; *Cien Años* at Amenábar 2075, in Belgrano; *De las Carretas* at Bethlem 427 on the Plaza Dorrego in the San Telmo district; *El Gato que Pesca* at Rodríguez Peña 159; the *Estragón* at Defensa 855 in the Southern Quarter; *Friday's* at San Martín 961; and *Hippopotamus* at Junín 1787, which doubles as a formal night-club. There are many other French restaurants in the city.

Italian & Spanish To cope with the sheer number of pizzerias and pasta houses you need a catalogue, not a guidebook. For other than their size Argentine pizzas are a disappointment, though they do surpass their emaciated cousins in Italy. If you're on your own, always order pizza by the portion, since even a medium-sized pizza is enough to stuff three famished people.

Despite the huge number of Italians in Buenos Aires, gourmets bemoan the lack of 'authentic' Italian restaurants, a fault which is difficult for the amateur to discern. It might be safer simply to talk of restaurants which specialise in pasta dishes. In the downtown area you can glutton out on assorted pastas at the *Salsa Bar-Restaurant*, a typical mid-range place on Córdoba near the corner with San Martín.

Other Italian restaurants include: *Temponés* at Junín 1727, which also serves Greek lasagna; *Tommaso* at Junín 1735 in the Recoleta district; *Subito* at Paraguay 640, which is said to be excellent; and *Robertino* at Vicente López 2158, also in the Recoleta. One of the best pasta places in the city is said to be *Cicerón* at Reconquista 647 in the Hotel Italia Romanelli.

La Casa de Esteban de Luca at Defensa 1000, on the corner with Carlos Calvo, in the San Telmo district is a friendly place with live piano in the evening. There's a lively café called the *Freria* opposite the Plaza Dorrego, and several other cheap but agreeable restaurants in the vicinity of this plaza.

Spanish restaurants include: *Cantabria* at Callao 1235, which specialises in seafood; *El Hispano* at Salta 20, which also has seafood dishes; *Laurak Bat* at Belgrano 1144, which has Basque-style food; *Sardis* at Vidt 1947, in the Palermo district; *Taberna Baska* at Chile 980; *Tasca Tancat* at Paraguay 645; and *Villarosa* at Hipólito Irigoyen 1389.

Northern & Central European For Swiss fondues and flambéed brochettes try *La Petite Fondue* at Libertador 2242, and *La Cave du Valais* at Zapiola 1779.

For goulash and sauerkraut try the *ABC* at Lavalle 545, which is a German restaurant.

The *Swedish Club* on the 5th floor, Tacuarí 143, is said to serve a fine, authentic, Swedish smorgasbord. Apparently the restaurant is only open to members but they do accept foreign visitors – could be worth a try.

The *Danish Club* at 12th floor, Alem 1074, is open for lunch only.

English The *Downtown Matias* at San Martín 979 is an imitation of a British/Irish pub and is reminiscent of similar ventures in Hong Kong. Like the Hong Kong version it has something of a misfit feel to it, rather like a square British peg in a round Latin American hole. Nevertheless the *Matias* has a homely feel and serves drinks, snacks and cold food at all hours and hot food for lunch. Other places with English style food include *Alexandra* at San Martín 774, which serves curries and seafood dishes; and the *London Grill* at Reconquista 455, whose menu includes curries and Yorkshire pudding.

Vegetarian If the full houses in the city's half-dozen vegetarian fast-food restaurants are anything to go by, vegetarianism appears to be firmly established.

Most vegetarian restaurants have a lunch-time and dinner-time smorgasbord. About US$3 gets you as much as you can eat plus one dessert. The best of these is *El Jardín* which has two branches, one at Suipacha 429 and the other at Lavalle 835.

Other fast-food vegetarian restaurants include *La Huerta* at the corner of Lavalle and Suipacha; *Verde Esmeralda* at Esmeralda 370; and *Verde Lavalle* at Lavalle 542. *El Jardín* probably has the widest selection.

Other veggie restaurants include the *Años Verdes* which has two branches – one at Santa Fe 1883 and the other at Corrientes 1219. Also try the *Granix* at Florida 126 and Florida 461; and *La Esquina de las Flores* at Córdoba 1599.

Asian For Chinese food try the *Cantina China* at Maipú 976, the *Restaurant Chung Kiu* at Paraguay 725, and the *Restaurant Tuen Huang* at Suipacha 544.

Moving up-market, other Chinese restaurants include: the *Asia* at Esmeralda 768 which serves Cantonese food; the *Gran Victoria* at Suipacha 783; the *Casa China* at Viamonte 1476 which has Shanghai-style food; and the *Oriente* at Maipú 512 which is Cantonese.

The *Persepolis* at Irigoyen 991 claims to be the first Iranian restaurant not just in Argentina but in all Latin America!

The *Seul* at Junín 548 is a Korean restaurant and the food is said to be authentic.

Fast Food The local greasy spoon chain is called *Supercoop*. These are open from around 11 am to 3 pm and are amongst the cheapest places to eat in Buenos Aires. There are branches at Lavalle 2530, Sarmiento 1431, Rivadavia 5700 and at the corner of Piedras and Rivadavia. Other fast-food chains include *Pumpernics* which is a McDonald's hamburger imitation.

Entertainment – The Tango

Buenos Aires has a string of night-spots devoted to keeping alive that peculiarly Argentine musical form, the Tango. Try the *Bar Sur* at Estados Unidos 299 in the San Telmo district; the *Caño 14* at Talcahuano 975; *El Viejo Almacén* at the corner of Independencia and Balcarce, which is generally rated highly; *La Casa de Carlos Gardel* at Jean Jaures 735; the informal *Los Dos Pianitos* at the corner of Giuffra and Balcarce; the *Taconeando* at Balcarce 725 in the San Telmo district; and the *Tanguería Corrientes Angosta* at Lavalle 750.

Things to Buy

Every Sunday afternoon the San Telmo market sets up at the **Plaza Dorrego**, on the corner of Defensa and Humberto I. You can find an extraordinary array of bric-a-brac including rusty firearms, mouldy banknotes, copper pots and hand-made jewellery. The nearby antique shops are like Aladdin's cave. Decorative bombillas and maté make good souvenirs. There's live jazz above the Café Feria and a smattering of clowns and buskers in the plaza.

Getting There & Away

Just as all Italian roads lead to Rome, so all the routes in Argentina wind up in Buenos Aires. Road, rail and air connections spread out from the Argentine capital like a giant spider web and sooner or later you'll be dragged in.

Air For details of international flights see the Getting There chapter earlier in this book.

Aerolíneas Argentinas (tel 3625008) is at Perú 2 on the corner with Rivadavia. There's a branch office at the corner of Santa Fe and Esmeralda.

Austral Líneas Aéreas (tel 499011) is at the corner of San Martín and Corrientes.

LADE (Líneas Aéreas del Estado) (tel 3610853) is at Perú 710 near the corner with Chile.

Buenos Aires is well connected by air to all parts of the country. For example, Aerolíneas has daily flights from Buenos Aires to Mendoza, Córdoba, Bariloche, Jujuy, Salta, Tucumán, Puerto Iguazú, Comodoro Rivadavia, Ushuaia, Río Gallegos and Río Grande. They have weekly flights to Resistencia, four days a week to Corrientes, and two days a week to Posadas.

Bus Almost all long-distance buses leave from the *Estación Terminal de Omnibus* which is at the junction of Ramos Mejia and Los Immigrantes near Retiro Train Station. To get there take subway Line C to Retiro Station and then walk the few hundred metres to the bus station.

From there you can get buses to almost everywhere in Argentina as well as to Uruguay, Paraguay, Brazil and Chile. Since there are so many companies and routes the information below is only meant to give you an idea of what's available.

Typical fares from Buenos Aires on domestic routes are:

Bariloche	US$40
Comodoro Rivadavia	US$40
Córdoba	US$14
Mar del Plata	US$9
Mendoza	US$22
Posadas	US$20
Puerto Iguazú	US$27
Puerto Madryn	US$29
Resistencia	US$16

La Estrella has daily buses to Bariloche.

TAC (Transportes Automotores Chevalier) have daily buses to Bariloche, Neuquén, Junín de los Andes and Mendoza.

La Estrella has daily buses to Puerto Madryn, Trelew, Rawson and Comodoro Rivadavia.

Also try Costera Criolla. From Comodoro Rivadavia you can catch connecting buses to southern Patagonia and from there carry on to Tierra del Fuego.

El Condor has over a dozen departures a day for Mar del Plata. Also try Micro Mar, Costera Criolla and Empresa Argentina. The trip takes about 5½ hours.

La Internacional Godoy has daily buses to Reconquista, Resistencia, Santa Fe, Formosa and Clorinda. Also try Empresa Central, El Rapido and General Urquiza.

Expreso Tigre Iguazú has daily buses to Puerto Iguazú. There are direct buses to Santiago in Chile.

Fenix Pullman Norte has buses twice a week with connections to Viña del Mar and Valparaíso.

TAC has daily buses to Santiago with connections to Viña del Mar and Valparaíso.

Expreso Gral Urquiza and Brazil Pluma have daily buses to São Paulo and Río de Janeiro in Brazil.

ONDA Buses de la Carrera has daily buses to Montevideo in Uruguay. The trip takes about eight hours.

Buquebus is at Suipacha 776 downtown and has daily buses to Montevideo.

Full details of transport between Argentina and Uruguay are in the Getting There chapter of this book.

Train The Railways Information & Booking Office (tel 3116411) is in the Galerias Pacifico at Florida 729. It's open Monday to Friday from 7 am to 9 pm and Saturday from 7 am to 1 pm. All trains leaving Buenos Aires can be booked here. You can also pick up copies of national train timetables and fare lists.

There are three national train stations in Buenos Aires. The routes they serve are:

Plaza Constitución for trains to Neuquén, Zapala, Bariloche, Mar del Plata, Miramar, Quequén, Olavarria, Bahia Blanca and San Antonio Oeste.

Lacroze for trains to Paraná, Concordia, Los Libres, Corrientes and Posadas.

Retiro for trains to Rosario, Santa Fe, La Banda, Tucumán, Villa Mercedes, Dolores, San Rafael and Córdoba.

Some examples of timetables and fares on major routes follow:

There are daily trains from Retiro to Tucumán. Fares are: coche cama US$40; pullman US$30; primera US$16; turista US$12. The trip takes about 20 to 21 hours, depending on the train.

There are daily trains from Lacroze to Posadas. Fares are: coche cama US$35; pullman US$27; primera US$15; and turista US$11. The trip takes 20 hours. From Posadas you can take a bus to Puerto Iguazú near the Iguazu Falls, or take a ferry across the Río Paraná to Encarnación in Paraguay.

There are daily trains from Plaza Constitución to Bariloche, Neuquén and Zapala. Fares to Bariloche are: coche cama US$66; pullman US$46; primera US$30; and turista US$23. The trip to Bariloche takes about 32 hours.

Boat Passenger and cargo ship schedules are listed daily in the *Buenos Aires Herald*. The pier at which each ship is docked is also listed. If you want to try your luck this is a good place to start. There are regular ferries from Buenos Aires to Montevideo; for details see the Getting There chapter of this book.

Getting Around

Getting around downtown Buenos Aires is easy enough. Walking will often suffice, and if not then most of that area can be covered by taxi and by short subway and bus rides. For anyone who doesn't live in Buenos Aires, getting beyond the downtown area to anywhere except the terminus of the subway lines requires a concerted plan of attack.

Airport Transport There are separate international and domestic airports in Buenos Aires.

The international airport is at Ezeiza, 35 km from the centre of the city. The best way to get to the airport from downtown is with the Servicio Diferencial coach Number 86 with the 'Aeropuerto' sign in the front window. This leaves from Avenida de Mayo on the block between Perú and Chacabuco, heading towards the National Congress building. The ride from downtown to the airport takes about 1¼ to 1½ hours.

Returning to the city the bus travels down Hipólito Irigoyen to the Plaza de Mayo. From downtown to the airport the bus runs between about 6 am and 10.15 pm on Monday to Friday, 6.30 am to 10.15 pm on Saturday, and 10 am to 10.30 pm Sunday. There are departures about every 20 minutes or half hour. The fare is about US$1.30

Remise taxis from Ezeiza Airport to the city centre cost about US$17 and take about 45 minutes. Buy a ticket before you leave the terminal at the Manuel Tienda León counter. There is also a taxi rank outside the Arrival Terminal where you can catch metered taxis into the city centre; these cost around US$10.

The airport for domestic flights is known as Aeroparque and is about four km from the city centre. This airport handles domestic flights and also those for Montevideo as well as some flights to Asunción, Santiago, Río de Janeiro and São Paulo, and Santa Cruz in Bolivia.

To get there take local bus No 33 from the Plaza Canada opposite the Ferrocarril General Belgrano, which is the train station next to Retiro. It's a 15 minute trip to Aeroparque and the bus drops you right outside the terminal building.

Coming back from Aeroparque, the No 33 bus stop is outside the airline booking office, next to the terminal building. There are two types of No 33 buses available from Aeroparque. The first has the sign 'BARRACAS' in the window and goes from Aeroparque to Retiro, Correo Central, Casa de Gobierno, Ministeros, Hospital Argerich, La Boca and onwards. The other bus has the sign 'DOCK SUD' and goes from Aeroparque to Retiro, Correo Central, Plaza de Mayo, Ministeros, Hospital Argerich and Dock Sud. Taxis from Aeroparque leave from outside the terminal building.

Train The Buenos Aires subway system actually predates many European subway systems. Old and rickety as it may appear this is a fast and efficient way of getting around the city and preferable to trying to decipher the bus routes.

The subway has five lines (*Linea A, B, C, D & E*) which link the downtown area to the suburbs. Several lines terminate at major national railway stations. This

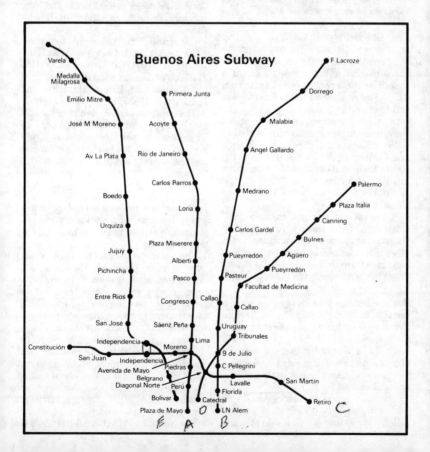

makes it easy to get to trains leaving Buenos Aires. The lines and destinations are:

Line A runs under Rivadavia from the Plaza de Mayo to Primera Junta. There are plans to extend this line from Primera Junta to Plaza Flores.

Line B runs under Corrientes from the Central Post Office on Alem to Lacroze Station. There are plans to extend this line.

Line C runs from the Plaza Constitución to Retiro Station and links all the other lines.

Line D runs from the Plaza de Mayo to Palermo via the North Diagonal, Córdoba and Santa Fe.

Line E runs from near the Plaza de Mayo to Varela via Moreno and San Juan.

The fare is about US$0.10 per trip regardless of distance. You buy tokens for the turnstiles at kiosks on each station. For convenience buy a few tokens at a time. The lines are open from 5 am to 1 am daily. You're allowed to take backpacks and bags on the trains.

In the downtown area the most convenient metro stations are located as follows: *Florida* is at the corner of Florida and Corrientes; *Retiro* terminates in the Retiro Train Station; *San Martín* is at the junction of Santa Fe and Maipú; and *Lavalle* is at the corner of Lavalle and Esmeralda.

Some subway stations are only 'half' stations. At these stations you can get on trains going in one direction but not in the other. For example, at Alberdi station you can catch trains heading towards Primera Junta but not towards the Plaza de Mayo.

Bus The Buenos Aires bus system is like a secret code and you'll probably have to live in the city for six months to crack it. Even if you do find the right bus it will probably be so crowded that you won't be able to see where you're going, and even if you can you'll soon be lost in the maze of unfamiliar streets.

The main guide to Buenos Aires' rust bucket buses is a pocket-sized booklet called *Guia Peuser* which is sold at many magazine kiosks. It's accompanied by a fold-out map of the city. The index of street names and map references allows you to pin-point your destination. About 190 bus routes are described. The number of the bus is never a good guide to its destination. You must look for signs in the window which state the final destination, as several buses of the same number will go to different places. Taxis are a fairly cheap alternative to struggling with the buses and you should use them, and the subway, as much as possible.

Car All the major international and local car hire firms have offices in Buenos Aires.

Car rental firms include: Automotores Sena (tel 3940522) at Maipu 867; A1 Rent-a-Car (tel 3110247) at Alvear 678; Avis (tel 3113899) at the Sheraton Hotel; National (tel 3113583) at Esmeralda 1084; and Hertz (tel 3116832) at Esmeralda 985.

The cheapest cars are usually Fiat 147s for US$18 per day plus US$0.25 per km. There are cheaper rates available if you hire by the week. For full details of car hire see the Getting Around chapter of this book.

Taxis Buenos Aires taxis have black bodies and yellow tops, with a luminous sign on the roof. When the red meter flag is up the taxi is for hire.

The taxi meter does not read in Australs but in units based on the time and distance covered. At the end of the trip the driver compares the meter reading to a table which lists the fare per unit. This saves having to adjust the meters to cope with constant inflation and price rises.

Fares are cheap by European or Australian standards. For example, the fare from the north end of Pellegrini to the San Telmo district will cost about US$2. There is a small additional charge for suitcases and other luggage. Drivers usually expect a small tip.

The company PIDALO SA (tel 934991)

has radio-controlled taxis which you can telephone day and night.

Tours There are several companies running tours of Buenos Aires. Try Buenos Aires Tur (tel 402304) at Lavalle 1444. They also offer three-hour city tours, half-day tours to La Plata and Tigre and night tours of Buenos Aires which include stopoffs in restaurants and night-clubs. City tours cost US$10; Tigre and La Plata are US$15 each; and the night tours vary from US$20 to US$45 depending on where you go.

Misiones & the North-East

Misiones is the small peninsula-shaped province at the north-east of Argentina. It's bordered on the west by the Río Paraná and on the east by Brazil and the Río Uruguay. At the northern tip of Misiones are the Iguazú Falls, best known as the backdrop to the film *The Mission*. The film portrayed the destruction of the Jesuit missions in the middle of the 18th century, and it is from these missions that the province takes its name. Several of the old mission stations can still be seen, one of which has been partially restored while others are overgrown ruins in the jungle.

History

When the Spanish first arrived at the Río de la Plata they saw that the local Indians wore ornaments of gold and silver, and concluded that the region must be rich in precious metals. In fact, the gold and silver had been looted from the Inca empire and had found its way downriver from what is now Paraguay. The Guaraní Indians of Paraguay had shown considerable zeal in raiding the Indian tribes on the borders of the Inca empire, and even those directly under Inca rule.

Around 1520 a band of white men joined a Guaraní raid against the Inca. Later accounts of this expedition spoke of them stumbling across a mountain kingdom ruled by a white king. The Indians of his domain were said to wear crowns of silver and gold plates hanging from their necks and ears, and strung out along their belts. Other reports spoke of Indians living along the Río Paraguay who traded gold and silver to the Guaraní in return for beads and canoes. The Spanish quickly came to believe that a southern El Dorado lay at their fingertips.

It was such reports which led to Pedro de Mendoza's great expedition to the Río de la Plata in 1536. Mendoza sent a contingent under Juan de Ayolas up the Río Paraguay to find a route to the gold-rich Indians. Ayolas ventured deep into Paraguay, left the river, crossed the Chaco, and reportedly returned with a large cargo of gold and silver to the Río Paraguay. There he and the other members of his expedition were killed by Indians.

In 1537 another expedition was sent upriver from the Río de la Plata settlement and established the city of Asunción, now the capital of Paraguay. The Spanish found the Guaraní friendly. It seems the Guaraní hoped the Spanish would support them in their raids against the Incas. From then on the Guaraní served as willing porters in all Spanish expeditions. Reports of the time speak of literally thousands of Guaraní accompanying the Spanish on their conquests, whether against the Incas or against the Indians of the Chaco.

The Guaraní were the only agricultural Indians the Spanish found in eastern Argentina who they considered to be even partially civilised. The Guaraní originally came from Brazil but had entered Paraguay

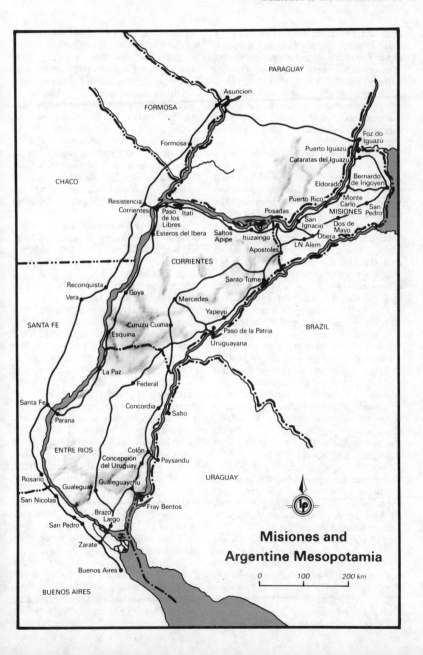

**Misiones and
Argentine Mesopotamia**

0   100   200 km

and the area around the Río Paraná. They had set up permanent settlements, growing corn, sweet potatoes, squash and manioc. They were skilled at fishing, pottery and at weaving cotton cloth. Aside from working for the Spanish as guides and porters, they also accompanied them on the expeditions which successfully established the cities of Santa Fe and Buenos Aires.

Within a few years the Spanish were firmly established in settlements around Asunción, some of them reportedly living with whole harems of Guaraní women as well as their relatives. However, the introduction of the encomienda system and forced labour eventually led to the decline of the Guaraní around Asunción. The mestizo descendants of the Spanish and Guaraní now comprise the main ethnic group in Paraguay, where the Guaraní language is still commonly spoken. Guaraní speakers can also be found in the Argentine provinces of Corrientes, the Chaco and Misiones.

Because of its relative isolation from the rest of Argentina and also because of its very different geography, vegetation and climate from the flat, open agricultural and grazing lands of the Argentine plains, Misiones lapsed into something of a wilderness after independence. Sovereignty of the region was disputed by Paraguay, Brazil and various Argentine caudillos. It was not until the 1870s and 1880s, after Argentina had consolidated itself as a nation, that much attention was paid by the central government to Misiones.

After the borders with both Brazil and the province of Corrientes were finalised, Misiones became subject to very extensive immigration in the later part of the 19th century. The Poles and Ukrainians seem to have been the earliest of the non-Spanish settlers, arriving in Misiones as early as 1890. They were followed by the Finns and Brazilian Germans, and after 1915 by the English, Swiss, Brazilians and European Germans.

Other immigrants included Swedes and Japanese although eventually Argentine immigration to the province predominated. Immigration was encouraged by land grants or by selling land very cheaply, and by co-operatives set up by the government to help overcome financial problems.

The story behind the Japanese settlement is an interesting one. Some Japanese had settled in the province early on, but the main colonisation occurred in 1959 backed by the Japanese government and a private Japanese colonisation agency. In that year a hundred Japanese families arrived in Misiones to start an agricultural colony about midway between Posadas and Puerto Iguazú.

Curiously, the Japanese made a conscious effort to abandon their Japanese customs and language. They first cultivated yerba mate, but then switched to a range of crops including corn, vegetables, tea, tobacco and rice. Others turned to lumbering and stock-raising.

Immigration and settlement in Misiones was based predominantly on agriculture. By the 1960s the province provided all of Argentina's yerba mate, and a large slice of its tobacco, citrus fruits, and cash crops such as tea and sugar cane. The north is important for its hardwood forests. Lumbering and related industries such as plywood and paper manufacturing are important. Some copper, iron ore and coal has been mined in Misiones. The only gold which has ever been mined here is tourist gold – with the development of the Iguazú Falls as a major tourist resort for both the Argentines and the Brazilians.

POSADAS

Posadas is the capital of Misiones. Situated on the Paraná River and on a train line to Buenos Aires, it is the chief commercial centre of the province.

The first settlement on this site was the Itapua Jesuit mission established in the 1650s, which soon moved across the river to Encarnación in Paraguay. The area around Posadas was largely neglected for the next two centuries until Paraguayan

Top: La Boca, Buenos Aires
Left: Buenos Aires
Right: Downtown Buenos Aires

Top: Iguazú Falls
Bottom: San Ignacio-miní

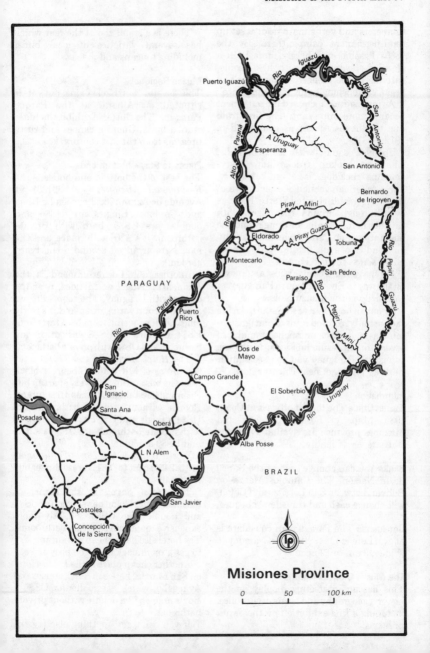

Misiones Province

0   50   100 km

lumberers and yerba mate traders set up semi-permanent camps there. By the 1880s Posadas was barely more than a glorified encampment with 4000 people, catering to the pioneer settlers who had began establishing farms in the province.

As immigration increased the settlement became more important. The first train line to Buenos Aires was completed in 1912.

Today Posadas, with its pool halls, Chevrolet pickup trucks and nasty-smelling truck dogs, is not unlike a sultry, Latin American version of a hick town in the south-western United States. Posadas is still rough around the edges, with gauchos in full regalia loitering round the bus station, and Paraguayans stocking up on bundles of fruit before heading back home across the Río Paraná.

For the visitor, Posadas is just a stop-over on the way to Encarnación in Paraguay, or to Brazil via the Iguazú Falls.

About an hour's drive from the town are the partially restored ruins of San Ignacio-miní, as well as the untouched remains of several other Jesuit missions. If you are going into Paraguay you can see similar ruins at Trinidad, near Encarnación.

Information

Tourist Office The tourist office is at Colón 1985. Maps of Posadas, Iguazú and Misiones province are available and the staff are very friendly.

Banks You can change cash at the Banco de la Nación. The Cambios Mazza on Bolivar, between San Lorenzo and Colón, will change cash and travellers' cheques.

Consulates The Paraguayan consulate is at San Lorenzo 1549. It's open Monday to Friday, 8 am to 12 noon.

The Museo Ciencas Naturales

This has an interesting display on the history, geography and fauna of Misiones, including a fine exhibition on the Jesuit missions.

There is a small zoo at the rear which has several varieties of local birds, including toucans and macaws.

Museo Regional

This is also worth checking out. It is situated on Alberdi at the Parque Paraguay. The clutter of exhibits includes stuffed birds, Guaraní canoes and rusty firearms from the last century.

Places to Stay – bottom end

The best of the bottom end hotels is the *Residencial Misiones* (tel 30133) at Avenida de Azara 1960, between La Rioja and Córdoba. Singles are US$6 and doubles are US$9, both with private bathroom. It's a friendly place and the rooms are arranged around a courtyard garden.

Another one I'd recommend is the *Residencial Nagel* on Mendez, near the corner with Uruguay. The rooms are set around a courtyard garden and it's fairly quiet and peaceful. Singles start from US$4. Doubles are US$6 without private bathroom and US$9 with private bathroom.

The *Hotel Horianski* (tel 22673) is at the corner of Mitre and Libano, a block from the bus station. It's very spartan but clean and habitable and it has a restaurant. Rooms without private bathroom are US$4 a single and US$7 a double. Rooms with private bathroom are US$5 a single and US$9 a double.

Worth trying is the *Hotel Familiar* at Mitre 2437, next to the Expreso Singer bus terminal.

The *Hotel Savoy* at the corner of Sarmiento and Colón has singles for US$3 and doubles for US$5. Slightly more expensive rooms have private bathrooms. The hotel also has a cheap restaurant. Try to get a room back from the busy street.

Another cheap place is the *Plaza Hotel* on San Martín, between San Lorenzo and Ayacucho, which has rooms for US$5 a single and US$7 a double without private bathroom.

If you can't get anything else try the

dank, dark and gloomy *Pension Argentina* at Sarmiento 274.

Places to Stay – middle
The *Gran Hotel Misiones* is two doors up from the *Horianski* and is a clean, modern building with double beds in fairly spacious rooms. Rooms with private bathrooms are US$7 a single and US$10 a double.

Another good place is the *Residencial Marlis* (tel 0752) at Corrientes 234. It's a bit out of the way, but it's modern, clean

and has a friendly manager. Singles are US$6 and doubles are US$7 without private bathroom.

Places to Stay – top end
The *Hotel Continental* (tel 38966) at Bolivar 314 has singles for US$13 and doubles for US$17.

The *Hotel de Turismo Posadas* (tel 31801) at Bolivar 167 is a modern, multi-storey hotel which may have some fairly cheap off-season rates.

The *Posadas Hotel* (tel 30801) at

1	Expreso Singer Terminal
2	Bus Station
3	Residencial Nagel
4	Gran Hotel Misiones
5	Hotel Horianski
6	Museo de Ciencias Naturales
7	Residencial Marlis
8	Hotel Cancillar
9	Hotel de Turismo
10	Post Office
11	Austral
12	Aerolineas Argentina
13	Plaza Hotel
14	Paraguayan Consulate
15	Pension Argentina
16	Savoy Hotel
17	Cathedral
18	City Hotel
19	Hotel Posadas
20	Hotel Continental
21	Tourist Office
22	Residencial Misiones
23	Train Station
24	Ferry to Paraguay

Posadas

Bolivar 272/76 has singles for US$15 and doubles for US$19, which includes private bathroom, television and breakfast.

Places to Eat

El Tronco is a parrillada set up under a dome-shaped tent at the corner of San Martín and Colón. *La Querencia* at Bolivar 322 is a rather up-market restaurant with prices to match. *El Tropezón* at San Martín 187 is a moderately priced parrillada which serves a fine peppered steak with mushrooms and creamed potatoes. There's a glut of hash-houses, snack joints and confiterias along Mitre, Bolivar, San Martín and Lorenzo and near the bus station.

Getting There & Away

At the time of writing there was a bridge under construction between Posadas and Encarnación, the Paraguayan river-town on the opposite side of the Río Paraná. This will change transport between the two countries, so use the information below as a guide only.

Air Aerolíneas Argentinas (tel 22036) is at San Martin 2031. They have daily flights to Buenos Aires and Puerto Iguazú.

Austral (tel 38069) is at Ayacucho 1728. They have daily flights to Buenos Aires, and flights three or four days a week to Rosario, Corrientes and Resistencia.

Bus Most buses leave from the bus station at the junction of Mitre and Junín. The companies Martignoni, COTAL and Empresa Iguazú each have daily buses to Puerto Iguazú.

Empresa Ciudad de Posadas has daily buses to Corrientes and Resistencia.

Empresa Tigre and Expreso Singer have a separate terminal at Mitre 2447.

Expreso Singer has daily buses to Buenos Aires, Córdoba, Paraná, Santa Fe and Asunción.

Empresa Tigre has daily buses to Puerto Iguazú.

Typical fares from Posadas are: to Buenos Aires US$24; Córdoba US$27; Corrientes US$9; Asunción US$4; and Puerto Iguazú US$9.

From Posadas it's a 5½ hour trip to Puerto Iguazú in a *bus rapido*, or a tedious eight hours in an ordinary bus. Posadas to Corrientes takes six hours, and another half hour to Resistencia. There will probably be direct buses from Posadas to Asunción by the time this book is out.

Train There are daily trains from Posadas to Lacroze Station in Buenos Aires. Fares are: coche cama US$35; pullman US$27; primera US$15; and turista US$11. The trip takes 20 hours.

Boat The ferry from Posadas to Encarnación leaves from the dock at the end of Guayucarari. There are a dozen departures a day Monday to Friday, and four or five on Saturdays and Sundays. The crossing takes ten minutes.

Getting Around

Posadas is quite small and you can walk around it easily. Local buses marked 'Centro' take you to the centre of town from the railway station and the Paraguay ferry dock.

You can hire cars from Tucan Car (tel 22436) at Bolivar 1620, Avis (tel 23483) at the corner of Colón and Bolivar, and A1 (tel 36901) at San Lorenzo 2208. Tucan is under licence from National.

THE JESUIT MISSIONS

The work of converting the Argentine Indian populations was carried out mainly by members of Roman Catholic religious orders. The first to enter Argentina were the Franciscans and Dominicans, followed by the Jesuits and others. The first Jesuits arrived in Asunción in 1588. Two priests went to a region called El Guairá, which now belongs to Brazil and is bounded in the west by the Río Paraná and in the south by the Río Iguazú. The Jesuits visited the

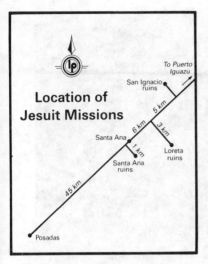

Location of Jesuit Missions

To Puerto Iguazu

San Ignacio ruins

5 km

6 km

3 km

Santa Ana

1 km

Loreta ruins

Santa Ana ruins

45 km

Posadas

Guaraní Indian villages but they did not establish any permanent missions.

In the early 17th century a number of Indian towns, the *reducciones*, were set up by the Spanish. It was thought that by grouping the Indians together in these towns, with priests as the only European residents, that it would be easier to 'civilise' and convert the Indians to Christianity. The Indians were meant to live as Europeans, learning European skills and customs. It was also thought that the reduccion system would be more humane than the encomienda.

In 1609, at the request of the Governor of Paraguay, the Spanish king gave the Jesuits permission to embark on a full-scale conversion of the Guaraní Indians to Christianity. That led to the building of the first Jesuit mission in Paraguay, San Ignacio Guazú, to the north of the Río Paraná.

In 1610 the Jesuits set up the first permanent missions in what is now the Argentine province of Misiones. These were San Ignacio-miní and Nuestra Señora de Loreto, both on the Río Pirapo. Such reducciones were exclusively under

religious leadership, and proved to be increasingly successful. Another dozen or so missions were founded in El Guairá between 1622 and 1629.

The Jesuits had a brief moment of glory in El Guairá. In 1630 their missions were attacked by the slave hunters from São Paulo in Portuguese Brazil, and the Guaraní were either killed or taken away in their tens of thousands to work in the Brazilian coffee plantations. Because of these attacks, in 1631 El Guairá had to be evacuated.

About 12,000 Indians rafted down the Río Paraná to the Guairá Falls. There they had to abandon the rafts and trek through the jungle until they reached a place where the river was once again navigable. New rafts were built and the river journey resumed. New settlements were eventually established, but only 4000 Indians had survived the forced migration.

Several missions in south-east Paraguay were also destroyed by the slavers, although at least two were later re-established. Attempts by the Jesuits to set up missions in Portuguese territory were also frustrated by the slave raids. After the destruction of the missions in Brazil the Guaraní Indians were given guns and on two occasions, in 1639 and 1640, they managed to rout the slavers.

The slavers were not the only problem which the Jesuits had to contend with. The Christianisation of the Guaraní was resisted by some Guaraní chiefs and shamans, and various Guaraní leaders who believed that the long period of turmoil would end only when the white men were thrown out.

The *encomederos* were angered by the loss of Indian labour to the missions. Hostile Indian tribes raided the southern missions. However, by the early years of the 18th century the Jesuits had secured several more missions in Paraguay, bringing the total there to about 30.

Each mission was organised like a small Spanish town, though power was almost entirely vested in the priests. The Jesuits

Ruins of the Jesuit mission, San Ignacio-mini

had a very paternalistic approach, but they were excellent administrators.

The Indians were trained as artisans, farmers, clerks and printers. The Indian children were taught to read and write. Yerba mate, tobacco and cotton were grown as cash crops, and livestock were maintained for the needs of the mission.

In 1750 a treaty between Spain and Portugal handed seven Jesuit missions (with 30,000 Indians), on the east side of the Río Uruguay, to the Portuguese in return for the colony of Sacramento. When the Indians refused to move, both Spain and Portugal sent in troops who defeated the Indians. Although the treaty was later annulled and several missions returned to the Jesuits, these had all been partially destroyed and the Indian populations substantially reduced.

The criollos demanded more and more land, and so around the mid-1700s the last of the secular reducciones was abandoned and the Indians dispersed. In 1767 the Jesuits were finally expelled from Latin America and their missions were given to the Franciscans. Settlers encroached on the mission lands and destroyed the cattle herds and plantations. The handicraft industries declined rapidly. Many Indians simply returned to the jungle.

The missions finally disappeared in the early years of the 19th century after most were destroyed or abandoned during the wars of independence. In 1848 the reigning Paraguayan dictator forced the last 6000 Guaraní Indians still in the missions to live in small villages like the rest of the Paraguayan population.

Had the missions survived, the Jesuits might have eventually established an independent theocratic state in the interior of South America, dramatically affecting the course of South American history.

San Ignacio-miní

Just off the road from Posadas to Iguazú are the ruins of San Ignacio-miní. There are buses to San Ignacio-miní from Posadas every two or three hours. The trip takes about an hour. Entrance to the site is free and there is a restaurant at the entrance. If you leave in the early morning you will have plenty of time to visit San

Ignacio-miní as well as the ruins of Loreto and Santa Ana.

San Ignacio-miní has been partially restored. In its heyday it was one of the most substantial Jesuit missions on the east side of the Río Paraná, but the ruins were only rediscovered in 1897. In 1943 the Argentine government set about restoring them. Today San Ignacio-miní, along with Trinidad and Jesús on the other side of the Paraná in Paraguay, is one of the few missions which still convey some of their former grandeur.

Built like a small Spanish town, the centre of the mission is the large plaza, with the remains of the cathedral decorated with bas-relief sculpture. As you enter the cathedral the baptistry and the remains of the base of the baptismal font are on the left. On either side of the main altar are engraved the names of Jesuit priests who died in the 17th and 18th centuries and who are buried in the cathedral. As you face the altar, the opening in the wall to the right leads to the cemetery.

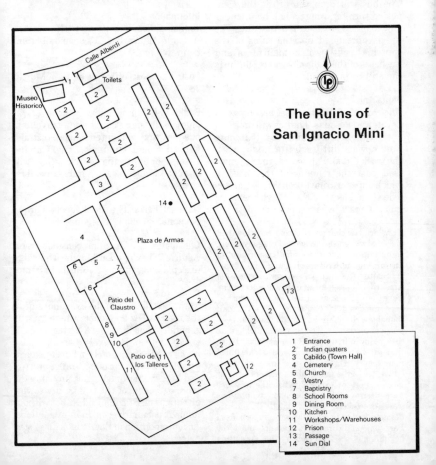

The Ruins of San Ignacio Miní

1 Entrance
2 Indian quaters
3 Cabildo (Town Hall)
4 Cemetery
5 Church
6 Vestry
7 Baptistry
8 School Rooms
9 Dining Room
10 Kitchen
11 Workshops/Warehouses
12 Prison
13 Passage
14 Sun Dial

Around the perimeter of the plaza you can still see the remains of buildings which were once living quarters, workshops and warehouses. The Indians lived in rows of stone buildings, each divided into separate compartments, with a verandah at the front. By the middle of the second decade of the 17th century some 2000 Indians lived in this mission.

Loreto

The ruins of Loreto are just off the road between Posadas and San Ignacio-miní. The bus will drop you off at the sign-posted turn-off, where a half hour trudge down a muddy road leads to the ruins. The site is unrestored but the ruins of the church, the outline of the main plaza, and the bases of the walls of various buildings can still be made out.

Santa Ana

The ruins of Santa Ana are between Loreto and Posadas. The bus will drop you at the turn-off. The ruins are a 15 minute walk down a dirt track (turn right when the track forks). Paths through the jungle lead past the remains of the mission, which appears to have been very extensive. The stone blocks of the church are being pushed apart by vines and tree roots.

If one drink is characteristic of Argentina then it's *yerba mate*. Also known as Paraguayan tea, yerba mate is made from a small tree or shrub of the same name. This tree is native to that part of South America where the borders of Argentina, Paraguay and Brazil meet. The leaves of the tree are dried, roasted, crushed and immersed in hot water. The Guaraní thought yerba mate had medicinal and even magical properties. The Spanish quickly took to drinking it. In time it became associated with the *gauchos* who always carried a satchel full of mate leaves. The Jesuit missions in Misiones cultivated yerba mate, which was one of their most important exports. When the missions were destroyed the yerba mate plantations were overtaken by the jungle. Domestic demand had to be satisfied with imports from Paraguay and Brazil. It was not until the beginning of the 20th century that Argentina

successfully re-established its yerba mate plantations (known as *yerbales*). Commercial plantations now operate in the northern provinces of Misiones, Corrientes and the Chaco. Walking around the ruins of the Jesuit missions you'll also come across wild yerba mate trees.

PUERTO IGUAZU

This town of 15,000 people lies on the bank of the Río Paraná overlooking Paraguay and Brazil. Visitors to the Iguazú Falls stay here or at Foz do Iguaçu.

Information

Tourist Office The tourist office is at Avenida Aguirre 396. It's open daily from 8 am to 8 pm.

Post The post office is at San Martín 780.

Banks The Cambio Dick, on Aguirre, will change foreign cash and travellers' cheques and will interchange Australs, Cruzados and Guaranis. The Cambio Ortega, opposite the tourist office, will change foreign cash and travellers' cheques.

National Parks The Intendencia Parque Nacional Iguazú is at Aguirre 66.

Consulates The Brazilian consulate is on Aguirre. They're open Monday to Friday (except holidays) from 8.45 am to 12.30 pm.

Places to Stay

Many people stay on the Brazilian side of the river at Foz do Iguaçu, where there is generally thought to be a better range of cheap hotels. However there are also many good, cheap hotels in Puerto Iguazú as well as a selection of mid-range and top end hotels. Puerto Iguazú is probably the more agreeable of the two border towns, although the Brazilian side is not without its own peculiarly Brazilian attractions. Accommodation in Puerto Iguazú is listed below.

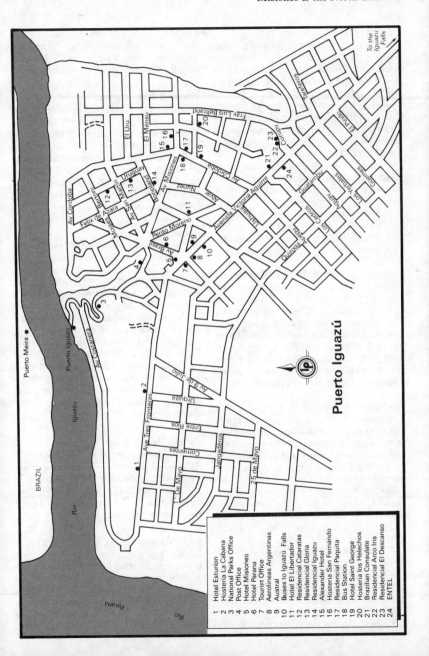

Puerto Iguazú

1 Hotel Esturion
2 Hosteria La Cabana
3 National Parks Office
4 Post Office
5 Hotel Misiones
6 Hotel Parana
7 Tourist Office
8 Aerolineas Argentinas
9 Austral
10 Buses to Iguazú Falls
11 Hotel El Libertador
12 Residencial Cataratas
13 Residencial Gloria
14 Residencial Iguazu
15 Alexander Hotel
16 Hosteria San Fernando
17 Residencial Paquita
18 Bus Station
19 Hotel Saint George
20 Hosteria los Helechos
21 Brazilian Consulate
22 Residencial Arco Iris
23 Residencial El Descanso
24 ENTEL

Places to Stay – bottom end

The *Hostería San Fernando* is very basic, but it's clean and pleasant with decent-sized rooms facing a small garden. Singles are US$6 and doubles US$8, both with private bathrooms.

The *Residencial Arco Iris* at Curupy 152 is clean but has very small rooms. The *Residencial Iguazú* at Bonpland 285 is motel-style on a quiet street opposite a small park. The *Residencial Paquita*, at Córdoba 731 opposite the bus station, is clean and modern, though not memorable. Rooms at all these places are about US$5 a single and US$7 a double.

Slightly more expensive is the *Residencial Cataratas* (tel 2610) at Uruguay 250 which has motel-style rooms with private bathroom and fans, set around a pleasant garden.

Similarly priced is the *Residencial Gloria* at Uruguay 344, which is a motel-style place on a quiet street. Also try *La Cabana* (tel 2564) at Tres Fronteras 434.

Camping is not allowed inside the National Park. The nearest campsite to the park entrance is at *Ñandú*. Three km outside Puerto Iguazú is *Camping Pindó* on Avenida Victoria Aguirre, which charges US$1 per day per person.

Places to Stay – middle

The motel-style *Hostería Los Helechos* has two rows of rooms set around a garden. It's a quiet, congenial place and definitely recommended. Rooms with private bathrooms are US$8 a single and US$13 a double.

Similar to Los Helechos are the *Hotel Saint George* (tel 2633) at Córdoba 745, and the *Alexander Hotel* (tel 2249) at Córdoba 665. Both have rooms for about US$13 a single and US$17 a double.

Slightly cheaper but not as good are the *Hotel Paraná* (tel 2399) at Brasil 335, and the *Hotel Misiones* (tel 2991) at the corner of Brasil and Aguirre. The front rooms of both hotels are likely to be very noisy.

The *Hotel El Libertador* (tel 2823) at Bonpland 475, on the corner with Perito Moreno, is an impressive building from the outside but many of the rooms are quite run-down. Singles are US$16 and doubles are US$21, with private bathroom.

Places to Stay – top end

Probably the best hotel in town is the *Hotel Esturión* (tel 2020) at Tres Fronteras 650. Rooms are US$38 a single and US$50 a double.

The luxury *Hotel International Iguazú* (tel 2790) is near the Visitors' Centre on the Argentine side of the Iguazú Falls. Rooms start from US$64 a single and US$86 a double.

Places to Eat

As Puerto Iguazú is a tourist town, there are plenty of restaurants about. *Los Troncos*, next to the Hostería San Fernando and diagonally opposite the bus station, is a cheap parrillada and pasta restaurant with ample helpings. Undercover at the bus terminal is *La Estancia* which is a moderately priced parrillada.

Slightly up-market is the *Restaurant Saint George* at Córdoba 745 which has fine food, although the restaurant itself is rather stark. There's a string of nameless confiterias, snack joints, pizzerias and parrilladas along Brasil and Bonparte in the town centre.

Getting There & Away

Air Aerolíneas Argentina (tel 2915) is at Avenida Aguirre 404. They have daily flights to Buenos Aires via Posadas.

Austral (tel 2644) is on Aguirre. They have flights to Buenos Aires five days a week, some via Rosario.

Bus Martignoni, COTAL, Empresa Iguazú and Empresa Tigre have daily buses from Puerto Iguazú to Posadas. It's a 5½ hour trip in a *bus rapido* or a tedious eight hours on an ordinary bus. The fare is US$9 on the ordinary buses and US$12 on a *bus rapido*. From Posadas there are buses to Corrientes, Resistencia, Buenos

Aires and Córdoba. There may be direct buses to some of these places from Puerto Iguazú.

Getting Around

Cars can be rented from Avis (tel 2020) at Tres Fronteras 650, and from A1 (tel 2748) at the Hotel International Iguazú.

IGUAZU FALLS

There is an Indian legend that, long ago, a god lived in the jungles near the Iguazú River. One day he noticed the beauty of a girl called Naipur and because of her beauty wanted to take her away. His plans went astray when a warrior called Caroba, who also loved the girl, fled with her downriver in his canoe.

The god's temper flared, and in order to stop the lovers he caused the earth to collapse, producing a line of waterfalls across the river. Naipur was hurled over the edge and was turned into a rock at the bottom of the falls. Caroba survived, but as punishment he was turned into a tree at the edge of the abyss, where he could look down helplessly at Naipur for eternity. This is said to be the origins of the Iguazú Falls.

The Spanish explorer Alvar Núñez Cabeza de Vaca is usually credited as having been the first white man to set eyes on the Iguazú Falls, while on a journey of exploration from the Brazilian coast to Asunción in Paraguay in 1541.

Others give credit to a Portuguese called Alejo García, who had been with the expedition of Juan Díaz de Solís. When García was shipwrecked in 1524 he headed inland, like so many after him, in search of a legendary kingdom of gold and silver in the jungles of South America. So many confusing stories surround García that some historians have suggested he never existed at all. However, it is generally accepted that not only did he become the first white man to cross central South America, but that he was also the first to set eyes on the Inca Empire. Alvar de Vaca's story is no less bizarre. On a Spanish expedition to Florida in 1528 he was shipwrecked off the coast of Texas. For the next nine years he and his companions wandered through Indian territory and found their way to Mexico City in 1536. After his return to Spain he was sent back to South America to take charge of the Río de la Plata settlement, only to find that the colonists had abandoned it and moved to Asunción. With some 200 men he trekked from the coast to Asunción, coming across the Iguazú Falls on the way. It is said that de Vaca was so impressed by the grandeur of the falls that he named them Santa María. Yet the first account of the expedition, published in Spanish in 1555, gives a matter-of-fact account of both the expedition and the 'discovery' of the falls. The narrator records that:

'Before arriving at the Río Iguazú . . . . they had learned from the local natives that it drops into the Río Paraná . . . . [Alvar de Vaca] with 80 men embarked in canoes and went down the Iguazú while the remainder of the people and horses carried on by land . . . . The current of the Iguazú was so strong that the canoes were carried violently downriver, because close to that point is a large fall, and the noise made by the water plummeting down the high rocks into the chasm can be heard a long way away . . . . It was therefore necessary to take the canoes out of the water and carry them on land past the waterfall . . . '

In time the name of the falls was changed to Iguazú, a Guaraní word which means Great Water. The great waters are, in fact, higher and wider than the Niagara Falls. They consist of some 250 waterfalls, some of them up to 70 metres high, stretched around a three km arc of the Río Iguazú. The most dramatic cataract is probably the one which claimed Naipur – the Garganta del Diablo or Devil's Throat.

The falls occupy a national park, one of the first to be set up in Argentina. For statistics enthusiasts the park contains 2000 species of butterflies and moths, 400 species of birds, 100 species of mammals,

40 species of reptiles and 60 species of frogs.

Getting There & Away

The Iguazú Falls are 20 km from the town of Puerto Iguazú. There are about 10 buses a day to the falls leaving from Puerto Iguazú. The first bus leaves at 7 am and the last at 5 pm. You can catch the bus either at the bus station or just near the tourist office. Entry to the falls is US$1 which you pay at the kiosk at the park entrance.

The bus drops you off at the Visitors' Centre, near the Hotel Iguazú and the falls. There is a connecting bus from the Visitors' Centre to Ñandú, where there is a walkway leading out to the Garganta del Diablo. These buses run at regular intervals throughout the day. There are also taxis from the Visitors' Centre to Ñandú.

Returning to Puerto Iguazú, the first bus leaves the Visitors' Centre at 7.45 am and the last at 6 pm.

The Visitors' Centre is open daily from 8 am to 6 pm and has a small museum. There is a bar and restaurant nearby.

Getting Around

Although it is hard to deny the power of the falls themselves, your final impression may be that they were created not by an angry god but by a team of architects and landscape artists. The hotels, snack bars, pedestrian paths and catwalks seem to fence the falls in, creating a tidy, manicured park – the ultimate Hemmeter Resort.

You can see the entire stretch of falls on the Argentine side from across the Río Iguazú in Brazil. There are helicopter rides over the falls from the Brazilian side. The Argentine side, however, is probably the more interesting as catwalks and pathways allow you to get right up the falls, including the Garganta del Diablo.

Many of the walkways on the Argentine side were destroyed several years ago by flooding and have not yet been repaired.

This splits the Argentine side of the falls into two halves. The first half is the area around the Isla Grande San Martín and the Visitors' Centre. The second half is around Garganta del Diablo. Signposts tell you where the various pathways lead, and though names have been given to the individual falls you'll have more fun making up your own.

Paths and catwalks take you over the top of the Salto Dos Hermanos (Two Brothers Falls), the Salto Bosseti and the Salto San Martín. From here you backtrack and walk down steps to the river bank where boats take you across to the Isla Grande San Martín. From here you'll get fine views of San Martín, Adán y Eva and the Salto Tres Mosqueteros (Three Musketeers).

Taking the boat back to the mainland you can then circle around to the Salto Alvar, named after Alvar Núñez Cabeza de Vaca. There is a plaque here to his memory. From here you return to the Visitors' Centre. From the Visitors' Centre you can catch a bus or taxi to Ñandú, where a walkway leads out to the Garganta del Diablo (Devil's Throat). From there you can also see the Brazilian falls on the other side: Union, Benjamín, Deodoro, Floriano and Santa María.

Near the Visitors' Centre there are two nature trails which have been marked out by the Parks administration. The first is the Macuco trail which is a cleared pathway which starts 200 metres from the Visitors' Centre and leads four km to the Salto Pozon and Salto Arrechea. The other area of interest is Bañado, which is a marsh where you can observe some of the birdlife in the area. In fact, there is so much wildlife in this area, in particular great swarms of stunningly coloured butterflies, that you almost expect David Attenborough to leap out of the jungle and burst into running commentary. A different type of commentary takes place several nights each month when a park ranger conducts a guided tour of the falls by full moonlight.

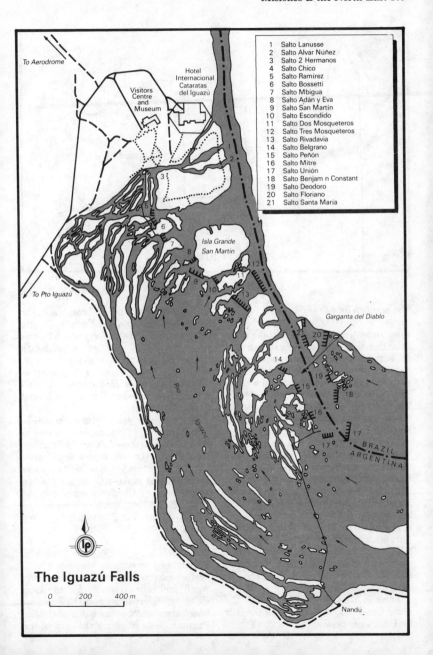

To Aerodrome

Hotel
Internacional
Cataratas
del Iguazú

Visitors
Centre
and Museum

1	Salto Lanusse
2	Salto Alvar Núñez
3	Salto 2 Hermanos
4	Salto Chico
5	Salto Ramírez
6	Salto Bossetti
7	Salto Mbigua
8	Salto Adán y Eva
9	Salto San Martín
10	Salto Escondido
11	Salto Dos Mosqueteros
12	Salto Tres Mosqueteros
13	Salto Rivadavia
14	Salto Belgrano
15	Salto Peñón
16	Salto Mitre
17	Salto Unión
18	Salto Benjam n Constant
19	Salto Deodoro
20	Salto Floriano
21	Salto Santa María

Isla Grande
San Martín

To Pto Iguazú

Garganta del Diablo

Río
Iguazú

BRAZIL
ARGENTINA

The Iguazú Falls

0   200   400 m

Nandu

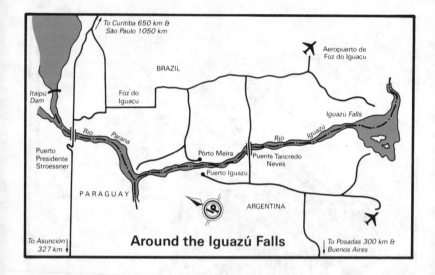

Around the Iguazú Falls

The Brazilian Side

To get to the Brazilian side of the falls from Argentina you have to take a bus from Puerto Iguazú to the Brazilian town of Foz do Iguaçu. These buses leave regularly throughout the day from the bus station in Puerto Iguazú and take you to Brazil over the Puente Tancredo Neves (the Tancredo Neves Bridge). The fare to Foz do Iguaçu is US$0.60 and the trip takes 30 minutes.

The bus pulls into the Terminal de Omnibus opposite the Mirante and Estoril Hotels. From here you catch a Transbalan bus marked *Cataratas* (Waterfalls) to the Brazilian side of the falls. These depart about every hour throughout the day; the trip takes about 30 minutes.

The bus drops you off outside the *Hotel Cataratas* where the pathway along the falls begins. At the end of the pathway is a tower with an elevator which takes you up to a bus station. You can catch the bus back to Foz do Iguaçu from there.

There is a helicopter pad outside the Hotel Cataratas, with rides over the falls for US$25 per person.

From the Terminal de Omnibus in Foz do Iguaçu you can get buses to Puerto Miera where there's a ferry which crosses the river to Puerto Iguazú, although there's really no point in taking this route. There are buses from Foz do Iguaçu to Puerto Stroessner in Paraguay, but no direct buses between Puerto Iguazú and Puerto Stroessner.

If you're only going from Argentina to Brazil to see the falls and then returning to Argentina, you shouldn't need a Brazilian visa. Even if you only have a single-entry visa for Argentina you shouldn't have any problem; just make sure no one stamps your passport. Change some Argentine Australs for Brazilian cruzados at the money-changers in Puerto Iguazú before you go.

CORRIENTES

If you head west from Misiones to the north-west provinces of Salta and Jujuy, you'll probably pass through the twin cities of Corrientes and Resistencia, which stand on opposite banks of the Río Paraná. These cities are the start of the long haul to the north-west, a sort of Old Patagonian Express by bus rather than train. The northern towns have few things to 'see'. By day, as people hide indoors from the fierce sun, they are virtual ghost towns, though the night-time street life can be lively.

Corrientes is the capital of the province of the same name. Corrientes is the northern province of what is referred to as 'Argentine Mesopotamia', the land between the Río Paraná and the Río Uruguay. The region was given its name by a French traveller in the 19th century, who compared it to the area between the Tigris and Euphrates Rivers of the Middle East.

Corrientes owes much of its prominence to the Río Paraná. The Paraná is one of the most important rivers in the Río de la Plata system. It originates in the mountains of Brazil and flows south to divide Paraguay from Argentina. The rich, alluvial soil and delta land allowed agriculture and grazing to be established along its banks, as well as the development of numerous towns such as Rosario, Santa Fe and Paraná. Ocean-going ships can navigate the river as far as Corrientes. The province is a land of rivers, marshes, lagoons, woodlands, and large areas of grazing and farming land. It has around 600,000 inhabitants, of whom a third live in the capital.

Banks The Banco de la Nación Argentina at the corner of Córdoba and 9 de Julio will change American Express and Citibank travellers' cheques. The Banco de Galicia at Córdoba 870 may change Thomas Cook travellers' cheques.

Things to See
The city of Corrientes was founded in 1588 and at that time was barely more than a fort with two dozen men and the blessing of god to defend it. When a force of 6000 Indians attacked the fort they were beaten off by the intervention of the 'Miraculous Cross', a cross put up by the Spanish to indicate their possession of the land.

It is said that burning sticks, hurled at the fort by the Indians, fell harmlessly at the base of the cross. Then in the course of the battle a lightning bolt struck, killing some of the Indians and driving the rest away in terror. The cross is now housed in the Iglesia de la Cruz (Church of the Cross) on Belgrano.

Places to Stay - bottom end
The *Hotel Colón* (tel 24527) at La Rioja 437, near the river, is basic but clean and habitable, with hot water showers and largish rooms with fans. There tends to be quite a bit of traffic noise, even in rooms at the back. Rooms without private bathroom are US$6 a single and US$7 a double. Rooms with private bathroom are US$6 a single and US$10 a double.

Places to Stay - middle
The *Hotel Caribe*, opposite the Estación Terminal de Transporte (the combined bus and train station) is a modern hotel with single rooms for US$11 and doubles for US$17, with breakfast and private bathroom. Unless you're planning on catching an early morning bus, this is really too far out of the centre for convenience.

The best place to stay in Corrientes is the *Hotel Buenos Aires* (tel 22065) at Pellegrini 1058. Though the rooms are quite basic, the hotel is an enormous double-storey stone mansion with a courtyard garden, a huge upstairs lounge and a pleasing restaurant. Rooms with private bathroom are US$10 a single and US$16 a double. Rooms without private bathroom are slightly cheaper.

Slightly more expensive is the *Hotel San Martín* (tel 65004) at Santa Fe 955/73, opposite the main plaza.

Places to Stay - top end
The *Hotel Hostal del Pinar* (tel 61089) at the corner of Martínez and San Juan is a multi-storey hotel with singles for US$19

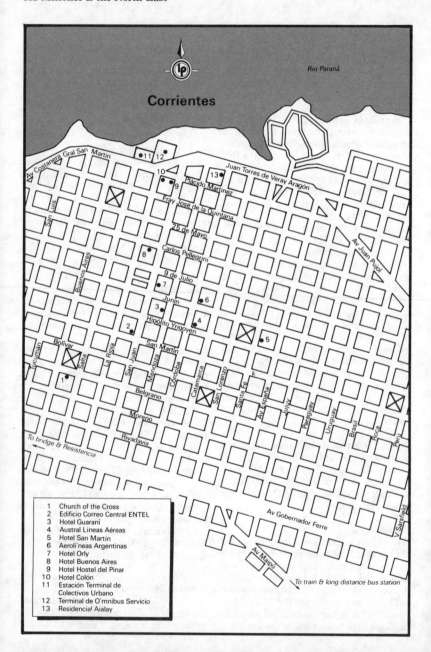

Rio Paraná

Corrientes

Av Costanera Gral San Martin
San Luís
Buenos Aires
Lucumán
Bolívar
Salta
La Rioja
San Juan
Mendoza
Córdoba
Catamarca
San Lorenzo
Santa Fe
Av España
Jujuy
Paraguay
Uruguay
Brasil
Roca
Perú

Juan Torres de Veray Aragón
Plácido Martínez
Fray José de la Quintana
25 de Mayo
Carlos Pellegrini
9 de Julio
Junín
Hipólito Yrigoyen
San Martín
Belgrano
Moreno
Rivadavia
Av Juan Pujol
Av Gobernador Ferre
Av Maipú

To bridge & Resistencia

To train & long distance bus station

V Sarsfield

1 Church of the Cross
2 Edificio Correo Central ENTEL
3 Hotel Guaraní
4 Austral Líneas Aéreas
5 Hotel San Martín
6 Aerolíneas Argentinas
7 Hotel Orly
8 Hotel Buenos Aires
9 Hotel Hostel del Pinar
10 Hotel Colón
11 Estación Terminal de
Colectivos Urbano
12 Terminal de O'mnibus Servicio
13 Residencial Aialay

and doubles for US$25. Similar is the *Hotel Guaraní* at Mendoza 970.

Places to Eat

One of the best places to eat in the evening is *Las Espueles* at Mendoza 847, a parrillada with an outdoor dining area. Servings tend to be a bit small but it's cheap and conducive to lingering. Also worth trying is the *Restaurante Italiana* on Carlos Pellegrini, on the block between Mendoza and San Juan, in the ornate mansion which houses the Italian Vice-Consul. At night Junín becomes a pedestrian mall with many restaurants and cafés.

Getting There & Away

The train station and the long-distance bus terminal are part of a complex called the *Estación Terminal de Transporte Gobernador Dr Benjamín S González.* This is on Maipú in the south-east of town. To get there take a local bus No 6, marked *Terminal*, from the local bus station on San Martín at the northern end of La Rioja.

Air Aerolíneas Argentinas (tel 23850) is at the corner of Córdoba and Junín. They have flights to Buenos Aires two days a week.

Austral is at Córdoba 981, near the corner with Yrigoyen. They have daily flights to Buenos Aires, and three days a week to Posadas and Rosario.

Bus From the Estación Terminal de Transporte you can get buses to various destinations in northern Argentina, although Resistencia is a better place for transport.

Expreso El Rayo has daily buses to Tucumán via Resistencia and Santiago del Estero.

EMP Central El Rapido has daily buses to Buenos Aires, and four days a week to Córdoba.

TA Chevalier has daily buses to Rosario, Santa Fe and Paraná.

Empresa Ciudad de Posadas has daily buses to Posadas.

Train There are daily trains from Corrientes to Lacroze Station in Buenos Aires. The trip takes about 21 to 22 hours.

Getting Around

There are buses to Resistencia which leave all through the day and night from the local bus station on San Martín at the northern end of La Rioja in Corrientes. In Resistencia they drop you off at the Plaza de Mayo before continuing on to the long distance bus station at the corner of Santiago del Estero and Santa María de Oro.

You can get the bus back to Corrientes from either of these stops. The trip takes half an hour.

RESISTENCIA

Across the Río Paraná from Corrientes is the city of Resistencia, capital of the Chaco. The province takes its name from a Quechua Indian word which refers to a hunting technique of encircling and then closing in on their prey.

The Chaco refers to the huge plain in central South America. This plain is bordered in the south by the Argentine pampas and the Córdoba mountains, in the east by the Río Paraguay and Río Paraná, in the west by the first foothills of the Andes, and in the north by a string of Brazilian mountain ranges. In Argentina it covers the provinces of Chaco, Formosa, Santiago del Estero and parts of Salta and Santa Fe.

This is a land of semi-arid plains, used for agriculture and cattle grazing, and a source of hard *quebracho* wood.

The first Spanish explorers entered the Chaco in 1528, though the Portuguese explorer and man-of-misfortune Alejo García may have come this way earlier, in his search for the southern El Dorado. Settlements were established by the Spanish later in the 16th century, but as the local Indians took to riding horses, became more aggressive and began raiding the Spanish settlements, the Spanish were forced to evacuate the area.

In the late 18th century peace treaties were made with several of the Chaco Indian tribes and attempts were even made to set up reducciones, but for the most part the few Spanish settlements never got more than a toe-hold.

The Chaco Indian problem was not settled until the middle of the 19th century. Indian raids against newly-established agricultural colonies and sheep ranches in Santa Fe, and the increased demand for quebracho wood, spurred the Argentine government into launching a series of military campaigns against the Indians in 1870-1883.

The city of Resistencia was founded on the site of the old settlement of the same name. With the Indian threat removed the population rapidly increased. The

Chaco became a major supplier of sugar cane, tobacco, cotton, cereal and other agricultural produce.

Places to Stay – bottom end

One of the best cheap hotels is the *Residencial Alberdi* at Alberdi 317, on the block between Ameghino and Obligado. It has clean, moderate sized rooms with wash-basins and double beds. Singles are US$4 and doubles US$7.

Another place I'd recommend is the *Residencial Aragon* at Santiago del Estero 154, near the corner with Santa María de Oro. It's fairly spartan, with small rooms, cot beds and fan, but it's clean and only costs US$3 per person.

An ideal place is the *Residencial San José* (tel 26062) at Rawson 304 near the corner with Obligado. The rooms are small, but each has a private bathroom. It's US$6 a double.

On Santiago del Estero, opposite the

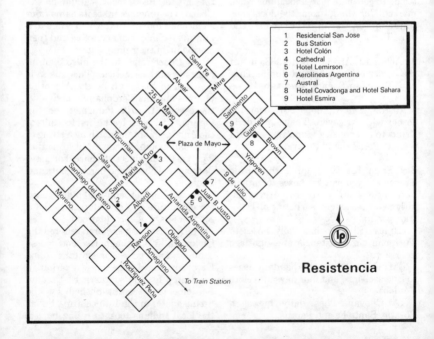

1 Residencial San Jose
2 Bus Station
3 Hotel Colón
4 Cathedral
5 Hotel Lemirson
6 Aerolineas Argentina
7 Austral
8 Hotel Covadonga and Hotel Sahara
9 Hotel Esmira

Plaza de Mayo

To Train Station

Resistencia

bus station, is the *Hospedaje Paraná* which will do if you can't get anything else. Rooms are US$6 per person.

Places to Stay – middle

There's a string of multi-storey, mid-range hotels in Resistencia, although there's not much to distinguish one from the other. They all charge about US$14 a single and US$20 a double.

The best of the lot is probably the *Hotel Covadonga* (tel 22875) at the corner of Güemes and Brown.

Others include the *Hotel Lemirson* (tel 22277) at Rawson 169/173; the *Esmira Hotel* (tel 22898) at Irigoyen 83 opposite the Plaza 25 de Mayo; and the *Hotel Sahara* (tel 22970) on Güemes next to the Covadonga. The Sahara tends to be a bit run-down.

Places to Eat

There are many cheap parrilladas and confiterias around the bus station, and many ice cream parlours, pizzerias and confiterias in the vicinity of the Plaza 25 de Mayo. There are some popular sidewalk confiterias on Güemes opposite the Covadonga and Sahara Hotels.

Try *La Estaca Parrilla* at the corner of Güemes and Brown, the *Restaurante Residentes Santafesinos* at Vedia 152, and the pizzas at the *Confiteria Zan En Pizzaria* on Rawson opposite the Plaza 25 de Mayo.

Getting There & Away

Air Aerolíneas Argentina (tel 25360) is on Juan B Justo, near the corner with Rawson. They have flights to Buenos Aires once a week.

Austral (tel 26235) is at the corner of Rawson and Juan B Justo. They have daily flights to Buenos Aires, four days a week to Rosario and once a week to Posadas.

Aerolíneas has a mini-bus to take passengers to the airports at Resistencia and Corrientes to catch their flights. This costs about US$2 per person.

Bus The long distance bus station is at the corner of Santiago del Estero and Santa María de Oro.

Empresa Godoy SRL has daily buses to Buenos Aires, and to Asunción in Paraguay via Formosa and Clorinda.

Transporte Central Sáenz Peña and La Estrella each have buses three or four days a week to Córdoba.

Empresa Ciudad de Posadas has daily buses to Posadas and Puerto Iguazú.

Transporte Central Sáenz Peña has daily buses to Salta in north-west Argentina. This is an overnight marathon trip of 17 hours.

La Internacional has its own terminal opposite the bus station. They have daily buses to Buenos Aires, Rosario and Santa Fe.

Typical fares are: to Buenos Aires US$23; Clorinda US$7; Asunción US$10; and Salta US$22.

Train There are no longer any passenger trains from Resistencia to Salta. If you want to cut across the north by train you have to first take a bus from Salta to Formosa.

From Formosa there are trains to Embarcación. These trains have only turista and primera class. From Formosa they depart every Wednesday and Sunday for Embarcación. The trip takes 22 hours.

From Embarcación the trains depart every Monday and Friday for Formosa.

Getting Around

If you're coming from Corrientes there are buses to Resistencia which leave all through the day and night from the local bus station on San Martín at the northern end of La Rioja in Corrientes.

In Resistencia they drop you off at the Plaza de Mayo before continuing to the long distance bus station at the corner of Santiago del Estero and Santa María de Oro. You can get the bus back to Corrientes from either of these stops. The trip takes half an hour.

The Andean Provinces

North-west Argentina was originally settled by various Indian tribes. They tended to be confined to the foothills of the Andes, unable to make much headway against the hostile, nomadic tribes of the pampas and the Chaco to the east. Although this was a dry, bleak land, streams provided enough water to grow crops and graze animals. The two main Indian groups were the Diaguita and the Atacameño.

The Diaguita inhabited a large area of north-western Argentina as well as parts of northern Chile. Like other Indian cultures of the north-west they relied on agriculture and hunting for their livelihood. Herding of domesticated llamas and alpacas was important. Their villages were quite large, with houses built of adobe or rough stones set in mud. Forts were built at strategic points. Stone-headed clubs, bows and arrows, and bronze knuckle-dusters were their main weapons. Copper and bronze weapons and tools such as axes, knives and agricultural implements were widely used. Pottery, weaving, basketry and wood carving were well developed.

The Atacameño lived in northern Chile and in Salta and Jujuy. They were displaced from Salta and Jujuy by the Diaguita in pre-Inca times. The Atacameño were a very old culture and isolated groups survived in north Chile in Spanish times. As with the Diaguita, agriculture and herding was important. The Atacameño were distinguished from the other Indians by the importance they placed on trade, often acting as intermediaries between other Indian tribes. Both northern Chile and north-west Argentina became part of the Inca Empire. Some tribes began to disappear as distinct groups after subjugation by the Inca. Others disappeared when the Spanish conquistadores entered their homelands.

Many of the towns of north-west Argentina have their origins in the 16th century, when Spanish explorers set out from Perú, Chile and Bolivia in search of gold and silver in the interior of Argentina. After the arrival of the Spanish the history of the north-west is a simple one of exploration, the building of forts, the herding of Indians into encomiendas, and a series of military campaigns to wipe out any threat from other Indians. The Spanish founded a number of what are now important cities, including Salta, Jujuy, Córdoba and Mendoza.

The Diaguita and other Indian groups were sufficiently numerous and 'civilised' for the Spanish to organise them into encomiendas. With a large labour force at the disposal of the Spanish, their settlements in the north-west grew rapidly. By the late 16th century wine and fruit was being exported from the Cuyo (the region centred on Mendoza). Not long after sugar cane plantations and vineyards were established at Tucumán.

The north-west settlements were also on the trade route from Buenos Aires to

116

Peru. Since the Spanish forbade the import or export of goods from Buenos Aires, most trade goods had to be carried by ox-cart through the interior to Lima. Settlements like Córdoba, Tucumán and Salta served as stop-overs on the route, where traders could rest and stock up on new provisions. It was an extraordinarily cumbersome system for the traders, though Spain's closed port policy meant that the settlements on the Argentine coast had to buy goods for their own needs from the settlements of the north-west.

For much of the colonial era the towns of the north-west were largely self-governing. The *cabildo* or town council, the basic unit of administration in the Spanish settlements in Latin America, was often the only source of authority. Cabildos in the more isolated areas became self-reliant, and were largely composed of criollos rather than Spanish-born administrators. They were staunchly independent, resenting the intrusion of any outsiders, including royal officials. It was not until the establishment of the Vice-Royalty of Río de la Plata, in 1776, that royal officials began to preside over the cabildos. Power became increasingly concentrated in Buenos Aires and the cabildos of the north-west towns became less important.

The towns of the interior prospered until independence from Spain. After that the coastal ports were opened to free trade. British demand for meat, hides and wool helped the coastal cattle and sheep grazing industry. The towns of the interior were hard hit by imported European goods, often cheaper and of better quality than Argentina could produce itself. Today, cattle grazing, sugar cane, vineyards, mining and oil extraction are important industries in north-west Argentina.

Travel in the North-West

To describe one town in the north-west is to describe them all. When the Spanish came to Argentina they built identikit towns, a sort of European colonial version of the modern-day department store or fast food chain where each member of the chain is indistinguishable from any other member.

In every town, from Buenos Aires on the coast to La Quiaca on the Bolivian border, they laid out a central plaza, hemmed it in with a cabildo (town hall) and other public buildings, and covered the land in the immediate vicinity with a neat grid of streets. The streets were named after the generals who led the campaigns against the Indians, and then later the heroes of the independence movement and past presidents of Argentina.

The towns are like identical beads strung out on a rough string – and that being the case it is mainly the string which is of interest to visitors. The towns need to be treated as they were meant to be in the 17th and 18th centuries – as stop-overs on the long haul from the coast to Peru and Bolivia. Using the towns as stepping stones you can side-trip to some of Argentina's strangest corners. These include the desolate *quebradas* (ravines) centred on Cafayate, and the mining town of San Antonio de los Cobres at the end of the rail-line which winds its way high into the Andes Mountains from Salta.

Getting There & Away

There are a couple of ways of approaching north-west Argentina. There are many flights from Buenos Aires to the major cities in the north-west. From Bolivia you can cross the border at Villazón/La Quiaca and then head south to Salta. From Brazil you can take the bus from Puerto Iguazú to Posadas, then cut across the north to Salta via the twin cities of Corrientes and Resistencia. From Buenos Aires you can take a direct train or bus to Tucumán, Jujuy or Salta. From Chile you can bus to Mendoza. From Mendoza there are buses to Tucumán and other cities in the north-west. There are buses from the northern Chilean city of Antofagasta to Salta, weather permitting.

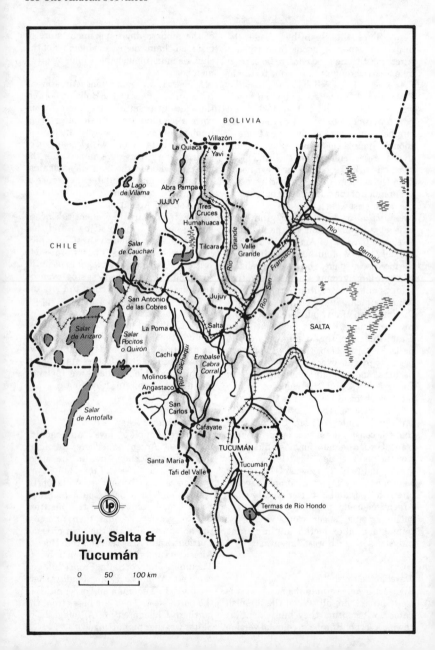

BOLIVIA

CHILE

SALTA

TUCUMÁN

Villazón
La Quiaca
Yavi

Lago
de Vilama

Abra Pampa
JUJUY
Tres
Cruces
Humahuaca

Salar
de Cauchari

Tilcara

Valle
Grande

Río Grande

Río San Francisco

Río
Bermejo

San Antonio
de las Cobres

Jujuy

Salta

Salar
de Arizaro

Salar
Pocitos
o Quirón

La Poma

Cachi

Embalse
Cabra
Corral

Molinos

Río Calchaquí

Salar
de Antofalla

Angastaco

San
Carlos

Cafayate

Santa María

Tafí del Valle

Tucumán

Termas de Río Hondo

Jujuy, Salta &
Tucumán

0   50   100 km

JUJUY

The extreme north-west of Argentina is a mountainous region comprising two distinct areas. The first is the Puna de Jujuy. The other is the Quebrada de Humahuaca.

The puna is a high plateau with an elevation of 3500 to 3800 metres, surrounded by mountains from which streams and rivers empty into salt marshes. Vegetation is very poor since the climate is dry and there is very little rainfall. There is, however, enough grassland to sustain large animals such as llama, vicuña and guanaco.

To the east of the puna is the Quebrada de Humahuaca. This is a narrow valley just 160 km long, through which the Río Grande runs. For centuries this valley has been the chief overland route from Argentina to Bolivia and Peru. The valley slopes downwards from north to south. The elevation in the north is 4000 metres. The southern end is just 1200 metres. Jujuy, the capital of Jujuy province, lies at the southern end of the Quebrada de Humahuaca.

Jujuy province probably takes its name from the Quechua word *xuxuyoc*, which referred to a particular type of Inca official who governed this area when it was part of the Inca empire. The Spanish called it the 'valley of the xuxuyoc', later shortening the word to Jujuy. Although the Incas were never able to fully exploit Jujuy, because of distance and because it had hardly any gold or silver, they did build a road through Jujuy to Mendoza. Ruins of their settlements can be seen at La Rioja.

Like the Incas before them, the Spanish organised encomiendas and moved unruly Indians to remote areas. During the 18th century the Indians along the frontier became more troublesome and frequently attacked Spanish settlements and outlying farms. The Spanish had to build forts and set up a special force of border guards for protection.

The chief towns of the north-west are

Salta and Jujuy, both capitals of provinces of the same name. The Spanish moved into the area in the early 1590s, establishing settlements in order to improve communication between Argentina and Bolivia and Peru. Jujuy's fertile farm land, its location on the route to Peru, and the development of sugar cane plantations by the Jesuit missions, helped its development. Jujuy became a prosperous settlement with a mixed population of Spanish, Indians, criollos, mestizos, black slaves, mulattos (of mixed white and black descent) and zambos (of mixed black and Indian descent).

The expulsion of the Jesuits in 1767 caused the sugar cane industry to decline (it would not be revived until a century afterwards). When Buenos Aires was opened to direct trade with Spain at the end of the 18th century, Jujuy was relegated to the role of a backwater town. The economic decline probably caused the provincial leaders to throw their lot in with the independence movement in Buenos Aires. Battles between Spanish and Argentine troops and then between troops of rival caudillos were fought on Jujuy's soil. Like Salta, Jujuy only began to make real economic progress in the latter half of the 19th century.

Information

Tourist Office The tourist office is at Belgrano 690, on the corner with Lavalle.

Banks Foreign cash can be changed at Noroeste at the corner of Otero and Belgrano, and at Dinar on Belgrano near the corner with Lavalle.

Consulates The Bolivian Consulate is at Aráoz 697, in the Ciudad de Nieva district.

Things to See

Jujuy is an agreeable enough city, but for visitors the real attractions are in the surrounding countryside. Many visitors use Jujuy as a base from which to explore the many interesting villages in the nearby mountains. One possibility is a hike from the Valle Grande to the small settlement of Tilcara, near Jujuy. Another possibility is to hike from the Valle Grande to Humahuaca. *Backpacking in Chile & Argentina*, by John Pilkington and Hilary Bradt, has a description of both these hikes.

Places to Stay - bottom end

The *Residencial Lavalle* (tel 22698) at Lavalle 372, between Alvear and Belgrano, is one of the few cheap hotels left in Jujuy. Rooms without private bathroom are US$4 a single and US$6 a double. Doubles with private bathroom are US$8. It's a fairly spartan place but it's clean and has hot water showers. The single rooms are quite claustrophobic.

Failing that try the *Hotel Chungking* (tel 28142) at Alvear 627, between Lavalle and Otero. Rooms without private bathroom are US$4 a single and US$7 a double. Rooms at the back are best as the front rooms are noisy. It's a spartan but reasonably pleasant hotel.

The *Residencial El Norte* (tel 22721) is at Alvear 444, near the corner with Urquiza and diagonally opposite the train station. It's basic but habitable, though women should beware of over-attentive management. Rooms without private bathroom are US$2/$4 for singles/doubles, and a bit more for a private bathroom.

Places to Stay - middle

A couple of good mid-range places include the *Hotel Avenida* (tel 22678) on 19 de Abril between San Martín and Belgrano. Singles are US$14 and doubles are US$18, both with private bathroom.

Similarly priced is the *Sumay Hotel* (tel 22554) at Otero 232 between San Martín and Belgrano.

Slightly cheaper is *Asors Hotel* (tel 23688) on Urquiza, diagonally opposite the train station. It's a good place but the front rooms are noisy.

Places to Stay - top end

The *Hotel Fenicia* (tel 27492) on 19 de Abril, between Sarmiento and Gorriti, has rooms for US$18 single and US$26 a double. It's within walking distance of the bus station.

Similarly priced is the multi-storey

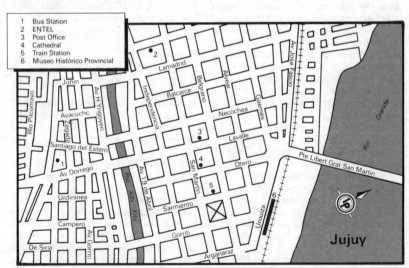

1	Bus Station
2	ENTEL
3	Post Office
4	Cathedral
5	Train Station
6	Museo Histórico Provincial

Jujuy

Hotel Internacional (tel 22004) at the corner of Belgrano and Sarmiento.

Also try the *Hotel Augustus* (tel 22930) at Belgrano 715, near the corner with Lavalle.

Places to Eat

Belgrano and Lavalle are the main streets of Jujuy. There's a pedestrian mall on Jujuy on the block between Lavalle and Necochea. There are several confiterias on the mall. Most of the restaurants are along Lavalle and Belgrano including a few established places such as *La Rueda* at Lavalle 320. There's no shortage of hash houses, ice cream parlours and pizzerias around the centre of town.

Getting There & Away

Air Aerolíneas Argentinas (tel 23897) is on Otero, near the corner with Belgrano. They have daily flights to Buenos, some via Salta and Tucumán.

Bus The long distance bus station is on Dorrego, on the south side of town.

Panamericana has daily buses south to Tucumán and Córdoba, and north to Tilcara, Humahuaca, Tres Cruces, Abra Pampa and La Quiaca. COTA Norte has daily buses to Humahuaca. Atahualpa has daily buses to Salta and La Quiaca.

Typical fares from Jujuy are: to Salta US$3; Humahuaca US$4; and La Quiaca US$9. The trip from Salta to Jujuy takes three hours.

Train There are trains three days a week from Jujuy to Retiro Station in Buenos Aires, via Rosario, Tucumán and Córdoba. Fares from Jujuy to Buenos Aires are: primera US$29; and turista US$21.

There are trains three days a week from Jujuy to La Quiaca on the Bolivian border, via Abra Pampa, Tres Cruces and Humahuaca. Fares from Jujuy to La Quiaca are: primera US$8; and turista US$5. The trip to La Quiaca takes about 9½ hours.

Getting Around

Cars can be rented from Avis (tel 22832) in the Hotel Panorama at Belgrano 1295, and from A1 (tel 29697) at Belgrano 580.

HUMAHUACA

The Quebrada de Humahuaca is a narrow valley running north-south through central Jujuy province. The valley is 160 km long and just three km wide at its widest point. The chief settlement is Humahuaca, barely more than a village of adobe houses and corrals topped with pieces of prickly pear cactus. Indian women herd donkeys, sheep and goats through the streets to pasture.

Things to See

The Spanish first settled at Humahuaca in 1594. Long before the area had been inhabited by agrarian Indians who had been ruled by the Incas. The Río Colorado supports agriculture but for the most part the quebrada is a formidable landscape of barren, rugged grey-brown mountains with shrivelled cacti.

One of the interesting features of this region is the tiny, white-washed churches which can be seen in Humahuaca and in nearby Uquía and Huacalera. All have fine examples of cactus wood panelling, doors and sculpture. Most were originally established in the 18th century. Their simple design, thick walls, and square towers are similar to churches in Peru.

In Uquía you can see the **Templo Santa Cruz y San Francisco**, originally built in 1691. This one is distinguished by its collection of 17th century paintings of winged angels in military costume – though if these really are the originals they're in surprisingly good condition!

Humahuaca to Uquía is 10 km, and from Uquía it's another 15 km to Huacalera. The bus trip from Humahuaca to Huacalera takes 40 minutes and costs US$1.

Places to Stay

The *Residencial Humahuaca* at Córdoba 401 is a very clean, comfortable place despite its rather humble appearance from the outside. Rooms with private bathroom are US$5 a single and US$7 a double. Rooms without private bathroom are US$4 a single and US$6 a double.

Cheaper, but extremely spartan is the *Hospedaje Río Grande*, at Corrientes 480, one street behind the bus station.

The *Residencial Colonial* at Entre Rios 110 is a very comfortable hotel with friendly people. It's similarly priced to the Residencial Humahuaca.

Top of the range is the *Hotel de Turismo Humahuaca* which is the large building at Buenos Aires 650. Like its swimming pool it's empty in the off-season, and rooms can be very cheap at that time.

Getting There & Away

Expreso Panamericano, Atahualpa SRL and Cota Norte LTDA have daily buses from Jujuy to La Quiaca via Humahuaca. Jujuy to Humahuaca is a three hour trip.

Atahualpa SRL has daily buses to Salta, Jujuy and La Quiaca.

LA QUIACA

From Humahuaca a long, dusty road climbs a thousand metres in altitude through bleak, barren mountainous desert. Here, the only signs of life are tiny adobe homesteads nestled in V-shaped valleys, or built on steeply sloping hillsides grazed by goats. By the time you get to Tres Cruces the sun may be shining and the sky cloudless, but a bitterly chill wind will be blowing across the puna. Around Abra Pampa the landscape changes to a dry pampa-like grassland grazed by herds of cattle, donkeys, llama and sheep. At the end of the journey you come to La Quiaca, the main border crossing between Argentina and Bolivia, connected to the Bolivian border town of Villazón by a bridge.

Information

Consulates The Bolivian Consulate will issue visas for Bolivia. They charge US$15.

Things to See

It's worth visiting Yavi, an Indian village of adobe houses 16 km from La Quiaca. The main attraction is the **Iglesia de San Francisco** with its ornate interior decorated in gold, with windows of translucent onyx. The figures on the main altar are (from left to right as you face the altar) San Francisco, Santa Rosario, San Juan and San Rafael. The original church on this site dates back to about 1680. To get into the church you need to find the caretaker who will open the church and show you around. It's open Tuesday to Friday from 9 am to 12 noon and 3 to 6 pm, and on Saturdays from 9 am to 12 noon. You can get to Yavi and back by taxi for around US$7.

Places to Stay

The *Hotel Cristal* is down an arcade on the main street, and has some cheap, box-like rooms at the rear for US$4 a single and US$6 a double. It's very spartan but will do for a night or two.

The *Grand Hotel*, opposite the train station, has rooms for US$3 per person. Like the Cristal it's very spartan but is probably the better of the two places.

Also worth trying is the *Residencial Victoria* which was being renovated at the time of writing.

The *Hotel Turismo* is the main tourist hotel, with cheap off-season rooms for US$6 a single and US$9 a double, both with private bathrooms.

Getting There & Away

Buses Panamericano by the Grand Hotel has daily buses to Jujuy.

Buses Atahualpa SRL, in the same arcade as the Hotel Cristal, has daily buses to Jujuy and Salta.

The fare to Jujuy is US$9.

VILLAZON

Villazón is the Bolivian border town opposite the Argentine border town of La Quiaca. The altitude is 3447 metres. Tres Cruces, on the road down to Humahuaca, is even higher at 3700 metres.

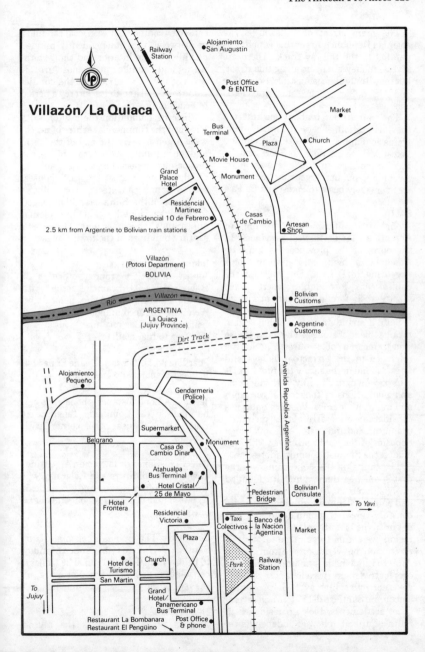

Villazón/La Quiaca

Railway Station
Alojamiento San Augustin
Post Office & ENTEL
Market
Bus Terminal
Plaza
Church
Movie House
Monument
Grand Palace Hotel
Residenciál Martinez
Residencial 10 de Febrero
Casas de Cambio
Artesan Shop
2.5 km from Argentine to Bolivian train stations
Villazón (Potosi Department)
BOLIVIA
Rio Villazón
Bolivian Customs
ARGENTINA
La Quiaca (Jujuy Province)
Argentine Customs
Dirt Track
Alojamiento Pequeño
Gendarmeria (Police)
Avenida Republica Argentina
Supermarket
Belgrano
Casa de Cambio Dinar
Monument
Atahualpa Bus Terminal
Hotel Cristal 25 de Mayo
Hotel Frontera
Pedestrian Bridge
Bolivian Consulate
To Yavi
Residencial Victoria
Taxi Colectivos
Banco de la Nacion Agentina
Market
Plaza
Park
Railway Station
Hotel de Turismo
Church
San Martin
To Jujuy
Grand Hotel Panamericano Bus Terminal
Restaurant La Bombanara
Restaurant El Pengüino
Post Office & phone

The main street of Villazón is the Avenida Republica Argentina which runs parallel to the railway track. There are several money-changers along this street, but they'll only change Australs, Bolivianos and US dollars cash – not travellers' cheques.

The train station is about one km from the bus station. There should be daily trains to Tupiza, Cotagaita, Vitichi and Potosí with connections to Sucre and La Paz. If not, go to the bus station on Avenida Republica Argentina from where there are daily buses to Potosí and La Paz.

SALTA

Along with Jujuy, Salta is one of Argentina's far north-west provinces. In the north of the province the Puna de Atacama, a high, cold plateau, joins Argentina to Bolivia. Due west of the capital are formidable deserts with bizarre rock formations and armies of cacti.

Salta is an Indian word which is said to mean a 'place of stones'. The name is also said to mean a 'place of rest', perhaps a reference to the attractive valleys and forests found in the east of the province. It is important agriculturally, with vineyards and plantations of tobacco, sugar, corn and many other crops. Western Salta has considerable mineral resources, including uranium, natural gas, oil, and even deposits of the gold and silver which so eluded the Spanish conquistadores.

The capital of the same name was the first Spanish settlement in Salta, founded in 1582. Even so, 70 years later the 'city' had barely 500 inhabitants and was under constant threat of Indian attacks. It was not until the 1770s that the Indians of this region were finally subjugated. Salta's position on the overland route from Buenos Aires to Lima made it an important stop-over for traders and travellers. The Spanish governor, presiding over Salta, Jujuy, Tucumán, Santiago del Estero and several other settlements, took up residence in Salta. Turmoil followed independence,

caused by conflicts between local caudillos, or between the independently-minded caudillos of the interior and the governments and caudillos in Buenos Aires. It was not until the 1870s that the conflict came to an end and Salta entered a period of peaceful progress.

Since its foundation the city of Salta has been the commercial centre of north-west Argentina. By the end of the 18th, and the beginning of the 19th century, the prosperous upper classes were able to indulge their tastes for fine houses, employing many architects, wood sculptors and silversmiths. Salta has still managed to preserve something of its colonial appearance and has many fine 18th century buildings in the town centre.

Information

Tourist Office The tourist office is at Buenos Aires 93, near the corner with Alvarado. The staff are very helpful and have a list of accommodation in private houses, as well as city maps, hotel lists and free tourist leaflets.

Post The post office is at Deáne Funes 140 between España and Belgrano.

Telephone Long distance phone calls can be made at the Compañia Telefonos at Belgrano 824, near the corner with Febrero.

Banks The Banco de la Nación Argentina, at the corner of Mitre and Belgrano, will change foreign cash and American Express and Thomas Cook travellers' cheques.

Consulates The Bolivian consulate is at Santiago del Estero 179. It's open Monday to Friday from 9 am to 1 pm. The Chilean consulate is at Ejercito de Norte 512, at the rear of the Güemes monument.

Things to See

A good place to start is the **Museo**

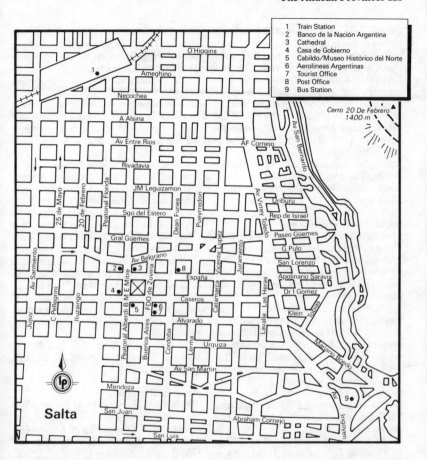

1 Train Station
2 Banco de la Nación Argentina
3 Cathedral
4 Casa de Gobierno
5 Cabildo/Museo Histórico del Norte
6 Aerolineas Argentinas
7 Tourist Office
8 Post Office
9 Bus Station

Salta

Provincial de Bellas Artes in the **Casa de Arias Rengel** at Florida 18. It's open Tuesday to Sunday from 9 am to 1 pm and 3 to 8 pm.

The museum's exhibition of modern art looks curiously out of place in this mid-18th century building but the remaining antique furniture gives an indication of the genteel flavour of upper class life in colonial Argentina. The key exhibit is a detailed painting of Salta as it appeared in 1854, showing dirt roads laid out in a neat grid, lined by red-roofed adobe brick houses and abundant trees. A close look at

the painting reveals bearded, top-hatted dandies on horseback, two-wheel ox carts, trains of pack donkeys, mestizos rugged up in ponchos, and tall poplar trees in the surrounding countryside.

With a bit of imagination it is not hard to capture something of the flavour of this era. A number of colonial buildings still stand in the town centre. Apart from the Casa de Arias Rengel, these include the late 18th century **Casa de Hernandez** at the corner of Alvarado and Florida, the **Casa de Leguizamon** (built in 1806 by a prosperous businessman) at Florida 8, and the building at **Caseros 417** which also houses a museum.

The **Cabildo**, which faces the main plaza, is of particular interest. The first cabildo of Salta was built in the 16th century. The current building owes its design to the cabildo which was built in 1676. It is very similar to the cabildo of Buenos Aires for which the plans were drawn in 1719. Both buildings show a simplicity of design with a plain arcade of two stories, capped by a bell tower in the centre. There is a good museum in the cabildo, open Wednesday to Sunday from 3 to 8 pm.

Places to Stay - bottom end

The *Residencial Viena* is upstairs at Florida 184, near the corner with Urquiza. It's very bare and basic with small rooms for US$4 per person. It is, however, very clean and well kept. The front rooms are very noisy.

The *Residencial Florida* (tel 212133) at Urquiza 722, on the corner with Florida, is probably the best place to stay in the lower price bracket. It's a modern building of several storeys with clean, basic but comfortable motel-style rooms. Rooms without private bathroom are US$3 a single and US$4 a double. Rooms with private bathroom are US$4 a single and US$7 a double. Rates during the tourist season may be higher.

The *Residencial Sandra* (tel 211241) is at Alvarado 630, between Buenos Aires and Alberdi. It's rather run-down and the downstairs rooms are dark and gloomy. Singles are US$5 and doubles US$9, both with private bathroom.

The *Residencial Centro* (tel 220132) at Belgrano 657 may not look like much from the outside but it's quite a pleasant place with friendly staff and a cool courtyard. The rooms are very basic but clean, though the front rooms tend to be noisy. Rooms without private bathroom are US$4 a single, and US$7 a double. Doubles with private bathroom are US$9.

The *Candilejas Hotel* is at Balcarce 980 near the train station. It's very simple but clean and habitable. Rooms are US$4 per person. Slightly more expensive rooms have private bathrooms.

The *Residencial Güemes* at Necochea 651, between Balcarce and Mitre, is rock-bottom accommodation but perhaps tolerable for a night. Singles are US$4 and doubles are US$6. It's fairly quiet but is definitely only for a short stay.

Places to Stay - middle

The *Hotel Italia* (tel 214050) at Alberdi 210 at the corner with Urquiza is a nice place. Singles are US$7 and doubles US$9, both with private bathroom.

One of the finest hotels in Salta is the *Hotel Elena* (tel 211529) at Buenos Aires 256, between San Martin and Urquiza. This is a colonial mansion set around a garden courtyard. The large rooms have double beds and private bathrooms. Singles are US$5 and doubles are US$9. If all the singles are full you should be able to get a double at a reduced rate if you're on your own.

The *Hotel Cabildo* (tel 224589) at Caseros 527, next to the Cabildo, has doubles for US$12.

Places to Stay - top end

The *Hotel Salta* (tel 211011) at the corner of Buenos Aires and Caseros is a large, semi-colonial style hotel with a charming downstairs dining room. Singles are US$21 and doubles are US$28.

The *Hotel California* (tel 216266) is at Alvarado 646. The California is a large hotel with singles for US$15 and doubles for US$20.

Similarly priced is the *Hotel Victoria Plaza* (tel 211222) at Zuviria 16, opposite the plaza. Slightly cheaper is the *Hotel Colonial* (tel 211740) at the corner of Zuviria and Caseros.

Places to Eat

You can satisfy your sweet tooth at the *Germania* at Caseros 356, a shop which sells, amongst others, *strudel de manzanas*

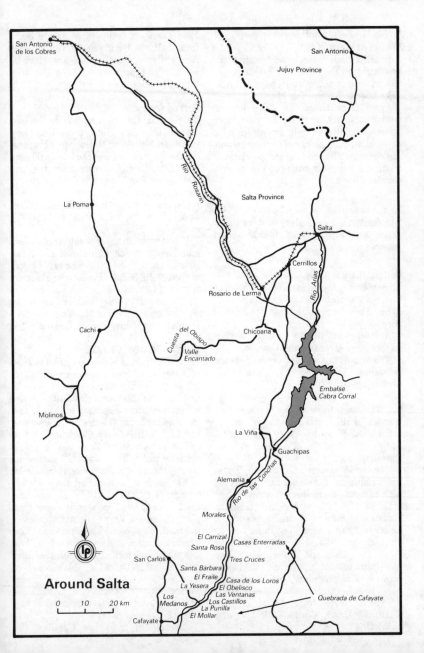

Around Salta

(apple strudel). Another sweet shop is *El Rincón* at Caseros 424.

Locally made sweets and biscuits can be bought at the Mercado Artesanal on San Martín at the western edge of town. Take bus No 3 from San Martín.

Apart from these there are lots of restaurants but nothing of particular interest in Salta. A walk downtown will, as usual, turn up plenty of confiterias and restaurants. The *Restaurant La Parla* is an up-market place with good pasta and parrilla dishes.

Things to Buy
The market is a good place to stock up on llama and alpaca wool blankets and ponchos.

Getting There & Away
Air Aerolíneas Argentinas (tel 214757) is at Caseros 475, near the corner with Buenos Aires. They have daily flights to Buenos Aires.

Austral (tel 224590) is at Buenos Aires 46, between Alvarado and Caseros.

The airport bus leaves from outside the Aerolíneas Argentinas office; ask inside about departure times.

Bus The long distance bus station is on Irigoyen at the eastern edge of town.

Empresa Bosio has daily buses to La Rioja via Rosario, Concepción and Catamarca.

Expreso Panamericano has daily buses from Salta to Tucumán and Córdoba, with connections to Buenos Aires.

La Veloz del Norte has daily buses to Resistencia, Paraná, Santa Fe, Mendoza, La Rioja, Córdoba and Tucumán.

Atahualpa SRL has daily buses to Jujuy, La Quiaca and Humahuaca. They have buses to Antofagasta in Chile during summer. Buses Andina Gemini also has buses to Antofagasta.

Typical fares from Salta are: to Tucumán US$8; Córdoba US$26; and Jujuy US$3.

Train There are trains three days a week from Salta to Retiro Station in Buenos Aires. Fares from Salta are: turista US$21; and primera US$29. The trip takes 24 hours.

Getting Around
To get from the train station to the bus station take bus No 5 from Necochea (between Mitre and Balcarce). This runs via the town centre and the Iglesia de San Francisco. Bus No 3 runs from the bus station, up San Martín to Florida; this is convenient for the town centre.

Cars can be rented from Avis (tel 220259) at Alvarado 537, and from A1 (tel 211877) at Córdoba 221.

If you want to meet some Argentines, and have a quick glimpse of the local sights, then there are plenty of tour operators in Salta. Typical is Turismo Saltur at Caseros 489, which has tours to the Quebrada del Toro, Cachi, San Antonio de los Cobres, Parque Nacional El Rey, Humahuaca, Jujuy and La Quiaca.

QUEBRADA DE CAFAYATE
West of Salta, the bizarre rock formations of the Quebrada de Cafayate are stretched out along the highway between Cafayate and La Viña. The most dramatic section is between two formations known as the Casa de los Loras (House of the Parrots) and Los Castillos (The Castles).

The aptly named Casa de los Loras actually looks like a waterfall turned to stone. One of the more obvious landmarks is El Obelisco, a pyramid-shaped rock formation by the roadside. Around the bend from El Obelisco stands a lone rock pinnacle which keeps silent watch over the road. Next come Las Ventanas (The Windows), huge solitary stone ridges. The last major rock formation before reaching Cafayate is Los Castillos, which looks like bundles of medieval castle towers. From the top of Las Ventanas you can overlook the Río Las Conchas winding its way through the quebrada.

Several km from Los Castillos the

Top: Village in the North-West
Left: Church at Yavi
Right: On the road from Cachi to Salta

Top: Near Cafayate
Bottom: House in which independence was declared in 1816

quebrada opens out on to a dry, flat plain and an army of cacti. Some have collapsed under their own weight, revealing their grotesque root system, and lie dried up on the desert like giant beached squids. Some of these monsters grow to over five or six metres high. Others stare down at you from mountain ridges like lines of Indians in old western movies. They produce large, white flowers which bloom from small buds on the arms of the cacti. Some people may find the area reminiscent of Arizona.

Getting There & Away

There a couple of ways of seeing this stretch of road. One is to hire your own car in Salta (you cannot hire cars in Cafayate). Another is to take a local bus from Salta, get off in the middle of the Quebrada, then walk towards Cafayate and pick up one of the buses going through later in the afternoon. There are tours available from Salta, but these seem more interested in getting their passengers to the souvenir shops in Cafayate than in seeing the scenery. See the Salta section for details of the tour operators.

Walking is a great way to get something of a feel for the desert. In a bus or car you miss the finer detail like the bird noises, the wind and the heat, and the strange feeling of being amidst the army of giant cacti. Walking is *hot* work here. You will need several litres of water, a hat and sun cream. It will take about five hours to walk the 20 km from the Casa de los Loras to the cactus army; from there it's another 10 km to Cafayate.

CAFAYATE

Cafayate is the chief township in the Quebrada de Cafayate and is noted for its vineyards. On the outskirts of town the Bodega La Banda is the oldest winery in the Cafayate Valley.

The valley has low rainfall, many days of sunshine and a high altitude (1700 metres above sea level) which provides a micro-climate with exceptionally good conditions for grape growing and wine production. You can sometimes go in and look at the processing plants. The **Museo de Vitiviniculture** on Güemes has an exhibition devoted to the history of wine production in Cafayate.

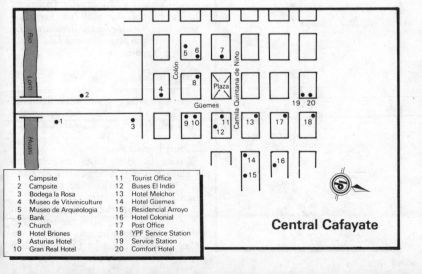

1 Campsite	11 Tourist Office
2 Campsite	12 Buses El Indio
3 Bodega la Rosa	13 Hotel Melchor
4 Museo de Vitiviniculture	14 Hotel Güemes
5 Museo de Arqueologia	15 Residencial Arroyo
6 Bank	16 Hotel Colonial
7 Church	17 Post Office
8 Hotel Briones	18 YPF Service Station
9 Asturias Hotel	19 Service Station
10 Gran Real Hotel	20 Comfort Hotel

Central Cafayate

Also interesting is the **Museo de Arquelogia** which is a private collection of Indian clay pots, vessels and funeral jars, pipes, amulets, arrow heads, stone tools and various other bric-a-brac.

Places to Stay

There are a number of cheap hotels near the plaza; see the map in this book for their location.

Two of the cheapest are the *Residencial Güemes* and the *Residencial Arroyo*. Both are very simple but are quite habitable.

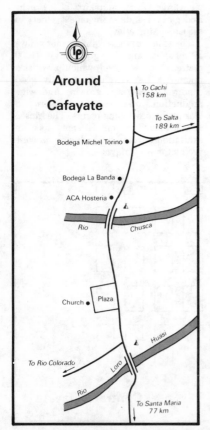

Around Cafayate

To Cachi 158 km

To Salta 189 km

Bodega Michel Torino ●

Bodega La Banda ●

ACA Hosteria ●

Rio   Chusca

Church ●   Plaza

To Rio Colorado

Huasi

Loro

Rio

To Santa Maria 77 km

Rooms are US$3 a single and US$4 a double without private bathroom.

Facing the main square is the *Hotel Briones* (tel 21270). It's clean and comfortable with single rooms for US$4 and doubles for US$6 both with private bathrooms. The rooms are set around a central courtyard and there's a confiteria attached. Similarly priced, if a bit rundown, is the *Hotel Colonial* (tel 21233) with rooms arranged around a central courtyard.

The *Hotel Melchor* (tel 21065) at the corner of Güemes and Almagro has small but comfortable rooms. There's a pleasant lounge area and the staff are friendly. Rooms with private bathroom are US$7 a single and US$9 a double. Similarly priced are the *Hotel Comfort*, the *Gran Real Hotel* (tel 21016) and the *Asturias Hotel* (tel 21040).

Two km from the centre is the *ACA Hosteria Cafayate* (tel 21296). Rooms are US$11 a single and US$15 a double.

Places to Eat

The *Restaurant La López Pereyra* makes an attempt at the wild west image with hide-covered wooden chairs and decorative wagon wheels and shotguns. Otherwise it's a run of the mill but agreeable parrillada. Similar are the *Restaurant La Apachoyo*, the *Miguelito* and *La Carreta de Don Olegario*.

Things to Buy

There are many souvenir shops in Cafayate, selling llama wool blankets, ponchos and scarves. Worth buying are the beautiful onyx jewellery boxes.

Getting There & Away

El Indio has daily buses from Salta to Cafayate. The trip takes four hours and the fare is US$5. The buses continue to Santa María.

From Cafayate there is a daily bus to Angastaco. The trip takes two hours and the fare is US$2. The road runs via San Carlos, an identikit of Cafayate, then passes through the jagged grey-brown rock of the Quebrada de Salta, the Quebrada de Estanque and the Quebrada de Flecha. At intervals there are tiny adobe Indian hamlets and vineyards which appear curiously out of place in the hostile environment. From Angastaco there is a bus every Friday to Cachi.

Empresa Aconquija has buses three days a week from Tucumán to Cafayate via Santa María.

ANGASTACO

Angastaco is an oasis amidst the mountains, set in a small river valley. Walk around here and you get the impression that nothing has changed much since Pedro de Mendoza's day. Angastaco is a settlement of squat mud brick, stone and thatch houses, and sandy roads, surrounded by fields of vines, onions and corn. Tall poplar trees and barren mountains form a backdrop to the village. Weather-beaten Indian women lead herds of sheep and bearded goats out to pasture. Donkeys stare at you from wooden corrals. Earthen bread kilns and primitive horse-drawn ploughs are still used by the farmers. The ACA Hosteria looks ridiculously out of scale.

Places to Stay

The *ACA Hostería* opposite the plaza is a simple but comfortable place with rooms for US$6 per person. In the off-season it's likely to be closed so find the caretaker who will give you a room. There's a small general store and one restaurant by the plaza.

Getting There & Away

Expreso Marcus Rueda has a bus every Friday from Angastaco to Cachi via Molinos. The bus continues from Cachi to Salta.

MOLINOS

On the road from Angastaco to Cachi, the village of Molinos is noted for its 18th century church. The church (coloured yellow by a preservative paste) stands opposite the restored mansion of the last Spanish governor of Salta, now used as a hotel and restaurant. Woollen cloth, woven by the local people, can be bought there. The body of the last Spanish governor is preserved in the church. Once exposed, it has now been encased in a crypt. The story goes that the dry climate preserved the body naturally and so it was kept on view until about 30 years ago.

CACHI

A dusty little settlement on the road from Angastaco to Salta, Cachi has an interesting archaeological museum on the main plaza. The museum houses a large collection of stones decorated with Indian petroglyphs, including images of animals, people and geometric patterns. Descending by road from Cachi to Salta you wind your way down barren, rugged mountains past armies of cacti to the flat plains below.

Places to Stay

The *Hostel Nevado de Cachi*, around the corner from the main plaza, has small rooms with private bathroom. It's very basic but clean and habitable. Rooms are about US$3 per person.

If you're coming in from Angastaco and want to stay at the *ACA Hotel Nevado de Cachi* get the bus to drop you off at the path leading up to the hotel. Rooms are US$12 a single and US$15 a double. It has a moderately priced restaurant.

Getting There & Away

Expreso Marcus Rueda has daily buses from Salta to Cachi. The trip takes four hours and the fare is US$6. The buses continue from Cachi to La Poma. In Salta the Expreso Marcus Rueda terminal is at Islas Malvinas 393, not at the main bus station.

SAN ANTONIO DE LOS COBRES

Heading north-west from Salta to the mountain settlement of San Antonio de los Cobres takes you through some of Argentina's starkest mountain territory,

San Antonio de los Cobres

littered with cacti, tiny homesteads of adobe houses, and deep river valleys. The bus passes through mountainous areas which look like huge piles of rubble dumped from giant pick-up trucks. Wild llama can sometimes be seen. Domesticated donkeys, sheep and goats are kept by the local people.

If you arrive at night, San Antonio appears over the hill as a bundle of lights in the middle of nowhere. Many of the inhabitants are Indian. Most of the houses are rough, adobe brick bungalows, yet even here there is the inevitable plaza with busts of the independence heroes. The air is thin (San Antonio is 3700 metres above sea level) and you may experience headaches and shortness of breath.

Places to Stay

The *Hospedaje Belgrano* on the main street has rooms for US$1.50 per person. It's a squat, adobe brick building with animal hide ceilings. Further up is the *Hospedaje y Restaurant Los Andes* which is similarly priced. There are a couple of bars in town and some general stores where you can stock up on food and drink. San Antonio is bitterly cold at night and in the morning; you need warm clothes!

Things to Buy

In San Antonio you can buy hand-made sheep's wool caps, gloves and socks.

Getting There & Away

Bus El Quebradeño has buses five days a week from Salta to San Antonio de los Cobres. The fare is US$5. Some of these continue on to Mina Tincalaya.

There is a road from San Antonio de los Cobres to La Poma, but there are no buses and if you're driving you may find it impassable or closed to traffic. La Poma is accessible by road from Cachi.

Train The so-called 'Train to the Clouds' runs daily from Salta to San Antonio de los Cobres. The fare in turista class is around US$4. Work on this extraordinary train line, with its 21 tunnels, 31 bridges and 13 viaducts, began in 1921 and took 27 years to complete.

The llama which you may see on the road to San Antonio de los Cobres are members of the camel family. Camels evolved around 40 to 45 million years ago in North America, but it has only been in the last two or three million years that they migrated into Asia and South America. The vicuña, guanaco and alpaca are also members of the camel family.

Unlike the double-humped Bactrian camel, the cameloids are graceful creatures. Like other members of the camel family the cameloids are extremely well adapted to the dry and often rugged environments in which they live. Soft pads on their toes help them walk on rocky trails.

The llama, with its thick coat, looks like a cross between a camel and shaggy deer. It can be found in north-west Argentina at elevations between 2300 and 4000 metres. An adult llama stands a metre or more at the shoulder and has a uniform or multi-coloured white, brown, grey or black coat.

The vicuña, which can be seen in the higher altitudes of the mountains of north-west Argentina, stands a metre at the shoulder. It has a cinnamon coloured coat with the underside, and sometimes also the chest, coloured white.

The guanaco lives in the Andes foothills of Peru and Chile and on the plains of Argentine Patagonia. About the same height as a llama but slightly lighter, it has a deep cinnamon coloured coat with white undersides.

The llama and alpaca were tamed by the South American Indians about 4000 to 5000 years ago, but the guanaco and vicuña have always been wild. The vicuña grazes on alpine grass at altitudes between 3700 to 4800 metres. The guanaco can live in more diverse habitats, including forests and open grasslands in elevations ranging from sea level to just over 4000 metres. Unlike the vicuña, the guanaco does not need to drink water since it's able to draw all it needs from what it eats.

About 90% of South America's alpacas and about 75% of its vicuñas are in Peru. About 70% of the continent's llamas are in Bolivia. Over 90% of all guanacos are in Argentina. In the Andean countries alpaca and vicuña are prized for their wool. Apart from their wool, llamas have traditionally been used as beasts of burden. Domestic cameloid populations declined drastically when the Spanish invaded South America. Uncontrolled hunting and the introduction of sheep decimated the guanaco populations, thought to have originally been around 35 to 50 million in Argentina alone.

SANTA MARIA

A dusty road leads from Cafayate to Santa María, past tiny adobe hamlets and vineyards. It's a dull, hot and tiring trip. Santa María is marginally bigger than Cafayate, and though lacking its character still has something of a backwoods feel to it.

Places to Stay

Most of the hotels are closed in the off-season. The only ones which are open all year are the *Plaza Hotel* opposite the main plaza and the *Hotel Provincial de Turismo* at the corner of San Martín and 1 de Mayo. Both charge about US$9 a single and US$12 a double for rooms with private bathroom. They're both modern, motel-style buildings with comfortable rooms.

1	Hotel Provincial de Turismo
2	Empresa Bosio
3	Hotel Plaza
4	Banco de la Nación Argentina
5	Hotel Alemán
6	Empresa Aconquija
7	Buses El Indio

Santa María

Places to Eat

There are several restaurants in town, including the *Restaurant El Rancho de Fredo* on Moreno, near the corner with Belgrano, which is pleasant and fairly cheap.

Getting There & Away

Empresa Bosio at Belgrano 415 has buses three days a week to Tucumán.

Empresa Aconquija at Belgrano 220 has buses six days a week to Tucumán.

El Indio at Belgrano 271 has daily buses to Cafayate and Salta.

TAFI DEL VALLE

Three hours drive out of Santa María, on the road to Tucumán, you pass through the township of Tafí del Valle, nestled in hilly, misty countryside reminiscent of the Scottish highlands. There is an ACA Hostería here, and a motel-style tourist complex with cabins outside the town on the road in from Santa María. From here the road follows a lush river valley which makes a startling contrast to the drier highlands. 'Tafí' is an Indian word which means 'the place of the cold wind'. It seems an unlikely place for settlement but, in fact, it was once settled by an Indian culture which came from the central Andes and entered Argentina before the 5th century AD. They terraced the slopes to plant their crops, made metal implements, built houses of stone, and erected monolithic stone pillars.

TUCUMAN

Tucumán was founded in 1565 and is the capital of the province of the same name, one of the smallest in Argentina. Nevertheless, it's noted for its prosperous sugar industry, one which has had a virtual monopoly on the Argentine market.

The Jesuits were the first to embark on the large scale production of sugar, with plantations around their missions worked by Indian labour. The plantations declined after the expulsion of the Jesuits in 1767, but 50 years later the Tucumán plantations were revived and new sugar mills were built. The building of railroads in the 19th century allowed access to the national market, while tariffs protected sugar production from foreign competition. Despite the wealth generated by sugar production, the money never reached the ordinary plantation labourers and the province remained one of the poorest in Argentina.

Tourist Office The tourist office is on 24 Septembre opposite the Plaza Independencia. They're friendly and helpful and have city maps and useful tourist leaflets to give away.

Post The main post office is at the corner of 25 de Mayo and Córdoba.

Telephone For long distance phone calls go to the Compañia Argentina de Teléfonos at Maipú 980.

Banks Foreign cash and travellers' cheques can be changed at Maguitur at San Martín 765.

Things to See

The **Casa Histórica de la Independencia**, on Congreso, is the building where Argentine independence was proclaimed in 1816. Portraits of the people who attended the Congress are hung on the walls.

Tucumán was chosen as the site of the Congress to avoid fear of domination by Buenos Aires. Nearly all the Argentine provinces sent delegates, of whom most were either lawyers or clergy. In effect, the Congress acted as a sort of makeshift Argentine government while Spain was preparing military expeditions to regain control of its colonies.

The independence movement aimed to expel Spain from Latin America, but it

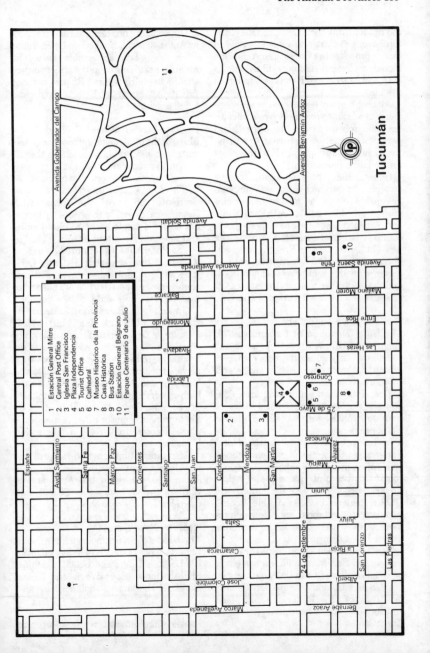

1 Estación General Mitre
2 Central Post Office
3 Iglesia San Francisco
4 Plaza Independencia
5 Tourist Office
6 Cathedral
7 Museo Histórico de la Provincia
8 Casa Histórica
9 Bus Station
10 Estación General Belgrano
11 Parque Centenario 9 de Julio

Tucumán

did not plan any social reform. One of the topics on the Congress's agenda was, in fact, a proposal to establish an Argentine monarchy. Prominent figures like Generals Jose San Martín and Belgrano supported the idea.

Although many leaders of the independence movement were staunch republicans, the monarchists gained the upper hand partly because it was felt that Argentina would get no support from Europe unless it also had a monarchy.

General Belgrano even advocated the crowning of an Inca prince to provide Argentina with a native American monarchy, which would unite Peru, Chile and Argentina as one Spanish-speaking country. Others considered offering the new throne to various French, Spanish, Portuguese and English princes. For one reason or another each proposal floundered, and the whole idea was put to rest by 1820 as Argentina fell into a period of anarchy.

Places to Stay - bottom end

The *Hotel Tucumán* at Catamarca 573, opposite the Plaza Alberdi, is basic but clean and fairly quiet. Its rooms without private bathroom are US$5 a single and US$6 a double.

The *Hotel Norte* at Catamarca 639, opposite the Ferrocarril General Mitre, is a rundown shack with box-like rooms for US$2 per person.

In the centre of town is the *Hotel Congreso* at Congreso 74, which has two levels of rooms set around a sort of indoor courtyard. It's quite gloomy and noisy. Rooms without private bathroom are US$6 a single and US$9 a double. Rooms with private bathroom are a few dollars more. Almost next door is the similarly priced *Hotel Astoria*.

The best place in Tucumán is the *Hotel Colonial* at San Martín 35, on the block between Avalleneda and Balcarce. Singles are US$6 and doubles are US$9 with private bathrooms. It's a clean, cool place and one of the best small hotels in Argentina.

Opposite the bus terminal and upstairs at Aráoz 40 is the *Hospedaje La Estrella*. It's a simple but comfortable place. The rooms are set back from the street so they should be fairly quiet. Rooms without private bathroom are US$5 a single and US$6 a double.

Places to Stay - middle

Many of the mid-range and top-end hotels will give considerable discounts in the off-season, so you can often get very good accommodation at very cheap prices.

The *Hotel California* (tel 229259) is at Corrientes 985 near the corner with Catamarca. Rooms with private bathroom are US$13 a single and US$18 a double, and most are air-conditioned.

The *Hotel Miami* at Junín 580 is a short walk from the Ferrocarril General Mitre. It's a modern, multi-storey hotel with air-conditioned rooms with private bathroom for US$14 a single and US$20 a double.

Opposite the Plaza Independencia is the *Hotel Plaza* at San Martín 435. Despite its fairly ornate facade, it is quite simple inside with two levels of rooms set around an indoor courtyard. Rooms with private bathrooms are US$10 a single and US$15 a double. Nearby is the modern high-rise *Hotel Corona* which is similarly priced. The *Hotel Metropol* is at 24 de Septembre 524, on the other corner of the plaza. Rooms are US$16 a single and US$23 a double.

There are a number of mid-range places on Alvarez between Congreso and 9 de Julio. These include the *Francia* (tel 229780), the *Versailles* (tel 229760), and the *Gran Hotel Premier*.

Places to Stay - top end

The *Hotel del Sol* is a modern high-rise on Laprida opposite the Plaza Independencia. It's US$23 a single and US$31 a double. Slightly more expensive is the *Grand Hotel del Tucumán* at Soldati 380.

Places to Eat

For something different try the *Restaurante*

Arabe Ali Baba at Junín 380. There are other Arabic restaurants at Junín 545 and Córdoba 700. For parrilla and fish try the *Gran Restaurant La Cantina* at San Martín 750. There are plenty of cheap and nasty hash houses around the bus station.

Getting There & Away

Air Austral (tel 224920) is at 24 de Septiembre 546. They have daily flights to Buenos Aires and Corrientes.

Aerolíneas Argentinas (tel 228747) is at 9 de Julio 112. They have daily flights to Buenos Aires and Córdoba, four days a week to Mendoza, three days a week to Rosario, and two days a week to Neuquén and Bariloche.

Bus The bus station is on Avenida Sáenz Peña.

La Estrella has daily buses to Mendoza. Panamericana has daily buses to Córdoba, Salta and Jujuy. El Rayo has daily buses to Sáenz Peña, Resistencia and Corrientes. TA Chevalier has daily buses to Buenos Aires, Rosario and Córdoba.

Typical fares from Tucumán are: to Mendoza US$23, and to Buenos Aires US$19. The trips from Tucumán to Mendoza or Buenos Aires take 20 hours.

Train There are two train stations in Tucumán.

The station on Sáenz Peña (opposite the bus station) handles trains which only have turista and primera classes. These include trains to Salta, Jujuy and La Quiaca, and some of the trains to Córdoba, Rosario and to Retiro Station in Buenos Aires.

Trains with pullman and coche cama class leave from the Ferrocarril General Mitre, opposite the Plaza Juan Bautista Alberdi.

Typical primera class fares from Tucumán are: to Salta US$7; Jujuy US$7; La Quiaca US$12; Córdoba US$10; and Buenos Aires US$23.

Getting Around

The most useful bus is the No 8 which connects the Ferrocarril General Mitre with the centre of town and the long distance bus station (Terminal de Omnibus).

From the stop on Catamarca outside the Ferrocarril General Mitre it runs down Corrientes, Maipú, Córdoba, Salta, Septiembre, Chacabuco, San Lorenzo, Congreso, Septiembre and Aráoz.

From the stop on Sáenz Peña outside the bus station it returns to the Ferrocarril General Mitre.

MENDOZA

Heading south from Tucumán and crossing the provinces of Catamarca, La Rioja and San Juan, you come to the province of Mendoza. The provinces of San Juan, San Luis and Mendoza comprise a region known as the *Cuyo* which is an Araucanian Indian word which means 'sandy land'.

The Spanish first came through the Cuyo around 1550, crossing the Andes between Argentina and Chile via the Uspallata Pass. A few years later the fertile land and large numbers of agrarian Indians encouraged them to settle the Cuyo. Many of the towns in this region were founded very early: Mendoza in 1561, San Juan in 1562, and San Luis in 1594.

The chief city of the Cuyo is Mendoza. It was named after Don García Hurtado de Mendoza, the governor of Chile who initiated Spanish settlement of the Cuyo with expeditions from Chile. Long before the Spanish arrived the local Huarpe Indians had well-developed agriculture, with irrigation systems, pottery and arts strongly influenced by the Inca. An Inca fort once stood on the site of modern-day Mendoza, and the Inca road from Cuzco ended in the Uspallata Pass.

For the first 150 years the 'towns' of the Cuyo were barely more than stockades. At first Mendoza had barely a dozen soldiers to defend it against Indian raids, and was cut off from Chile for six months each year when the mountain passes were buried in deep snow. Although trade with Chile continued, the settlements of the Cuyo became much more closely tied to Buenos Aires and the northern Andean settlements.

The Cuyo developed early as a fruit-growing and vineyard centre. Fruit was dried or conserved and either sold in Argentina or exported to Chile. Fruit was first grown in small orchards. It was not until the present century, with a big increase in population and demand, that fruit was grown in large quantities. Today the Cuyo, Misiones Province, the Río Negro valley and the area around Buenos Aires are all important fruit growing regions.

With the building of railways (which reached Mendoza from Buenos Aires in 1885) and the introduction of refrigeration it was possible to export fresh fruit from the interior to Buenos Aires and abroad. The region began to attract vineyard farmers from Italy. French capital was used to set up wineries. Tariffs protected the industry from foreign imports. Chilean and European immigrants were allowed to establish small farms in the province. Aside from fruit and wine, Mendoza is an important oil producer, and also has deposits of uranium, copper and other valuable ores.

Information

Tourist Office The tourist office (tel 242800) is at San Martín 1143. They have free maps of the city and lists of hotels and are very helpful.

Post The main post office is at the corner of San Martín and Colón. ENTEL is at Chile 1574.

Banks There are several money-changers along San Martín between Catamarca and Garibaldi which will change foreign cash and travellers' cheques. There is a money-changer at the bus station which changes American dollars cash and Chilean pesos.

Consulates The Chilean Consulate (tel 255024) is at Civit 296.

Things to See

The city of Mendoza was destroyed by earthquake and fire in 1861, and hardly any colonial buildings survive. Mendoza is, however, the departure point for the journey over the Andes to Santiago, in Chile.

Cerro de la Gloria

In 1817 General José San Martín led his revolutionary army from Mendoza over the Andes to liberate Chile from Spanish rule. A monument to San Martín stands atop Cerro de la Gloria in the Parque San Martín on the edge of the Mendoza.

By modern standards San Martín's army seems absurdly small. It comprised just 4000 soldiers (mainly Chilean exiles and Argentines), 1400 militia to help transport supplies, 9000 mules, 1500 horses and a mere 18 cannon. Most of the army marched through the Paso Uspallata and Paso de los Patos. It took 18 days to get through the passes, battling both Spanish units and altitude sickness. After crossing the mountains, the main army crushed the Spanish at the Battle of Chacabuco, while other units captured the settlements of Copiapó, Talca and Coquimbo.

Places to Stay – bottom end

There are cheap hotels near the train station and the bus station, although those near the train station are more convenient and are close to the town centre.

The *Hotel Terminal* on Alberdi, oppsite the bus station, has very small rooms but is clean and habitable. Rooms without private bathroom are US$5 a single and US$7 a double.

There are several cheap residencials on Martin Güemes behind the bus station, a short walk from Alberdi. These include the *Residencial Betty* at Güemes 456; the *Residencial San Fernándo* next door; the

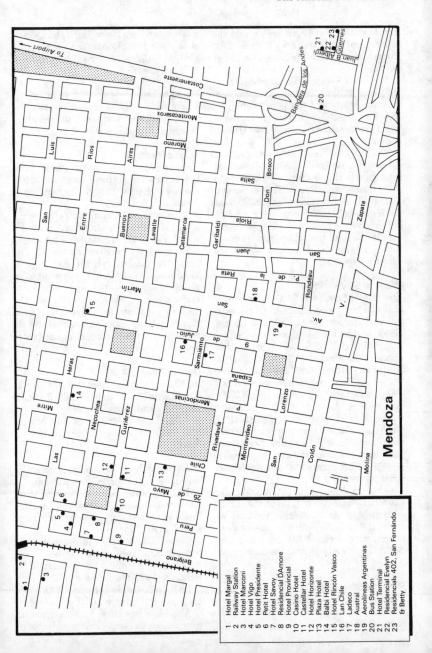

Mendoza

1 Hotel Margal
2 Railway Station
3 Hotel Marconi
4 Hotel Vigo
5 Hotel Presidente
6 Petit Hotel
7 Hotel Savoy
8 Residencial D'Amore
9 Hotel Provincial
10 Casino Hotel
11 Castellar Hotel
12 Hotel Horizonte
13 Plaza Hotel
14 Balbi Hotel
15 Hotel Rincón Vasco
16 Lan Chile
17 Ladeco
18 Austral
19 Aerolíneas Argentinas
20 Bus Station
21 Hotel Terminal
22 Residencial Evelyn
23 Residencials 402, San Fernando
   & Betty

Residencial 402 at Güemes 402; and the *Residencial Evelyn* at Güemes 294. Rooms at all these are about US$3 per person.

The *Hotel Savoy*, at Belgrano 1377 near the train station, is very basic but has friendly staff and is good value by Mendoza standards. Rooms with private bathroom are US$4 a single and US$6 a double.

The *Hotel Vigo* is on Necochea, near the corner with Belgrano. With its pleasant front garden this is quite a good place to stay. Rooms start from US$4 per person.

The *Hotel Horizonte* (tel 253998) at Gutiérrez 565 has rooms with private bathroom from US$6 a single and US$8 a double. Despite the rather dim interiors this is a fairly quiet, comfortable place with friendly staff.

Places to Stay - middle

The *Hotel Margal* (tel 252013) at Juan B Justo 75 has air-conditioned rooms with private bathrooms from US$7 a single and US$9 a double. Similar is the *Hotel Marconi* (tel 233636) which is roughly opposite the *Margal*.

Also try the *Hotel Presidente* (tel 234808) on Perú, near the corner with Las Heras and the *Petit Hotel* (tel 232099) across the road.

The *Hotel Provincial* (tel 258284) at Belgrano 1259 is a very respectable hotel with comfortable little rooms. It's a short walk from the train station. Rooms with private bathroom are US$10 a single and US$13 a double.

Other mid-range places include the *Castellar Hotel* (tel 234245) at the corner of 25 de Mayo and Gutiérrez; the *Castillo Hotel* (tel 257370) which is almost next door; and the *Hotel Rincón Vasco* (tel 233033) on Las Heras near the corner with 9 de Julio.

Places to Stay - top end

The *Hotel Balbi* (tel 233500) at Las Heras 340 has singles from US$15 and doubles from US$20.

The grandiose *Plaza Hotel* (tel 233000) is at Chile 1124. Rooms in this imposing old-style edifice are US$21 a single and US$29 a double.

Places to Eat

There's a formidable range of restaurants, cafés, snack bars and other eateries along San Martín and Las Heras.

Around Mendoza

Though Mendoza is dry and arid, irrigation networks have drawn on the five rivers which pass through the province to create rich farmland.

Mendoza is well known for its vineyards, and produces over two-thirds of Argentina's wine. There are a number of *bodegas* outside the city which can be visited. The grape harvest festival, the *Fiesta de la Vendimia*, is in March. If you want to go skiing or hiking in the Andes there are many shops in Mendoza which sell the necessary equipment. Travel agencies on Las Heras and San Martín organise ski tours, city tours and tours to the places around Mendoza.

Getting There & Away

Air Aerolíneas Argentinas (tel 245146) is at San Martín 850. They have daily flights to Bariloche and Buenos Aires.

Austral (tel 293167) is at San Martín 921. They have daily flights to Buenos Aires.

Bus The new bus station is on Bandera de los Andes at the corner with Alberdi.

TAC has daily buses to Buenos Aires, Bariloche, Zapala, Córdoba, and Santiago in Chile with connections to Valparaíso and Viña del Mar.

Chile Bus and Fenix Pullman also have buses to Santiago and Valparaíso.

Coitram has daily taxi colectivos to Santiago and Viña del Mar.

La Estrello has daily buses to San Juan, La Rioja, Catamarca and Tucumán.

Alto Valle has buses to Neuquén with connections to Bariloche, San Martín de

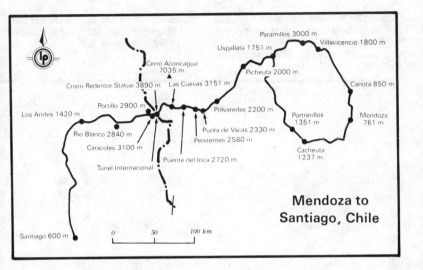

Cerro Aconcagua 7035 m
Cristo Redentor Statue 3890 m Las Cuevas 3151 m
Los Andes 1420 m
Portillo 2900 m
Río Blanco 2840 m
Caracoles 3100 m
Tunel Internacional
Puente del Inca 2720 m
Paramillos 3000 m
Uspallata 1751 m Villavicencio 1800 m
Picheuta 2000 m
Canota 850 m
Polvaredas 2200 m
Punta de Vacas 2330 m
Penitentes 2580 m
Portrerillos 1351 m
Mendoza 761 m
Cacheuta 1237 m
Santiago 600 m
0 50 100 km

Mendoza to Santiago, Chile

Los Andes, Zapala and Junín de los Andes. Also try Empresa de Sur.

Typical bus fares from Mendoza are: to Buenos Aires US$30; Bariloche US$30; Zapala US$24; Córdoba US$13; Santiago US$11; and Neuquén US$14.

Train The *Aconcagua* departs Mendoza daily at 4 pm and arrives in Buenos Aires the following morning around 8.30 am. A bit faster is the twice-weekly *El Libertador* and the weekly *El Condor*. Fares on the *Aconcagua* are: turista US$11; primera US$15; pullman US$22; and coche cama US$29.

Chile to Mendoza

The journey from Santiago over the mountains to Mendoza is one of the most striking bus rides in Latin America. You start in Santiago in the morning, travelling east through a landscape of tattered farmland, hovels and poorly cultivated land. The road passes over hilly country, through the Chacabuco Tunnel and drops out onto a barren, rugged landscape of scrub, cacti and vineyards.

You begin to climb into the Andes Mountains following the road to the Portillo Ski Resort.

After leaving Portillo the road by-passes the statue of **Cristo Redentor**, and carries on to Punta del Inca and the Argentine customs post.

The road then follows the dry Río Vaca valley to the eastern side of the Andes Mountains. The mountains seem to tumble out onto the Argentine plains, with their rows of tattered poplar trees, sprawling shanty towns and endless highways.

Getting Around

To get from the town centre to the bus station take the local trolley bus marked 'Villa Nueva' from Lavalle, between San Martín and San Juan. The 'Villa Nueva' bus leaves the bus terminal from the stop on Alberdi. It runs along España, Gutiérrez, past the Plaza de San Martín to Lavalle. Buses 5, 6 and 9 from the bus terminal will take you to Juan B Justo near the train station.

Taxis are also available.

Turismo La Cumbre has daily tours to

various places around Mendoza, including the mountains and the wineries. For public buses to some of these places enquire at Expreso Uspallata at the bus station.

Cars can be rented from National (tel 231420) at Sarmiento 127, and from Avis (tel 257802) at Espejo 228.

Patagonia

'Patagonia' refers to the huge area of land occupying the southern cone of South America, generally considered to be the area south of the Río Colorado and north of the Straits of Magellan, the strait which separates the island of Tierra del Fuego from the mainland. Most of Patagonia belongs to Argentina and encompasses the provinces of Nuequén, Río Negro, Chubut and Santa Cruz. On the other side of the Andes is a thin slice which belongs to Chile.

History

Patagonia was given its name by Magellan, but whatever romantic visions it may conjure up it's probably derived from the word *pata*, Spanish slang for 'foot'. This might be a reference to a race of large Indians who once inhabited these parts and who wrapped their feet in animal skins, making them seem very large. An Italian, Antonio Pigafetta, who survived the Magellan expedition, recounts seeing giants in Patagonia and describes one as:

> . . . so tall that the tallest of us only came up to his waist. He was very well built and when he was brought to the captain he was clothed with the skin of a beast. The skin was very skilfully sewn. He had his feet covered with the skin of this animal. The captain named these people Pataghom . . . .

There is another story that Magellan named the land after Gran Patagón, a monster in the *Primaleon of Greece*, a romance of chivalry published in Spain several years before Magellan set sail. In this story the hero, Primaleon, sails to a remote island. There he captures a monster called the Gran Patagón which he takes back to his own land to present to his queen.

While wintering at San Julián, Magellan, perhaps inspired by the story, decided to kidnap two giants to take back to the Spanish king. Pigafetta recounts that this was done by treachery:

> . . . we gave them knives, scissors, mirrors, bells and glass, all of which they held in their hands. Meanwhile the captain sent for large iron fetters, like those which are put on the feet of prisoners. The giants took great pleasure in seeing these fetters . . . the captain had the fetters put on the feet of both of them . . . but then seeing the trick which had been played on them, they began to blow and foam at the mouth like bulls . . .

In Greek *patagos* means 'a roaring' or a 'gnashing of teeth'. Since Pigafetta describes the Patagonians blowing and foaming at the mouth like bulls it's possible that Magellan had actually given the land of the giants a Greek name.

One of the Indians escaped. The other was got on board a ship but eventually died in the Pacific. A hundred years later William Shakespeare drew on Pigafetta's account for *The Tempest*. In this play, first performed in 1611, the servant Stephano contemplates the economic gain to be had from the savage Caliban:

If I can recover him and keep him tame, and get to Naples with him, he's a present for any Emperor that ever trod on neat's leather.

Shakespeare's play had alluded to the rape of the New World, as fortune seekers of one type or other sought to carry off the wealth of El Dorado. In the centuries to follow even the continent's most distant corner, Patagonia, would not escape depredation. Aside from the voyages of Magellan and other mariners (whose primary purpose was to find a southern route around the American continent) the first European excursions into Patagonia were inspired by the search for Trapalanda.

Trapalanda was a southern El Dorado, supposedly inhabited by the Spanish-speaking mestizo offspring of Spanish soldiers and American Indians. The existence of this city was first reported by Francisco César, Sebastian Cabot's pilot, who in 1528 wandered up-country from the Río de la Plata, crossed the Andes and returned with stories of a civilisation where gold was in common use. For the next four centuries expeditions and lone wanderers set out in search of this city, sometimes reported to be in the Andes Mountains of southern Patagonia.

Pillaging Patagonia was not, however, an easy task and it caused later writers to wax lyrical on the hardships of adventure. The voyage to Patagonia by the English navigator John Davis, in 1591-93, might even have inspired Samuel Taylor Coleridge. Though Davis survived the long voyage home his crew were ridden with scurvy and burrowing worms ate the timbers, ropes, clothes and human flesh. In *The Rime of the Ancient Mariner* Coleridge could have been paraphrasing Davis:

The many men, so beautiful!
And they all dead did lie:
And a thousand thousand slimy things
Lived on; and so did I.

Despite the early forays by Europeans,

the whole of Patagonia and a good slice of the pampas remained firmly under Indian control right up until the middle of the 19th century. The Patagonian Indians lived by hunting the rhea (a bird similar to an ostrich or emu), the seal, and the guanaco (a variety of llama) with bow and arrow, and by collecting shellfish from the rocky shoreline. They wore fur clothes and made tools and weapons from sea shells, stone and wood. In 1741 a European visitor reported for the first time that the Patagonian Indians were riding horses – probably influenced by the horse-riding Araucanian (Mapuche) Indians who had invaded the plains on the eastern side of the Andes that century.

When Darwin visited Patagonia in 1833 he shed some light on earlier reports of giants inhabiting the area. He wrote:

We had an interview at Cape Gregory with the famous so-called gigantic Patagonians, who gave us cordial reception. Their height appears greater than it really is, from their large guanaco mantles, their long flowing hair, and general figure; on an average their height is about six feet, with some men taller and only a few shorter; and the women are also tall; altogether they are certainly the tallest race which we anywhere saw . . .

The coming of the Europeans spelt the end of the Indians. If there ever truly was a race of giant Indians in Argentina, they disappeared in the exterminations of the 19th century. In his diary Darwin recorded the destruction of the native people, and in one instance writes of the massacre of Indians by a force of 200 soldiers:

They first discovered the Indians, by the dust of their horses, in a wild mountainous country . . . The Indians were about 112, women, children and men, in number. They were nearly all taken or killed, very few escaped. The Indians are now so terrified, that they offer no resistance in body, but each escapes as well he can, neglecting even his wife and children. The soldiers pursue and sabre every man. Like wild animals, however, they fight to the last instant. One Indian nearly cut off with his teeth, the thumb of a soldier, allowing his own eye to be nearly pushed out of the socket. Another who was wounded, pretended death, with a knife under his cloak, ready to strike the first who approached ... Every one here is fully convinced that this is the justest war, because it is against Barbarians. Who would believe in this age in a Christian civilised country that such atrocities were committed ... Great as it is, in another half century I think there will not be a wild Indian in the Pampas North of Río Negro ...

For centuries Patagonia seemed too remote and barren to warrant settlement or even exploration by the European settlers further north. Occasionally, Jesuit missionaries made forays into hostile Indian territory, but it wasn't until a group of Welsh immigrants set themselves up at Chubut in 1865 that any large European settlement was established.

The final solution to the Indian problem was carried out under the command of General Julio Roca. In 1879-80 he led a military expedition to the Río Negro Valley, destroyed the Indian settlements and either killed or dispersed their inhabitants. Many of the survivors were sent to work as slaves in private houses in Buenos Aires. The Indian threat to the *estancias*, railroads and European settlements was removed.

With the Indians out of the picture Patagonia became a stamping ground for explorers, outlaws, missionaries, *gauchos* and finally, tourists. In his book *In Patagonia*, Bruce Chatwin describes the eccentric, violent and sometimes tragic characters who have found their way to Patagonia, including the North American bank robbers Butch Cassidy and the Sundance Kid.

Economy

Two decades after the extermination campaigns had removed the Indians, sheep herders began to move southward to the good, short grazing grass of the plateaus and the water of the streams and canyons. The border with Chile was finalised in the 1880s, Argentine military outposts were established, railroads were built, and farming and sheep and cattle grazing gained a foothold along the Río Negro and the Río Colorado.

Pedigree cattle were imported from Britain. Following the introduction of refrigerated ships in 1877 the export of fresh beef took off. Sheep raising is still the major occupation of Patagonia. Huge ranches, covering thousands of square km, pasture millions of animals but only employ a handful of people.

After Mexico and Venezuela, Argentina is now Latin America's largest petroleum producer, although all its natural gas and almost all its oil is used for domestic consumption. A large percentage of its oil production comes from the Comodoro Rivadavia and Chubut fields in Patagonia. Most of the rest comes from San Sebastián in Tierra del Fuego and from the Mendoza fields 50 km south of the city of Mendoza.

Coal production is restricted to the Río Turbio district, but by 1960 these mines provided the country with almost a fifth of its coal needs. These industries have their origins during and after WW I when Argentina was short of metal ores and cheap sources of power.

Geography

Geographically Chilean Patagonia is quite unlike Argentine Patagonia. The coastline of southern Chile is a wild and beautiful land of virtually unspoilt mountains, glaciers, forests and lakes. It has many national parks, including the spectacular Torres del Paine park near Puerto Natales.

In contrast, most of Argentine Patagonia is an arid land where the prevailing westerly winds leave a haze of dust in the air as they sweep incessantly across the plain. It makes up a quarter of the country's land area but contains only a few per cent of the population.

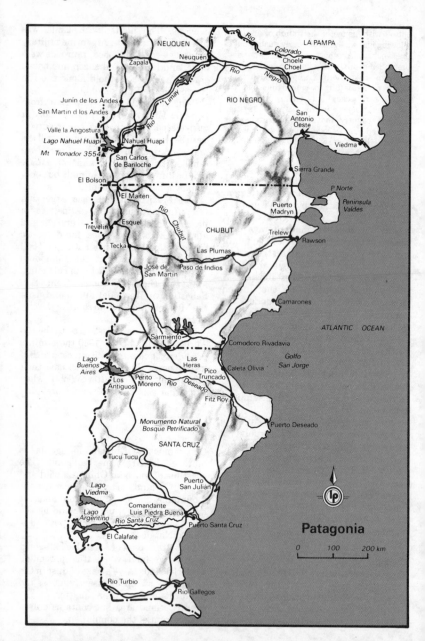

Patagonia

0   100   200 km

Climate

The few cm of moisture which Argentine Patagonia gets each year falls mostly as snow in the winter. The climate is moderate for the most part, except in the far south where the temperature dips below freezing during winter.

Books

Books on Patagonia and Tierra del Fuego are listed in the Books & Bookshops section in Facts For the Visitor, earlier in this book.

Travel in Patagonia

Patagonia has an enchanting pull which has endeared it to many visitors. Charles Darwin writes in *The Voyage of the Beagle* of how he found the vast, empty Patagonian landscape so irresistible:

In calling up images of the past, I find that the plains of Patagonia frequently cross before my eyes; yet these plains are pronounced by all wretched and useless. They can be described only by negative characters; without habitations, without water, without trees, without mountains, they support merely a few dwarf plants. Why then, and the case is not peculiar to myself, have these arid wastes taken so firm a hold on my memory?

In the 1860s the naturalist William Henry Hudson travelled to the Río Negro to look for the birds that migrated to La Plata (near Buenos Aires) in winter. Years later he wrote *Idle Days in Patagonia* in which he partly answers Darwin's question. Hudson concluded that time spent in the vast, open spaces of Patagonia causes visitors to 'go back' to a sort of primitive mental state characterised by an intense alertness. Given that the effect was so profound it was not so strange that Patagonia could make such a lasting impression on a visitor's mind.

Although foreigners have been fascinated by Patagonia and Tierra del Fuego for the last hundred years, the majority of Argentines do not seem to share their enthusiasm. The Argentines seem to think of these huge plains as a place to pass through on their way to tourist resorts such as Bariloche, Calafate or Ushuaia.

Tell an Argentine that you are going to Patagonia and the chances are they will reply 'Oh, nobody goes there!'. Wages in Patagonia are two or three times what an Argentine can scrape up in Buenos Aires, but even that hasn't been sufficient encouragement to induce a mass exodus to the south. Many of those who do go seem to count the days until they've served their sentence. The romance of Patagonia is something to be exported in tourist brochures.

Aside from the oil towns, like Río Gallegos and Comodoro Rivadavia, or a few tourist resorts like Ushuaia and Calafate, life in Patagonia is hidden from view on the estancias.

The last of the gauchos can still be seen wearing traditional clothing including long, baggy trousers called *bombachas* and the wide belts called *rastras* decorated with silver coins – sometimes with a long bladed dagger tucked in behind. Usually referred to as Argentine 'cowboys', the gauchos have been as much a part of the romance of Argentina as the Australian drovers and North American trail-riders were in their respective countries.

Those who have come to shun the tarted-up appearance of Argentine confiterias and cafés, with their jacketed waiters and yuppie clientele, will find the towns of Patagonia a godsend. In many places you can still find a raw edge – or at least a raw appearance – to life. Seek out the rustic bars with their high-ceiling bar rooms, tarnished wooden furniture, peeling yellow paint, pendulum clocks with Roman numerals hanging from the walls, and men in faded jeans and rolled up shirt sleeves knocking back swigs of liquor.

Patagonia offers some of the most monotonous scenery in Latin America. Through the plains of Nuequén, Río Negro, Chubut and Santa Cruz the only variable seems to be the density of the sheep population and the distances between roadside stops. The constants are the endless barbed wire fences and power lines, the thin gravel roads and the occasional bundle of buildings comprising an estancia far away in the distance.

Patagonia also offers some of the most spectacular sights in Argentina. It includes the picture-postcard scenery of the lake district around Bariloche. Near Calafate the Moreno Glacier stands 60 metres high and stretches four km across a lake. On the Valdés Peninsula there are colonies of penguins, sea elephants and sea lions, and in the middle of the year right whales and killer whales appear off the coast.

From Río Gallegos you can bus to Río Turbio and over the mountains to the Chilean town of Puerto Natales. From Calafate you can bus to Puerto Natales via the eerie Torres del Paine mountains. From the Chilean city of Punta Arenas you can cross the Straits of Magellan to Porvenir in Tierra del Fuego.

Río Negro & Nuequén Provinces

Over 400 years ago the Spanish Captain Francisco César led an expedition into western Argentina where, it was rumoured, silver could be found in great quantities. Rumour had it that César's expedition stumbled upon a kingdom of incredible wealth. Rumour built on rumour and before long the Europeans had acquired visions of a great city of gold, a southern El Dorado, somewhere in the depths of Patagonia. The city came to be known as the City of the Ceasars. As the central pampas area was explored and settled the search for the city moved southward.

Some of these expeditions passed through that part of Argentina now known as Nuequén province. While they never

found the city they did (no doubt to their great disappointment) set eyes on what would one day be one of Argentina's great tourist attractions, Lago Nahuel Huapi. Some time in the mid 17th century a missionary-explorer established a mission on the shores of the lake, using it as a base to explore the area in the continuing search for the lost city.

Until the horse-riding Araucanian Indians invaded the Argentine pampas in the late 18th and early 19th centuries, the Indians around Nuequén were mainly hunters and gatherers who lived by the rivers and lakes. Although the Spanish and Argentines sent many exploratory expeditions through this region, it was not until a group of Germans went there in 1856 that any attempt was made by Europeans to establish permanent settlements. San Martín de los Andes was originally an army base established in 1898. The capital, Nuequén, was founded as recently as 1904.

Today, the chief attraction of Nuequén province is San Carlos de Bariloche, or Bariloche for short. Its coniferous forests, thermal springs and ski resorts have turned the southern end of the province into a giant tourist park. Otherwise most of Nuequén is turned over to cattle grazing, fruit growing, coal mining and oil extraction in the bleak, arid plains.

Nuequén is an Indian word which means turbulent. The name probably refers to the Río Nuequén. To the south lies the province of Río Negro, which takes its name from the river. Like Nuequén this is an area of typically 'Patagonian' landscape with plateaus and pampas rising to the Andes in the west. It's an important agricultural province with large fruit farms along the Río Negro, and sheep grazing on the plains.

NUEQUEN

The city of Nuequén is the capital of Nuequén province. It's a pleasant enough city but, for visitors, is only a stop-over on the way to Bariloche or to Chile.

Tourist Office The tourist office is at Feliz San Martín 182, at the corner with Río Negro.

Places to Stay – bottom end

Hotels are plentiful but surprisingly expensive even in the off-season.

The *Hotel Imperio* (tel 22488) at Yrigoyen 65, near the corner with San Martín, has tiny, gloomy rooms for US$6 a single and US$7 a double without private bathroom. Rooms with private bathroom are US$8 a single and US$9 a double.

The *Premier Hotel*, at the corner of Alcorta and Corrientes, has singles for US$7 and doubles for US$10. It's clean, but overpriced and rather gloomy.

The *Hotel Buffet* on Feliz San Martín, on the block between Chubut and Río Negro, has clean, comfortable but rather murky double rooms with private bathroom for US$8. Similarly priced are the *Residencial Monza* (tel 24317) at Feliz San Martín 552 which is clean but a bit ramshackle, and the *Residencial Ingles* (tel 22252) at Feliz San Martín 534 which is bright, clean and comfortable.

The *Residencial Nuequén* at the corner

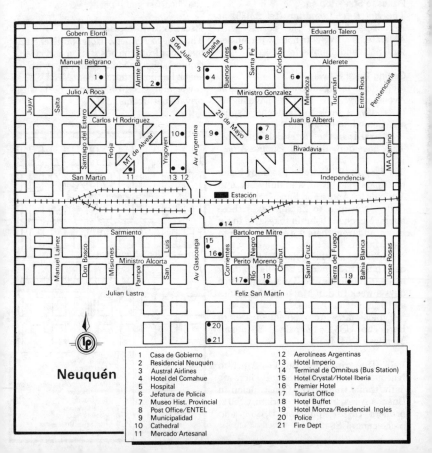

Neuquén

1	Casa de Gobierno	
2	Residencial Neuquén	
3	Austral Airlines	
4	Hotel del Comahue	
5	Hospital	
6	Jefatura de Policía	
7	Museo Hist. Provincial	
8	Post Office/ENTEL	
9	Municipalidad	
10	Cathedral	
11	Mercado Artesanal	
12	Aerolíneas Argentinas	
13	Hotel Imperio	
14	Terminal de Omnibus (Bus Station)	
15	Hotel Crystal/Hotel Iberia	
16	Premier Hotel	
17	Tourist Office	
18	Hotel Buffet	
19	Hotel Monza/Residencial Ingles	
20	Police	
21	Fire Dept	

of Roca and Yrigoyen is a very respectable place with small but comfortable rooms. Rooms without private bathroom are US$7 a single and US$10 a double. Rooms with private bathroom are also available. Get a room at the rear since those facing the street are likely to be noisy.

Places to Stay – middle

Try the *Hotel Crystal* and the *Hotel Iberia*, both on Avenida Olascoaga, between Perito Moreno and Mitre. Both have doubles for US$15.

Places to Stay – top end

The *Hotel del Comahue* (tel 22439) at Argentina 387, on the corner with Alderate, is a five-star hotel with singles for US$20 and doubles for US$27.

Getting There & Away

Air Aerolíneas Argentinas (tel 22337) is at Avenida Argentina 16. They have flights three days a week to Bariloche, Esquel and Comodoro Rivadavia.

Austral is in the Hotel del Comahue. They have daily flights to Buenos Aires

Bus Empresa El Petroleo has daily buses to Zapala via Cutral, and daily buses to Junín de los Andes and San Martín de los Andes. Nuequén to Zapala takes three hours. Nuequén to Junín takes five to six hours, and from there it's another hour to San Martín.

Andesmar and La Union del Sud have daily buses to Mendoza. El Valle has daily buses to Bariloche and Zapala, and three days a week to San Martín de los Andes and Junín de los Andes.

Typical fares from Nuequén are: to Bariloche US$15; Zapala US$4; and Mendoza US$14.

Train The trip from Buenos Aires to Nuequén takes about 21 hours. There are daily trains from Plaza Constitución in Buenos Aires. Fares are: turista US$12; primera US$27; pullman US$36; and coche cama US$43.

ZAPALA

Zapala is a smaller version of Nuequén, and is likewise only a stop-over on the way to the lake district or to Chile.

Tourist Office The tourist office is on San Martín near the plaza.

Places to Stay – bottom end

On Zeballos and next to the *Restaurant Don Hector* is an unnamed hospedaje with rooms without private bathroom for about US$4 a single and US$7 a double. It's clean and reasonably comfortable and the cheapest you'll get.

Places to Stay – top end

The *Nuevo Pehuean Hotel* on Etcheluz, one block from the bus station, is a clean, comfortable, modern building with a snack bar downstairs. Rooms are US$9 a single and US$16 a double, both with private bathrooms.

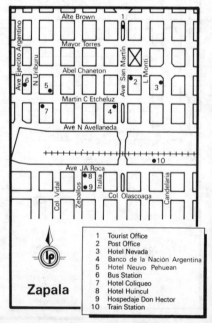

1	Tourist Office
2	Post Office
3	Hotel Nevada
4	Banco de la Nación Argentina
5	Hotel Neuvo Pehuean
6	Bus Station
7	Hotel Coliqueo
8	Hotel Huincul
9	Hospedaje Don Hector
10	Train Station

Zapala

Opposite is the *Hotel Coliqueo* which is slightly cheaper than the Pehuean.

The *Hotel Nevada* on Chile has singles for US$6 and doubles for US$9. It's a nice place with largish rooms.

The *Hotel Huincal* on Avenida Roca, has rooms without private bathroom for US$7 a single and US$9 a double. Slightly more expensive rooms have private bathrooms.

Getting There & Away

Bus All buses leave from the main bus station. El Petroleo has daily buses from Zapala to San Martín de los Andes, Junín de los Andes and Nuequén, and buses two days a week to Buenos Aires. El Valle has daily buses to Nuequén. TAC has daily buses to Bariloche and Mendoza. La Unión del Sol have daily buses to Temuco in Chile; the fare is US$14.

Train Train information for Zapala is similar to Nuequén; see that section for details.

SAN CARLOS DE BARILOCHE

San Carlos de Bariloche, or Bariloche for short, is the centre of the Argentine Lake District and one of the largest population centres in the area. Set amid deep blue lakes, forested mountains, glaciers and pine forests it has an almost Bavarian alpine appearance. During summer the meadows are ablaze with yellow wildflowers.

Although you can fish, climb and trek in this region, Bariloche is probably most famous outside Argentina as the country's chief ski resort. A huge ski village graces Cerro Catedral above the town. Many visitors spend their time in Bariloche on walks and treks, amidst the lakes and mountains.

Yet despite the inherent beauty of the scenery, it is probably only fair to say that, like the Iguazú Falls in north-east Argentina, the lake district has been stripped of its rough edge, tamed and turned into something resembling a giant, manicured park. You'll probably find the

areas to the south, around El Bolsón, Esquel, and the Parque Nacional Los Alerces, more appealing.

Information

The Centro Civico is on Mitre. The post office, tourist office and the Museo de la Patagonia are all here. Note; there are two O'Connor streets, Viceamirante Eduardo O'Connor and John O'Connor.

Books *Bariloche y Aéreas de Influencia* (Guías Almar, 1987) is a useful guide to the area and is published in both English and Spanish. If you're interested in trekking buy *Las Montañas de Bariloche* (Guías Regionales Argentinas) by Tonçvek Arko and Irina Izaguirre.

Tourist Office The tourist office is open Monday to Saturday from 9 am to 8.30 pm. They have a list of all accommodation in the town and will telephone hotels and book rooms for you.

Post The post office is next to the tourist office.

Telephone Long distance phone calls can be made from ENTEL at Elflein 554 on the corner with Frey.

Banks Foreign cash and travellers' cheques can be changed at the Casa Piano at Mitre 131.

National Parks The National Parks office is at San Martín 24. You can get information on treks into the mountains from the Club Andino Bariloche, at the corner of Morales and 20 de Febrero. There are a number of shops in Bariloche which specialise in outdoor equipment, selling everything needed for trekking, camping, fishing, hunting (including rifles and, to add a touch of medieval pretension to the sport, bows and arrows).

Consulates The Chilean consulate is on

the 3rd floor at Villegas 239. It's open Monday to Friday from 9 am to 2 pm.

Things to See

Those expecting a Bavarian alpine village will be taken aback. Bariloche can barely be distinguished from any other Argentine town, except by the profusion of hotels and restaurants. Most of what there is to see and do in the area is outside, not in, Bariloche.

The best way to see something of the surrounding area is to hike and camp. Failing that there are tours organised by several tour companies in Bariloche, which is a quick and painless way of taking in the views. It also gives you an opportunity to meet some of the Argentine visitors to the area. These companies are listed in the 'Getting Around' section. Some possible excursions are listed on the following pages.

Museo de la Patagonia

This museum, in the Civic Centre, has some interesting exhibits on the fauna and flora of the area; it's open Tuesday to Friday from 10 am to 12 noon and from 2 to 7 pm, and on Saturday from 10 am to 1 pm.

Flora & Fauna

In the winter it's sometimes possible to see puma in the lake district, since they catch large fish in the rivers. Woodpeckers and red and grey foxes can also be seen. Several species of deer, included the Axis or Spotted Deer which is a native of India, have been introduced. Others include the red deer and Dama deer, both of European origin. A native of South America is the *huemul*, a tiny brown deer which stands just one metre high when fully grown. Wild boar were introduced from Europe.

It's also worth looking out for the yellow-coloured mushrooms which resemble perforated sponges or brain coral. These attack trees but will fall to the ground and turn yellow as they decay. The Indians who once inhabited this area would pulverise the mushrooms when they were green to make flour, from which the colloquial name 'Indian bread' is derived.

Lago Nahuel Huapi

The town lies on the shores of Lago Nahuel Huapi, a glacial lake about 60 km long, averaging around 10 km wide, and over 300 metres deep in places. This rather peculiarly-shaped lake with its sprawling arms is set amidst heavily forested, rugged mountain scenery. In winter the region is buried in snow. Sometimes snow falls are so heavy that they bury the mountain *refugios*, the roofs of which make small hills which skiers can zip over.

You'll notice that the upper reaches of some hills have great patches devoid of trees or other vegetation. This has been caused by forest fires which have also burnt underground, destroying the tree roots so that the trees have never grown back. Other steep areas have no forests because of erosion, and because the weight of the snowfalls pushes vegetation over so it cannot grow. Many tree trunks litter the ground, toppled by the weight of the snow.

Circuito Chico

Despite the name the Circuito Chico offers some of the biggest views in the Lakes District.

The circuit begins with a chairlift ride up to the peak of Cerro Campanario which provides you with a panoramic view of Lago Nahuel Huapi, Lago Moreno and Laguna El Trebol.

After coming down the mountain you carry on along the perimeter of Lago Nahuel Huapi to the Hotel Llao Llao, a Central European looking affair in a setting which some may find reminiscent of Austria or Switzerland.

From here you follow a road to a panoramic look-out point where you can look down on Moreno, El Trebol and Nahuel Huapi. This road takes you past Colonia Suiza, so called because the first Europeans to settle it were Swiss. Their descendants still live there today.

The Little Circuit is a good half day excursion out of Bariloche. The chairlift

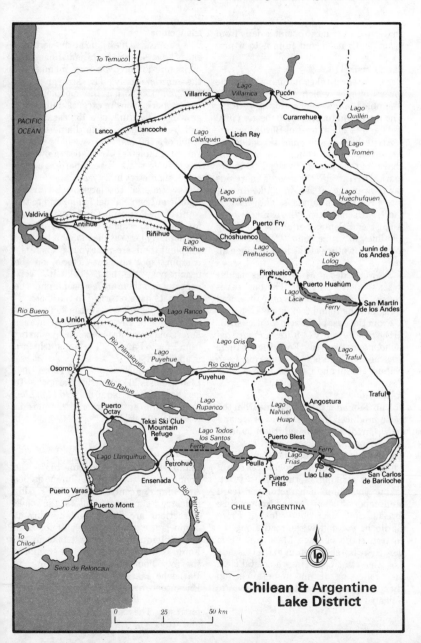

Chilean & Argentine Lake District

on Cerro Campanario operates daily from 9 am to 12 noon and from 4 to 6 pm.

Cerro Catedral

Cerro Catedral takes its name from the towers of rock which crown it, said to resemble the towers of gothic cathedrals. The mountain touches 2400 metres (7800 feet) and is 20 km west of Bariloche.

At its base is the chief ski village of Argentina from which an array of chairlifts take you up to the 2000 metre mark. Driving into the resort's enormous car park in the off-season is like driving into a K-Mart on Sundays. The season is short, with enough snow for skiing in July, August and September and some skiing possible in June and October. The information office at the resort is open all year.

TA Mercedes at Mitre 161 has regular buses to Cerro Catedral. The bus leaves hourly from the corner of Mitre and Quaglia. The round trip fare is US$3.

From the base of the resort the chairlift to the *Restaurant y Confiteria Piedra del Condor* operates daily. From the top there are spectacular views overlooking Lago Nahuel Huapi and Lago Moreno.

Volcán Tronador

Volcán Tronador takes its name from the noise produced by avalanches of ice and snow. On the Argentine side the mountain rises in an almost sheer wall of rock and it's possible to walk up to the snow line. The journey to Volcán Tronador is one of the most striking in the lake district, taking you through a picture postcard landscape of snow-capped mountains, forests and deep blue lakes. From Bariloche you follow the road along the eastern shore of Lago Mascardi. From here there is a short detour to the Cascada Los Alerces at Lago Hess, a crystal clear lake reflecting distant mountains. You then backtrack and follow a dirt road to Volcán Tronador.

Isla Victoria

The Península Quetrihué at the northern end of Lago Nahuel Huapi, is distinguished by its forest of *arrayan* trees, members of the myrtle family. The arrayan is an evergreen tree with a cinnamon coloured, papery bark. They're exceptionally slow-growing. The trunk of a 15 year old tree will be only three cm in diameter. The trunk of a 150 year old tree will be only 30 cm in diameter. Arrayanes grow one metre in 25 years. By comparison a pine grows six metres in 25 years.

Isla Victoria, the large island in the middle of Lago Nahuel Huapi and to the south of the Península Quetrihué, is noted for its giant sequoias – which are not particularly large at the moment because the plantations are quite young. There is a camping spot on Isla Victoria, on the beach near the boat dock. It's very peaceful and there are few people once the tour boats have returned to Bariloche.

Turisur has tour boats to Isla Victoria and the Bosque de Arrayanes (the Arrayanes Forest on Península Quetrihué) departing from Puerto Pañuelo. The round trip fare is about US$11.

Puerto Pañuelo is near the Hotel Llao Llao which is 26 km outside Bariloche. To get there take bus No 20 marked *Llao Llao* from the stop at the corner of Moreno and Rolando in Bariloche.

Junín de los Andes

Established as a fort in 1883, the nondescript township of Junín de los Andes is now a centre for the cattle-raising industry. For most visitors the chief attractions are fishing and hunting as Junín is the jumping off point for Lago Huechulafquen, the largest lake in the Lanín National Park. The last stretch of the four hour bus ride from Junín to Bariloche takes you through the Valle Encantado, a region of jagged rock towers which look like devastated mountain fortresses. The road follows the Río Limay and runs via La Rinconada, Alicura,

Confluencia, Rincón Chico and past Alicura.

San Martín de los Andes

San Martín de los Andes is a pancake-flat grid of hosterías, restaurants, houses and apartment blocks. With several lakes in the vicinity, such as Lago Lacar, Curruhue and Lolog, it's a popular destination for Argentine fishing enthusiasts. The winter attraction is Cerro Chapelco, where there is a sizeable ski run. Otherwise the circuit from Bariloche to San Martín via Villa La Angostura is unmemorable. Only the areas around Confluencia in the Paso Córdoba and the Valle Encantado, both with strange pinnacles and shattered rock formations, are of any interest.

Hiking

If you're after solitude then it's best to visit the mountains outside the January/February tourist season. Some people have found the area to be overcrowded and often abused (littering, cutting down trees for firewood) during the tourist season. One possibility is to hike from the National Park outpost at Pampa Linda over the Paso de las Nubes to Puerto Peulla on the eastern shore of Lago Todos los Santos in Chile. This is a 2½ day hike. The eastern slopes of the mountains are carpeted in beech trees and bamboo. There are lots of good camping spots but the trails tend to be overgrown in parts and can be hazardous in bad weather.

Fishing

The fishing season is during summer, from 15 November until 15 April. Fishing permits can be obtained from the National Parks office and can be issued for two weeks, one month or the whole season. The tourist office has a leaflet, in English, which details where and when you're allowed to fish in the national park.

The lakes are well-known for trout fishing. Brown trout, otherwise known as European trout, were introduced to the lakes. River trout, originally from the eastern United States, were also introduced. Other species which inhabit the lakes and rivers are rainbow trout, land-locked salmon, perch and Patagonian mackerel. Trout can be seen in the streams during winter, which is the breeding season, before they move downstream into the lakes.

Places to Stay

At last count there were 76 one to five-star hotels, 71 hosterías, 37 hospedajes, 39 bungalow complexes and 15 camping grounds in or around Bariloche.

The cheapest accommodation is usually in private houses. In the high season however, cheap accommodation can be difficult to find, either in hotels or private houses. It is best to contact the tourist office in Bariloche, which keeps a list of all accommodation.

There are many hotels on the outskirts of Bariloche and by the lakes. These can be fine alternatives to staying in the town but you'll really need your own car to make it practical. Some of these, such as the Hotel Tronador, offer some of the finest settings in the Lake District.

Places to Stay – bottom end

El Mirador (tel 22221) at Moreno 658 is a private home converted into a hotel. Rooms without private bathroom are US$3 per person, and around US$4 per person with private bathroom.

The *Residencial Nogaré* (tel 22438) at Elflein 58, between Morales and Rolando, charges US$5 per person in the off-season for comfortable, carpeted rooms with private bathroom. Rooms at the rear should be quiet.

The *El Ciervo Rojo* (tel 23810) is at the corner of Quaglia and Elflein, and is similar to *Nogaré*.

Other places in this block include *Nikola* (tel 22500) at Elflein 49 and *La Casa de Noguiera* at Elflein 205.

The house at Frey 635 has also been recommended and is one of the cheapest in Bariloche at US$2 per person. It's

San Carlos de Bariloche

1   Club Andino de Bariloche
2   National Parks Office
3   Post Office
4   Tourist Office
5   Museo de la Patagonia
6   Casa Piano
7   Aerolineas Argentinas & LADE
8   Chilean Consulate
9   Austral
10 Local Bus Station
11 ENTEL
12 Cathedral
13 Train Station

Lago Nahuel Huapi

RR. STA Airport
Villa Angostura

clean, friendly, has hot water showers and is popular with foreign visitors.

Places to Stay - middle

The *Residencial Tito* (tel 24039) at Eduardo O'Connor 745, between John O'Connor and Goedecke, has comfortable motel style rooms with private bathroom. Off-season rates are US$7 a single and US$14 a double.

The *Hotel Pilmayquen* (tel 26175) at the corner of 12 de Octubre and John O'Connor is on a fairly quiet street with fine lake views from the front rooms. Off-season rates are around US$7 a single and US$13 a double for rooms without private bathroom.

The *Hotel Restaurant Cabaghi* (tel 22697) at the corner of Quaglia and Gallardo is a modern building. Rooms with private bathroom are US$6 per person.

Places to Stay - top end

Top end hotels include the *Edelweiss* (tel 26165) at San Martín 202, and the *Panamericano Bariloche* (tel 25846) at San Martín 536. Both charge about US$37 a single and US$50 a double. Both are in the town centre.

If you really are interested in up-market accommodation you should try to get value for money by staying at one of the lakeside hotels outside of town.

One possibility is the *Hotel Tronador* on the road to Cerro Tronador, by the shores of the strikingly beautiful Lago Mascardi. Rooms are US$30 a single and US$50 a double, which includes all meals, though you'd need your own transport to make staying there practical.

Places to Eat

Like hotels, there are so many restaurants in Bariloche that it's difficult to recommend any one in particular. A few words of vocabulary are worth knowing since you can rake up some interesting fish and wild game dishes. *Jabali* is wild boar. *Ciervo* is deer. *Ciervo macho* is stag.

Fish dishes include *trucha* which is trout.

The *Restaurant El Jabali* at San Martín 130 is a moderately priced restaurant which serves wild boar, trout and rabbit. It has a passable Chinese smorgasbord lunch and dinner, which is a cheap and filling meal.

The *Restaurant Villegas* at Villegas 363 specialises in trout. It's a cosy place but though they make a fine dish it does tend to be rather expensive.

I'd recommend the *Restaurante Parrilla 1810* at Elflein 167 for its cosy atmosphere and enormous servings at moderate prices. Very good value is the *Parrilla La Vizcacha* at Rolando 279, which serves trout. The *Nikola* at Elflein 49 is good, with a mixed menu which includes very large pasta dishes.

The *Pizza Via Roma* at Mitre 5 has typically huge pizzas. *La Andinita* at Mitre 56 is more agreeable. Indistinguishable from the Via Roma is *El Mundo Pizza* at Mitre 370.

For vegetarian food try *La Huerta* at Morales 362, between Elflein and San Martín.

For chocolates you should try two stores; one on Mitre between Rolando and Villa, and the other at the corner of Mitre and Villegas.

Confiterias abound in Bariloche. The *Caffe Status* is probably the liveliest of the lot although it's relatively expensive. The *Confiteria La Marmita* at Mitre 319 is a fine place with a cosy atmosphere and a large selection of cakes.

Getting There & Away

Air Austral (tel 22454) is at Rolando 157. They have daily flights from Bariloche to Buenos Aires.

Aerolíneas Argentinas (tel 22591) and LADE are at the corner of Villegas and Mitre. Aerolíneas has flights three days a week to Buenos Aires.

Catedral has a bus between the town centre and the airport. The fare is US$1 and the trip takes about 20 minutes.

Bus Tickets for Buses El Valle, TAC, Bus Norte and Don Otto can all be bought at the office at Mitre 10.

El Valle has daily buses to Nuequén, Buenos Aires, Junín de los Andes and San Martín de los Andes.

TAC has daily buses to Zapala and Mendoza.

Buses Norte has daily buses to Osorno, Puerto Montt, Valdivia, Temuco and Santiago (all in Chile) via the pass at Puyehue. They have daily buses to Nuequén, El Bolsón, Esquel and Buenos Aires.

TA Mercedes, at Mitre 161, has daily buses to Nuequén, Esquel and El Bolsón. They have buses four days a week to Osorno and Puerto Montt via Puyehue.

La Estrella at Palacio 246 has daily buses to Nuequén and Buenos Aires. Transportes Chevalier SA at Moreno 107 has daily buses to Buenos Aires.

Catedral Turismo, at the corner of Mitre and Palacio, has bus/boat combinations to Puerto Montt in Chile via Lago Todos los Santos. On the first day you depart Bariloche at about 9 am. You bus to Puerto Pañuelo, then take a ferry across Lago Nahuel Huapi to Puerto Blest. From Puerto Blest you bus to Puerto Alegre, and then take a ferry to the Argentine customs post at Puerto Frías. You then bus across the border to Peulla in Chile and stay one night at the Peulla Hotel. Next morning you take a ferry from Peulla to Petrohué at the other end of Lago Todos los Santos. From there you bus to Puerto Montt via Ensenada and Puerto Varas. In summer, between mid-November and mid-March, it's possible to do the whole trip in one day, without spending a night at the Peulla Hotel.

Typical fares from Bariloche are: to San Martín de los Andes US$10; to Junín de los Andes US$8; Nuequén US$15; Buenos Aires US$53; Esquel US$15; El Bolsón US$6; Puerto Montt and Osorno via Puyehue US$20.

Train There are daily trains to Bariloche

from Plaza Constitución in Buenos Aires. Fares from Buenos Aires are: turista US$23; primera US$30; pullman US$46; and coche cama US$58. The trip takes about 24 hours.

Getting Around

Bus The main local bus stop is at the corner of Moreno and Rolando. Take bus No 20 marked *Llao Llao* to the Hotel Llao Llao, via Playa Bonita, Puerto Moreno, Campanario, El Trebol, Península San Pedro and Puerto Pañuelo. On its return trip it goes down Elflein to the train station; you can pick up the bus at the corner of Elflein and Morales.

Car Cars can be rented from: Open Car (tel 26325) at Eduardo O'Connor 213; Hertz (tel 26534) at San Martín 295; National (tel 24404) at Libertad 114; and A1 (tel 24869) at Mitre 26.

Tours There are a number of tour operators in Bariloche including Catedral (tel 25443) at Bartolome Mitre 399; Tur Acción (tel 22276) at Quaglia 219; and Martín Tour (tel 24163) at San Martín 453.

Typical tour prices per person are: Cerro Catedral US$7; Circuito Chico US$7; Tronador, Lago Hess and the Cascada Los Alerces US$15; El Bolsón US$15; San Martín de los Andes US$20; Isla Victoria and the Bosque de Arrayanes US$15. Some of the tours are described below. The tourist office and tour operators will fill you in on others.

If you want to make a quick side-trip to Chile, Martín Tour has two-day excursions from Bariloche to the Chilean lake district, costing US$96 per person. These leave from Bariloche, and take you by bus and boat to Petrohué on the Lago Todos Los Sandos. From Petrohué you bus to Puerto Montt. The following day you bus to Bariloche via Osorno, Puyehue, El Rincon and Villa La Angostura.

EL BOLSON

El Bolsón is a one horse town which lies in

Tours Around Bariloche

1	Cascada los Alerces
2	Cerro Tronador
3	Cerro Catedral
4	Piedras Blancas, Cerro Otto
5	Colonia Suiza, Cerro López
6	Puerto Pañuelo, Llao Llao
7	Isla Victoria
8	Península de Quetrihué
9	Cascada los Cántaros

the shadow of the massive phalanx of Cerro Piltriquitron. The town itself is of no interest but the surrounding countryside has splendid scenery – though you need to trek and camp to make it worthwhile.

Tourist Office The tourist office is on the square facing San Martín, but is closed in the off-season.

Places to Stay

The cheapest place is the *Residencial Salinas* at Roca 641, with rooms for US$3 per person.

The *Amancay Hotel* at the corner of San Martín and Hernandez has singles for US$7 and doubles for US$10. It's a very pleasant place with comfortable motel-style rooms with private bathrooms. The *Arrayanes Hotel* opposite is similar. Also try the *Piltriquitron Hotel* a few blocks down the road.

Places to Eat

There's a string of cheap and moderately priced parrilladas along San Martín. The *Restaurant Achachay* is cheap, with generous servings.

Getting There & Away

Buses TA Mercedes on Perito Moreno, near the corner with Esquel, has daily buses from El Bolsón to Bariloche and Esquel. Fares from El Bolsón are: to Esquel US$10; to Bariloche US$5.

Getting Around

If you're having trouble getting around, try a tour of the local area with Pulmari Turismo at San Martín 2995. Also enquire about trekking and horse-riding expeditions into the local mountains at Adventuras Patagonicas on Pablo Hube. Tour operators in Bariloche have day trips to the El Bolsón area.

Chubut Province

Centred round the Río Chubut, Chubut province is an expanse of windswept plains, divided up into giant sheep farms and occasionally broken by canyons. There are two ways you might approach Chubut. The first is by road travelling south from Bariloche to Esquel via El Bolsón. The other is from Buenos Aires either by bus or plane to Puerto Madryn or Trelew.

Although Magellan sailed along the coast in 1519 it was not until 350 years later that the area attracted European settlers. Before then the cold climate, arid landscape and remoteness had deterred settlement. However, in the 1850s it was just this isolation which attracted, of all people, the Welsh.

The idea of a Welsh settlement in Argentina has its origins in the political and social developments in Wales in the 18th and early 19th centuries. In the 19th century a number of Welsh nationalist leaders, influenced by socialist ideas, Marxism and various European nationalists, once again raised the issues of enfranchisement, education and freedom of religion and language for the Welsh.

Many Welsh had already gone to North America. It was believed they would be able to live there free from constraints imposed on them by English rule, and free from the threat of complete cultural absorption by the English. For the most part the Welsh settlers in North America were quickly assimilated and tended to lose their native language and culture. Welsh leaders in both North America and Wales began to search elsewhere for a land where Welsh colonies could be established, but which would have political autonomy and allow the Welsh identity to be retained.

By the 1850s Welsh leaders had decided on Patagonia as an ideal place to establish such a venture. Attempts in 1852 and 1855 to found colonies both failed. In 1862 the Argentine government was approached for help but Congress was wary of allowing a large Protestant colony to establish itself in the predominantly Catholic country, and also feared British and North American territorial ambitions under the guise of colonisation.

At first the Welsh were sent away empty-handed. However, the following year the decision was overturned by the Minister of the Interior Guillermo Rawson, who gave the Welsh a grant of land in the coastal region of the Río Chubut valley.

Back in Wales the Chubut valley was bandied about as a 'farmers' paradise' where land was free for the taking. In 1865 the first contingent of 153 people (including 78 children) set sail for Argentina. History has the first colonists sailing off into the Atlantic Ocean singing hymns, bound for the Welsh Eden. It does not seem to record what they thought when they first set eyes on the coast of Patagonia.

After a two month voyage they sailed into the Golfo Nuevo to the south of Península Valdés. Those who expected to find a Wales beyond Wales could not have found anything less like the green, wet landscape of their homeland than the arid plains of Patagonia.

The trouble began immediately. Because of a dangerous sand bar near the mouth of the Río Chubut, the colonists had to be landed on the beaches 60 km to the north, near the site of modern-day Puerto Madryn. For several days they camped in the caves in the cliffs, drinking brackish water. Then the men set out on a five day walk to the river. While they were gone another ship arrived and took the women and children south. The voyage was expected to take two days, but because of storms they spent 17 days at sea. Five children died.

The Welsh established their first settlement on the site of the modern-day town of Rawson – named after the Argentine Minister. Few knew how to

Top: Cerro Catedral
Bottom: Around Bariloche

Top: Somewhere in Patagonia
Bottom: Gauchos (EA)

farm. Of the men four were farm labourers. The rest included a tailor, a soldier, a bookseller and a motley array of other professionals – most of them unsuited to the work of carving out an agricultural colony in virgin land.

At first they tried to farm the dry land, but because they didn't know how to, they had to rely for food on the Argentine government and passing ships. The local Indians traded meat, and taught the Welsh how to hunt the rhea, guanacos and small animals of the plains. No doubt because of this kindness, the Welsh did not join in the extermination campaigns (1879-80) under General Roca.

It was only when the Welsh devised irrigation systems that they were able to grow their crops successfully and the threat of starvation receded. By 1873 the colony was stable enough for new immigrants to join them. By the middle of the 1880s the Welsh had spread out through all the arable land in the Río Chubut valley and by all accounts appear to have developed a happy and prosperous life. By 1885 there were about 1600 Welsh living in the Chubut valley and their farms were exporting surplus wheat to Buenos Aires and the Falklands.

Roca's campaigns finally removed the Indians and opened up Patagonia to Argentine settlement. The Argentine government established its own administration in Chubut, presided over by a governor. Catholic missionaries began entering the province to convert the remaining Indians.

In 1886 the company of Lewis Jones, one of the leaders of the 1865 colony, started building a train line from Chubut to Bahía Blanca. Gradually the sense of isolation was broken down and new towns were established in the province, including Puerto Madryn, Colonia Sarmiento, Trelew, Esquel and Comodoro Rivadavia. In the early 1900s more settlers began arriving in Chubut, including Argentines, Scots, English, Italians and South African Boers.

Welsh immigration did not end until the start of WW I. Despite the high hopes of the founding fathers to create a Wales beyond Wales only 3000 Welsh immigrants went to the Chubut settlements in half a century of colonisation. In the late 1950s the central government began to encourage industrialisation and settlement in the province, and since then the prominence of the Welsh in Chubut has declined.

Today, only a few of the original settlements have retained anything of their 'Welsh' appearance, but there are many people who still speak and consider themselves Welsh. A Welsh eisteddfod (folk festival) is held once a year at Gaimen. City names also recall the Welsh influence. Puerto Madryn is named after Parry Madryn, one of the leaders of the 1865 colony.

Trelew is the Welsh for 'Lewis' City', in honour of Lewis Jones, another leader of the 1865 colony. Original Welsh settlements include Gaimen, which still has many old Welsh buildings and many people of Welsh descent. Welsh settlements were also established at Dolavon near Gaimen, and at Trevelin to the south of Esquel.

Books

For an overview of British settlement in Argentina read *The Forgotten Colony* (Hutchinson, London, 1981) by Anglo-Argentine journalist Andrew Graham-Yool. It includes a chapter on Welsh settlement.

The Desert and the Dream: A History of the Welsh Colonisation of Patagonia, 1865-1915 (University of Wales Press, Cardiff, 1975) by Glyn Williams deals specifically with Welsh settlement and is the most comprehensive work available.

The Welsh in Patagonia: An Example of Nationalistic Migration by John Baur gives a good overview of the reasons for Welsh settlement in Patagonia. The essay was published in the *Hispanic American Review* (Vol 3, No 4, 1954).

World Minorities in the Eighties

(Quartermaine House Ltd, 1980), edited by Georgina Ashworth, has a short section on Welsh settlement in Argentina and the problems which the Welsh have faced in that country.

If you can read Spanish then you may find a guide book called *Turismo por Chubut*, published by Chubut's Sub-secretaria de Informacion Publica y Turismo, quite useful. It has a lengthy section on Welsh settlement in the province. You should be able to buy it in the larger bookshops in Puerto Madryn and Buenos Aires.

PUERTO MADRYN

From across the plains, Puerto Madryn looks like a toy town casually dumped on the edge of nowhere. Any traces of its Welsh past have been completely erased. For visitors it's mainly just a jumping off point for the Península Valdés with its colonies of sea elephants and penguins, and herds of killer whales and right whales. September and October are the best months to visit to see the whales. Further south, at Punta Tombo, there is a huge penguin colony which can be visited from September/October to February/March, prior to the penguins migrating further south.

Information

Tourist Office The tourist office is at Sarmiento 386 (tel 71514) and has information about the wildlife reserves as well as city maps. It's open Monday to Friday from 7 am to 1 pm. There is a second office on Roca near the corner with 9 de Julio. It's open Mondays to Fridays from 8 am to 12 noon and from 5 to 7 pm, and on Saturdays, Sundays and holidays from 10 am to 12 noon.

Banks The Banco de la Nación is at the corner of 9 de Julio and 25 de Mayo and will change American Express travellers' cheques.

Places to Stay – bottom end

Because it has been developed as a holiday resort, hotels in Puerto Madryn are on the expensive side. The cheap hotels are definitely bottom of the barrel and it's hard to recommend any of them.

The *Hotel Paris* at the corner of Sáenz Peña and 25 de Mayo has singles for US$4 and doubles for US$9 without private bathroom. It's a fairly depressing flop-house and I wouldn't recommend it. It does, however, have one of the best seafood restaurants in town.

Of a similar price and standard are the *Hotel El Antiguo* at 28 de Julio 147, between 25 de Mayo and Mitre, and the *Aguila Hotel* at the corner of Zar and Sáenz Peña.

The *Hotel Vaskonia* at 25 de Mayo 43 is very spartan with box-like rooms for US$3 per person. It's marginally better than the other cheap hotels. There are some rooms with private bathroom for US$5 per person.

There are a few places with single rooms for US$6 and doubles for US$9. These are *El Dorado* at San Martín 545 which is similar to the Aguila Hotel; the *Petit* at Alvear 845 which is very ugly and depressing; and the *San Francisco* at Sarmiento 1290.

Places to Stay – middle

The best of the cheaper hotels is the *Residencial La Posta* near the corner of Roca and Irigoyen. Single rooms are US$9 and doubles US$13. The rooms are very compact with bunk beds, but they do have private bathrooms and are clean. The staff are fairly friendly.

The *Hostel del Rey* (tel 71156) at Brown 681 is a large place fronting the beach, with singles for US$16 and doubles for US$20 with private bathrooms. It's quite comfortable and you may get cheaper rates in the off-season. It tends to get quite a lot of traffic noise.

Similar in standard and price to the Hostel del Rey are the *Hotel Yanco* (tel

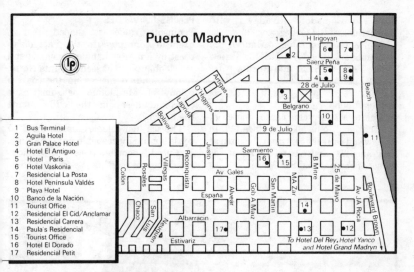

Puerto Madryn

1 Bus Terminal
2 Aguila Hotel
3 Gran Palace Hotel
4 Hotel El Antiguo
5 Hotel Paris
6 Hotel Vaskonia
7 Residencial La Posta
8 Hotel Peninsula Valdés
9 Playa Hotel
10 Banco de la Nación
11 Tourist Office
12 Residencial El Cid/Anclamar
13 Residencial Carrera
14 Paula's Residencial
15 Tourist Office
16 Hotel El Dorado
17 Residencial Petit

71581) at Roca 627, and the *Hotel Grand Madryn* (tel 71728) on Lugones near the corner with Brown. Also try *El Cid* (tel 71416) at 25 de Mayo 850 which is on a quiet street. Both have rooms for around US$10 a single and US$13 a double.

Others include the *Carrera* (tel 71531) at Zar 852 which is a bit out of the way, and the *Gran Palace Hotel* (tel 71009) at 28 de Julio 390 which is good apart from the downstairs rooms, which are rather shoddy. Both have singles for US$16 and doubles for US$20.

Places to Stay – top end
The high-rise *Península Valdés* (tel 71292) at Roca 163, near the corner with 28 de Julio, has singles for US$30 and doubles for US$40.

Places to Eat
There are several confiterias along 28 de Julio, most with videos showing gun-slinging and kung-fu movies. Parrilladas include the *Hueney* at Sáenz Peña 38 and the *Zenon* at Zar 752. Cheap eats include the rustic *Restaurant Español* and *Loco's* on San Martín near the corner with 28 de

Julio. The *Hotel Paris* at the corner of Sáenz Peña and 25 de Mayo has one of the best cheap restaurants in town, with particularly good seafood dishes.

Getting There & Away
Air The nearest airport is at Trelew. LADE has flights to Esquel two days a week. Aerolíneas has daily flights to Buenos Aires and flights several days a week to Esquel, Comodoro Rivadavia, Río Gallegos, Río Grande and Ushuaia.

Bus The long distance bus station is at the junction of Zar and Irigoyen in Puerto Madryn.

Buses 28 de Julio have frequent buses all through the day between Puerto Madryn and Trelew. If you have to catch a plane take one of these to the airport which is on the way to Trelew.

La Puntual has daily buses to Comodoro Rivadavia and Buenos Aires. Don Otto has daily buses to Buenos Aires, Comodoro Rivadavia and Esquel.

Empresa Chubut has buses four or five days a week to Esquel.

Transportadora Patagonica has daily

buses to Comodoro Rivadavia with connections to Río Gallegos.

Typical fares from Puerto Madryn are: to Comodoro Rivadavia US$13; Trelew US$2; Esquel US$22; and Buenos Aires US$29.

Getting Around

In Puerto Madryn cars can be rented at International Rent-a-Car at Roca 117. In Trelew you can rent cars from National at Belgrano 471, and A1 (tel 21371) at the corner of Fontana and San Martín.

PENINSULA VALDES

Península Valdés is shaped like an axehead connected to the Patagonian coast by a narrow handle. Penguins and sea elephants can be seen at Punta Norte. A few hundred metres up the coast a colony of Magellanic penguins have burrowed nests in the cliffs facing the beach.

The sea lion colonies are on the west coast but are inaccessible from the cliffs. You need binoculars to see the sea lions clearly but the coastline itself is impressive.

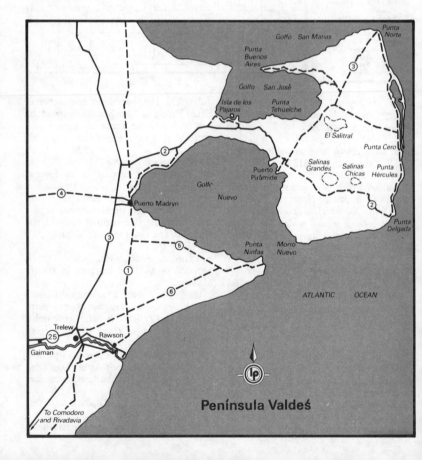

Península Valdés

The coast also sports Antarctic gulls and oyster catchers amongst many other species of birds.

At Puerto Pirámide on the south coast there is a hostería where you can eat, then take a launch out into the bay to see the right whales. If the weather is good, the boats can get within a few metres of the whales.

On the way back to Puerto Madryn you can stop on the coast opposite the Islas de Pájaros. The island is a bird sanctuary and you're not allowed on it. There are telescopes set up on the beach but it would require a trained eye to identify the species of individual birds. Near the lookout point is a replica of an old Spanish church which was once part of a settlement destroyed by Indians. Several survivors of the attack then walked several hundred km along the coast to the Spanish settlements in the north.

There is a huge penguin reserve at Punta Tombo, 120 km south of Trelew. There is another penguin colony at Punta Loma just to the south-east of Puerto Madryn.

Books There are some good books on the fauna of the peninsula, available in both Spanish and English from bookshops in Puerto Madryn. These are: *La Ballena Franca de Península Valdés* (The Right Whales of Península Valdés) by G Harris and C Garcia; *Fauna costera de la Patagonia* (The Fauna of the Patagonian Coasts); and *El Elefante Marino* (The Sea Elephant).

Getting There & Away

Trying to hitch to the reserves is hopeless. There are few vehicles and considerable distances between the reserves. The peninsula is flat grazing land, not trekking country.

The only alternatives are to take a tour or to hire your own car in Puerto Madryn. The latter is best since you can then stay as long as you like at the reserves. Tours stay about an hour at each place.

Getting Around

Tours For tours try Turismo Puma at 28 de Julio 44 and Tur Mar at 25 de Mayo 157. Day tours cost about US$17 per person. The boat ride to see the right whales off Puerto Pirámide costs an extra US$10.

For tours to the penguin colony at Punta Tombo try the agency in the Hotel Yanco at Roca 626, and the Receptivo Puerto Madryn at the corner of Belgrano and Roca. These cost US$14 per person.

Fauna of the Península Valdés

Penguins The Italian, Antonio Pigafetta, one of the few survivors of Magellan's expedition, recorded seeing penguins on the voyage, either in the Straits of Magellan or somewhere on the coast of Argentine Patagonia. How these peculiar birds got their name is unknown. It may have come from the Welsh name *pen gwyn* which means 'white head'. By Pigafetta's time the name was already applied to similar birds which lived in the North Atlantic until they became extinct in the mid-19th century. An account of Thomas Cavendish's voyage around the world in 1586-88 is one of the first to use the word 'penguin'. It's possible that English (or Welsh?) sailors who knew about the northern bird gave the same name to the southern species.

In any case, penguins have been around a lot longer than European sailors – by about 45 million years. The first fossil penguin bone, from a bird which probably stood about 1½ metres tall, was found last century on the South Island of New Zealand. The species of penguin which you can see on the peninsula in Argentina and at Punta Tombo just south of the peninsula, is the *Spheniscus magellanicus*. Its common name is the Magellanic penguin. It's sometimes called the jackass penguin because, like other species of *Spheniscus*, it makes a loud braying sound.

This particular species breeds from the Península Valdés southwards, around the tip of South America and up the Pacific side almost to Valparaíso in Chile. They spend April to August at sea, then return to their nesting grounds from September to March which is the breeding season. They incubate their eggs in burrows which they dig near the shoreline. Until the chicks loose their fluffy plumage, develop adult feathers and are able to swim and catch food for themselves, they must be fed by their parents. Both the male and female parents incubate the eggs and feed the chicks. When frightened the penguins run on all fours, using their flippers as front legs, and dive into their burrows.

The penguin is extremely well-adapted to its environment. Webbed feet work as rudders. Heavily muscled wings propel them through the water. They cannot remain submerged for long periods and therefore have to live on marine animals found at shallow depths. They eat small fish, crustaceans and squids. Because they have special salt-secreting glands they can drink sea-water without any harmful effects. Their small scale-like feathers overlap and lie flat to make a barrier which is almost water and wind proof. Penguins also have a thick layer of insulating fat beneath their skin.

Penguins have a number of predators. Large birds like giant petrels take their eggs and occasionally kill the penguin chicks. Leopard seals attack penguins in the water. Killer whales eat larger species like the emperor penguins. The Indians of Tierra del Fuego once hunted penguins for food and for their skins. The Maoris of New Zealand may have eaten them. However it was not until the Europeans arrived in the southern oceans that penguins were hunted *en masse* for their blubber, which could be boiled down to make oil. Penguins are now a protected species world-wide.

Whales It was only in the 18th century that whales, commonly thought by Europeans to be large fish, were finally identified as mammals. They are warm blooded, breathe air with lungs, give birth to live young and feed them on milk which is secreted from mammary glands. Since they breath air directly they regularly have to surface. They get rid of foul air, accumulated while submerged, by forcing it out through their blowholes in sprays of water.

Despite their great size (the largest whale species is the blue whale which can grow up to 27 metres long from head to tail, and weigh as much as 30 elephants) whales are well adapted for life in the ocean. They have streamlined bodies, and a layer of fat (blubber) beneath the skin which insulates them from cold water. Their small flippers are used for steering. Their large tail is used for propulsion.

Whales are divided into two different groups, the toothed whales and the baleen whales. The toothed whales, which include dolphins, porpoises and killer whales, have teeth and feed mainly on fish and squid. In contrast the baleen whales, which include the right whale, are virtually vegetarian. They have a series of 'baleen plates' instead of teeth. These plates strain plankton, tiny fish and krill (a creature resembling a tiny shrimp) from mouthfuls of water. The organisms are trapped on the bristles of the plates and are licked off by the whale's tongue. The baleen whales feed by skimming the surface of the water with their mouths open, letting water filter through the plates.

Killer whales (*Orcinus orca*) grow up to nine metres long. Female killer whales are only half the weight of the males and slightly shorter. The killer whale is easily distinguished by its black body and white underbelly, and its tall, narrow triangular dorsal fin. Their prey includes fish, squid, penguins, dolphins and seals. They've even been known to attack right whales. Surprisingly, they don't normally prey on people, perhaps because they have yet to identify these spindly creatures as edible. Killer whales are the wolf-packs of the oceans. They travel in groups and hunt in teams, herding fish into shallow water near the coast and then picking them off one by one.

The right whale got its name because it was the 'right' whale to kill. It swims relatively slowly, floats after it's been harpooned, and produces a large amount of oil which can be made into soap and other products. The right whales are dark with white patches on the chin and belly. They grow up to 18 metres long from head to tail. Their head and jaws have large skin callosities. These are raised and thickened patches of skin, infested with parasitic worms, barnacles and 'whale lice' which are pale, spider-like creatures about two cm long.

For some reason, right whales need shallow coastal bays in fairly warm waters in which to mate. The whales mate in winter, and calves are born in spring and early summer. The female produces one calf every two to three years. The right whales visit the Península Valdés from May to December each year, where they mate and give birth to their calves. Around mid-November they start moving away from the coast to feed in the oceans which, in summer, are rich in plankton and krill.

Sea Elephants & Sea Lions At Punta Norte, on the peninsula, you can walk down to the beach to within a few feet of the sea elephants. They slumber on the sand looking a bit like giant, mud encrusted slugs, occasionally lifting a clawed fin to scratch themselves before falling back into a doze. They burp and gurgle and occasionally lift their heads to rasp at people who get too close.

South American sea lions can be seen on the west coast of the peninsula, as well as in the Beagle Channel between Tierra del Fuego and Navarino. The male sea lions are distinguished by a thick shag of fur around their neck like a lion's mane.

Sea elephants and sea lions are members of the *Pinnipedia* order. This order encompasses three families. The walrus family has only one member. The family of eared seals includes the South American sea lion. The family of true or hair seals includes the sea elephant.

Male sea elephants are at least three times the weight of females and grow up to 6½ metres long (twice the length of the females). The males are also distinguished by their large, elephantine snout. In fact, the males are so unlike the gentler looking females that it's hard to imagine they belong to the same species.

Pinnipeds are extremely well adapted to life in the ocean. They have sleek, tapering bodies which glide easily through the water (apart for the walrus, which is a clumsy swimmer). When a seal dives, muscles close its nostrils and water pressure helps to hold them closed. When the seal opens its mouth to seize its prey, the larynx and oesophagus are closed off to prevent water from entering them. A seal's blood contains an abundance of oxygen-carrying haemoglobin, giving them an oxygen capacity much greater than a human's. When they dive their heart rate slows down and most of the blood is diverted to the brain. Sea elephants can stay submerged for up to 30 minutes. They live mainly on squid.

Pinnipeds breed in spring and early summer. Some species breed on ice, while the sea elephant breeds on land. The males start coming ashore on the Península Valdés in July, and stake out their territory before the females arrive in August. The females, carrying foetuses conceived in the previous season, come ashore just before they're due to give birth. Female elephant seals suckle their pups after giving birth. At the end of lactation the female mates once more and then quickly severs her relationship with the first pup. Male sea elephants mate with numerous females, gathering 'harems' of dozens of females.

GAIMEN

For visitors, Gaimen is the chief place of interest and the one which still retains something of its older, Welsh appearance.

First impressions of the hot, dusty main street may suggest a town which is barely different from any other in outback Argentina, but a closer look reveals quite a lot of the town's past.

One street back from the main street is 28 de Julio along which the railway line once ran to Puerto Madryn, although the track was was ripped up after the trains stopped running in 1959. The former **train station** is now used as a museum and contains an interesting collection of memorabilia and photos from the early days of the Welsh colonies.

The Welsh-built stone houses are the oldest in Gaimen; the red brick houses are more recent.

The school on the main street was once the site of the cemetery; the graves have been moved to the top of a hill overlooking the town. The cemetery contains many graves with inscriptions in Welsh. Those of members of the 1865 colony have a small plaque which indicates that they were the first colonisers.

Places to Eat

The more obvious sign of a Welsh presence are the tea houses which cater to the tourist trade. Most of these are in private homes of people of Welsh descent, and serve a genteel Welsh country tea and sweets. I'd recommend the *Casa de Té Plas y Coed* run by a friendly couple who speak Welsh, Spanish and English. Their house is over a hundred years old.

Getting There & Away

There are buses to Gaimen and Dolavon from the main bus station in Trelew; Buses 28 de Julio have about nine buses daily.

ESQUEL

In *The Old Patagonian Express*, Paul Theroux describes the landscape around

Esquel as looking like a 'backdrop for a dinosaur skeleton in a museum'. It is hard to disagree with his description and harder to better it. Driving south from El Bolsón the bus turns away from the lush forest of southern Río Negro and heads out into the endless expanse of Patagonian plains.

Trees are conspicuous by their absence. Even sheep are scarce. People carrying large bundles occasionally get off the bus and wander out into the plains, or wait by gas stations for vehicles to materialise and carry them away. On the horizon the last sprinklings of snow whiten the higher peaks of the mountains almost until the end of the year. Besides the Andes, the only conspicuous features of this land are the rail tracks, barbed wire fences, the thin threads of gravel road and the endless power lines.

Esquel is a dusty town, a grid of streets flanked by barren mountains that glow a strange orange in the setting sun. The sun glares off the uniformly rectangular buildings. Truck-dogs, with ferocious eyes and teeth, peer at strangers from the backs of Chevrolet pick-up trucks. This quiet town is, however, the jumping off point for the Parque Nacional Los Alerces, one of the wildest national parks in Argentina –largely untamed, lightly touristed and (unlike the Bariloche area) ragged around the edges.

Information
The post office, tourist office and the bus terminal are all at the corner of Fontana and Alvear.

Banks The Banco de la Nación at the corner of Alvear and Roca will change American Express travellers' cheques and foreign cash.

Places to Stay - bottom end
Esquel has a number of moderately priced hotels but nothing particularly cheap.

The *Residencial Huentru Niyeu* (tel 2576) is at the corner of Chacabuco and Perito Moreno, a quiet street away from the centre of town. Rooms are relatively expensive at US$9 a single and US$13 a double.

Similarly priced is the *Hotel Vascongada* (tel 2361) at the corner of 9 de Julio and Mitre. The rooms are clean though rather stark. They also have single rooms without private bathroom for US$5.

The *Hospedaje Beirut* on 25 de Mayo near the corner with Chacabuco is a clean, friendly, bright little hotel with singles for US$5 and doubles for US$10, both without private bathroom.

Places to Stay - middle
The *Residencial Esquel* (tel 2534) at San Martín 1042 is US$11 a single and US$17 a double with private bathroom. It's a comfortable if nondescript place run by friendly people.

Others include the *Residencial Ski* (tel 2254) at San Martín 963, which is pretty much on par with the Residencial Esquel, and the *Residencial La Tour d'Argent* (tel 2530) at San Martín 1063.

The *Hotel Huemul* (tel 2533) at the corner of 25 de Mayo and Alvear has small rooms and tiny bathrooms, but is otherwise clean and comfortable with quiet rooms at the rear. Singles are US$9 and doubles US$14, with private bathrooms.

On par with the Huemul is the *Residencial Maika* (tel 2457) at the corner of 25 de Mayo and San Martín.

Places to Stay - top end
The *Hotel Tehuelche* (tel 2420) at the corner of 9 de Julio and Belgrano, has singles for US$21 and doubles for US$29.

Places to Eat
There are a number of nondescript restaurants around the centre of town, including pizzas at *Don Pipo* on Rivadavia near the corner with Roca; *Restaurant*

Jockey Club at Alvear 949 which is moderately priced but dull; the *Parrilla La Estancia* on 25 de Mayo near the corner with San Martín; and the *Restaurant Vascongada* at the corner of Mitre and 9 de Julio which serves a mean curried steak. *Las Mutisias* at Alvear 1025 is a genial confiteria.

Getting There & Away

Air Aerolíneas Argentinas (tel 2539) is at the corner of San Martín and Sarmiento. They have flights to Trelew four days a week and to Bariloche three days a week.

LADE (tel 2227) is at 25 de Mayo 777. They have flights to Trelew two days a week, and to Bariloche three days a week.

Esquel Tours, on Fontana, has a mini-bus to the airport. Its departure times are linked to the flights.

Bus TA Mercedes has three routes from Bariloche to Esquel. The first is the direct route via Río Villegas, El Bolsón, Hoyo de Epuyen, Epuyen and Leleque with buses four days a week. The second is via El Bolsón, Epuyen and Cholila with buses three days a week. The third is via El Bolsón, Cholila and Lago Futalaufquen with daily buses. The fare to Bariloche is US$15.

Angel Giobbi has buses once a week to Comodoro Rivadavia via Sarmiento, Manantiales, Tamarisco, La Laurita, San Martín, Gobernador Costa and Tecka.

Don Otto has buses twice a week to Puerto Madryn. The fare is US$22.

PARQUE NACIONAL LOS ALERCES

West of Esquel lies the wild and relatively untouristed Parque Nacional Los Alerces. The park takes its name from the slow-growing alerce trees which are found here. A tree which is 2500 years old may only stand 60 metres high and be two metres across the trunk. The oldest alerce tree, 4600 years old, is in Nevada in the USA. Apart from the alerces the park also has many arrayanes, the slow-growing trees

with the cinnamon-coloured bark which you see in the forests around Bariloche.

Geography

This is an area of sharply contrasting variations in climate and relief. The mountainous areas of the park range from 2500 to 3500 metres in altitude, with many snow-capped mountains. As a result of the accumulation of ice there are important glaciers in this region.

Glacial lakes resembling shattered mirrors are strewn out along the Patagonian mountains that border the park. These include Lakes Menéndez, Futalaufquen, Cisne, Verde and a dozen others. All are of unknown depth. There are many rivers and streams connecting these lakes to each other.

Some of the features of this region have names from Mapuche Indian languages. For instance, Futalaufquen means 'big lake' and Futaleufú means 'big river'.

Climate

The climate of the region ranges from hot and humid in summer to bitterly cold in winter. There are extreme temperature variations ranging from –17°C to 30°C.

These variations in altitude, terrain and climate produce distinct patterns in the dispersal of flora in the park.

On the western side of the park, where the climate ranges from moderate to warm and humid, are the Patagonian forests.

On the eastern side of the park, where the climate and terrain is arid, there is insufficient water for forest to grow. Instead this area is characterised by scrubby, grassy plains.

Flora of the Los Alerces National Park

Conifers The forest areas are characterised by coniferous trees, including cypress and southern beech. Conifers are a very old group of trees. Fossils date back 300 million years ago. They prefer cool climates, either high latitudes or high altitudes, and

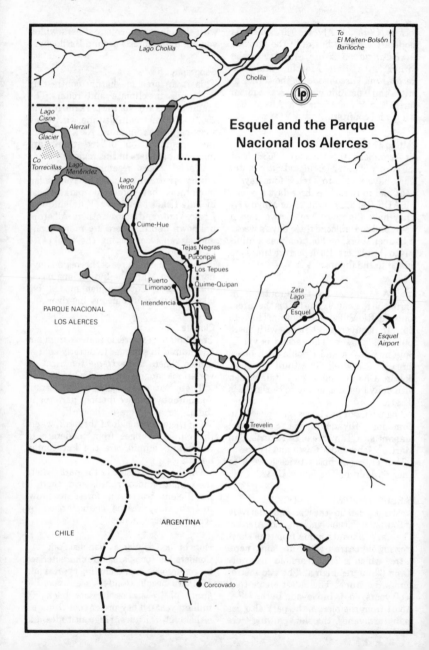

Esquel and the Parque Nacional los Alerces

have been logged extensively for their fine timber.

One of the main types of coniferous trees in the Los Alerces National Park is the alerce (*Fitzroya cupressoides*). This tree is also known as the Patagonian cypress. They live only in Chile and Argentina. They are exceptionally slow growers. Some of the trees alive today are between 3000 and 4000 years old. They reach a height of 45 to 50 metres and a diameter of up to five metres. Most of the alerces grow on the north and south side of Menéndez Lake, and around Lake Cisne. Their wood is similar to redwood and was once used for housing.

Usually, in a forest of alerces, you will find the ciprés de las guaitecas (*Pilgerodendron uviferum*). This tree grows up to 25 metres and has reddish wood. It is similar in appearance to the alerce. This is one of the most southerly conifers in the world, and is now a protected species because of the degree of logging that it has suffered. It grows only in Chilean and Argentine Patagonia and in Tierra del Fuego.

Also found in the park is the ciprés de la cordillera (*Austrocedrus chilensis*) which is conical in shape and is distinguished by its wrinkly bark. It's known as the Chilean incense cedar because it has a scented and hardy wood, which is used in carpentry. It grows up to 25 metres high and is native to Chile and Argentina.

Southern Beeches The other family of important trees in the park are the *Nothofagus*, or southern beech trees. The southern Beeches are members of a group known as the 'broadleaves' and are characterised by their flattened leaves.

Unlike the conifers, these are a flowering plant. The reproductive structures of the broadleaves are located in flowers, whereas in conifers the reproductive structures are located in cones. Like cypresses, the broadleaf trees are logged for hardwood timber, which is used for building, fencing and furniture. They are evergreen and grow up to 50 metres high.

Southern beeches are found in South America, New Zealand, eastern Australia, New Guinea and New Caledonia. Fossil southern beech trees have been found in Antarctica. Their wide dispersal appears to have been caused by continental drift – the species was scattered when the original continent, Gondwanaland, broke into separate pieces.

The main southern beech found in the park is the coihue (*Nothofagus dombeyi*). It has strong, well shaped branches, with greyish bark. It can grow up to 35 metres in height. It lives at altitudes of around 900 to 1000 metres above sea-level. This is an evergreen tree. Its leaves are dark green and very shiny and thick – so thick that it's hard to distinguish the flowers and fruits. The word coihue is a Mapuche Indian word meaning 'new fruit'.

The Yellow Woods Growing around coihues you often find the mañiu macho (*Podocarpus nubigena*). This is a conifer which belongs to a group of evergreen trees and shrubs known as 'yellow woods'. They are found in many parts of the world and are important for their timber.

Another type of yellow wood found in the park is the ñire (*Nothofagus antarctica*). It grows up to 15 metres high. It's characterised by its wrinkly bark and fruits which develop in groups of three. This tree is also found as a bush. Both trees and bushes are often found mixed with the related species known as lenga (*Nothfagus pumilio*).

The lenga tree ranges in size from a small tree to a shrub. Trees grow at lower altitudes and shrubs at high altitudes, so the lenga marks the timberline in the park. In autumn its leaves change to dark red, giving the landscape an exceptionally colourful and attractive appearance.

Also found growing around the coihues is another type of tree which is cut for timber, the mañiu hembra (*Saxegothaea conspicua*). This tree is known in English as the Prince Alfred yew. It can grow up to 20 metres high. Its bark is a brown, reddish colour. It generally grows in the areas with high rainfall where it can reach its greatest height and girth.

The Arrayanes Another distinctive tree found in the park is the arrayán (*Luma apiculata*). This ranges in size from a tree to a small bush. It grows up to five metres high. It has smooth, reddish or cinnamon coloured bark and produces white flowers. Within the national park it can be found along both sides of the Arrayanes River, which connects Lake Verde with Lake Futalaufquen. Its wood has traditionally been used only for producing ornament-ation. It is now a protected species.

Laurelias The hua-huán is a member of the *Laurelia* family. This is a big or medium sized tree. It's distinguished by its leaves which are quite tough and leathery. There are three species of Laurelias. One is found in New Zealand, one in the Philippines and the other in Chile and Argentina. It's commonly known in South America as the Chilean laurel, and its greenish coloured wood is used for making furniture.

Native Bushes & Shrubs There are a number of interesting bushes and shrubs in the park.

The palo piche (*Fabiana imbricata*) is an evergreen bush found only in Chile and Argentina. It grows up to 1½ metres high, has a thick mass of branches, scale-like leaves and white or violet tube-shaped flowers. If eaten, it can have a diuretic effect.

The calafate (*Berberis buxifolia*) is more commonly known as a barberry. The barberry bush is found in Central Asia, China, Japan, Europe and the Americas. This particular variety grows to 1½ metres high, and has thorns and pricking leaves. Its flowers are yellowish. Its fruit is edible. According to traditional stories, those

who eat the fruit of this bush will never be able to leave Patagonia.

The michay (*Berberis darwinii*) is a thorny barberry bush which grows up to 2½ metres high. It has rhomboid shaped leaves, and orange flowers. The fruit is a deep blue and about half a cm in diameter. The fruit is edible and is used to make jams and jellies.

The fuinque (*Lomatia ferruginea*) is a small tree which belongs to the protea family. It lives in very humid areas. Its leaves are dark green , and it produces flowers which are greenish-yellow on the outside and reddish inside.

The espino negro (*Colletia spinosissima*) is a bush which grows from half to one metre high. It has branches covered in fine, deep green hairs and produces pinkish-white flowers. It also grows in groups on the arid plains in the east of the park.

This plant is a member of the buckthorn family. Plants which are grown from seeds, or from grafts of the branches, begin as round spines – thus the name *spinosa*.

Native to Chile and Argentina is the retamo (*Diostea juncea*) which produces bright yellow flowers.

Another plant which is also responsible for the fiery appearance of the Patagonian landscape in spring and summer is the mutisia (*Mutisia decurrens*) which produces brilliant orange flowers. This is a climber, wrapping its tendrils around other trees and shrubs.

Non-Native Plants There are a number of non-native species of plants found in, or in the vicinity of, the park.

The common ajenjo (*Artemisia absith-irum*) is a member of the group known, incorrectly, as the Japanese chrysanthemums. These are found in Europe and Asia and are actually derived from two Chinese species. They reached Europe in the 18th century. In ancient times they were used as a medicinal plant.

The lupino (*Lupinus polyphillus*) originated in the west of North America and has long been grown as an ornamental plant. You see these growing wild and in the gardens of hotels and houses in western Patagonia. They have metre high spikes which produce masses of small flowers. Originally only pale blue or white flowers would grow, but cultivation has now allowed the production of all sorts of different coloured flowers.

The mosqueta (*Rosa englanteria*) is a variety of rose known as the sweet briar, because of its fragrant leaves.

Places to Stay

There are several camping grounds and hosterías along the road from Esquel to Lago Futalaufquen to Bariloche.

Possibly the best of the hosterías is the *Hostería Cumé Hué* which charges US$20 per person per night, which includes breakfast, lunch and dinner. It's set back from the road but is easily identifiable in the spring by the blaze of flowering lupins in the front garden. The hostería is set on a small beach on the lake and it's a popular place for fishing, especially for brown and rainbow trout.

Other places include the *Hostería Quime Quipan* and the motel-style *Hostería Puconpai*.

Getting There & Away

There are a couple of ways of getting to the Parque Naciónal Los Alerces from Esquel.

TA Mercedes has a daily bus to Bariloche via Lago Futalaufquen, Lago Verde and Lago Rivadavia. You can do this as a day-trip. In the late afternoon take the bus coming through from Bariloche back to Esquel.

There are few cars on the roads during the off-season so hitching will be difficult.

Esquel Tours at Fontana 754, Esquel, has day tours along the north-east coast of Lago Futalaufquen and then on to Lago Verde, Lago Menéndez and Lago Cisne.

The tours are US$20 per person. This trip is usually done entirely by boat, but sometimes they'll take you by bus to a river crossing just after the Hostería Cumé Hué. A pedestrian suspension bridge crosses Río Verde and a path leads to the eastern shore of Lago Menéndez. From there you catch a launch to Alerzal at the northern tip of Lago Menéndez, then follow a trail to Lago Cisne (Swan Lake).

COMODORO RIVADAVIA

Comodoro Rivadavia was founded at the turn of the century. In 1907 it became an overnight boom town when a group of workers drilling for water struck oil instead. This was the first major discovery of oil in Argentina and led to the government setting up the YPF (Yacimientos Petrolíferos Fiscales) to exploit the reserves.

Today, Comodoro Rivadavia is one of the largest towns in Patagonia, with over 100,000 people. The reserves to the west and south of the town provide about a third of Argentina's crude oil supply. There is not much of interest for visitors in Comodoro Rivadavia but you may have to stay there overnight on your way to or from the southern tip of Argentina.

Information

Tourist Office The tourist office is in the bus station.

Banks You might be able to change travellers' cheques at the Banco de la Nacion at San Martín 102 and the Banco Londres y America at Rivadavia 270.

Consulate The Chilean Consulate is at Sarmiento 936.

The Petrified Forest

Comodoro Rivadavia is the jumping off point for visits to the Reserva Geológica Bosque Petrificado, the Petrified Forest. The petrified forest is about 30 km from the town of Sarmiento, which is due west

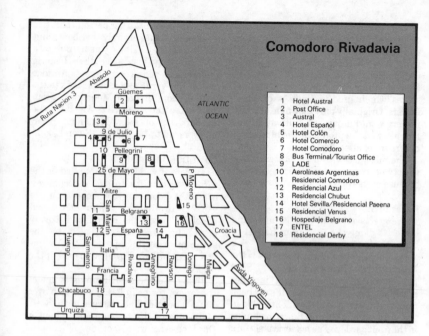

Comodoro Rivadavia

1 Hotel Austral
2 Post Office
3 Austral
4 Hotel Español
5 Hotel Colón
6 Hotel Comercio
7 Hotel Comodoro
8 Bus Terminal/Tourist Office
9 LADE
10 Aerolineas Argentinas
11 Residencial Comodoro
12 Residencial Azul
13 Residencial Chubut
14 Hotel Sevilla/Residencial Paeena
15 Residencial Venus
16 Hospedaje Belgrano
17 ENTEL
18 Residencial Derby

of Comodoro Rivadavia and can be reached by daily bus.

Places to Stay – bottom end

The *Residencial Chubut* at Belgrano 738, between Rivadavia and Ameghino, has some dark, gloomy rooms for US$7 a single and US$13 a double, with private bathroom. The *Hotel Sevilla*, around the corner on Ameghino, is similar. Next door the *Residencial Paeena* has a rather forbidding appearance from the outside but is not bad all things considered.

Most foreign visitors seem to head to the *Hotel Comerica* on Rivadavia, between Pellegrini and 9 de Julio, with its rustic bar and restaurant. Rooms are US$4 a single and US$9 a double.

The *Residencial Venus* on Rawson, near the corner with Belgrano, is a modern building. Rooms with private bathroom are US$5 a single and US$10 a double.

The *Hotel Colón* on San Martín is

worth trying. Rooms without private bathroom are US$7 a single and US$11 a double. Rooms with private bathroom are a few dollars more. There's a rustic bar downstairs which is a cross between a wild west saloon, pool hall and Parisian café.

The *Hospedaje Belgrano* at Belgrano 546, on the corner with Dorrego, is spartan but clean, quiet and cheap. The *Hotel Español* on 9 de Julio is basic, clean, but may be noisy.

Places to Stay – middle

The *Residencial Azul* at Sarmiento 724 has singles from US$15 and doubles from US$20.

The *Residencial Comodoro* (not to be confused with the Hotel Comodoro) at España 919 is worth trying though front rooms are noisy. Rooms with private bathroom are US$16 a single and US$21 a double.

Places to Stay – top end

The *Hotel Comodoro* (tel 22061) is the high-rise building in the centre of town at 9 de Julio 770. Singles are US$20 and doubles are US$26. Similarly priced is the *Hotel Austral* (tel 21021) at Rivadavia 190.

Places to Eat

The *Comercio* does adequate meals for a few dollars per person.

There's a bunch of restaurants, confiterias, rustic bars (try the one in the Hotel Diana at the corner of Belgrano and Rawson), pool halls, hash houses and pizzerias along Rivadavia but it's not really worth mentioning any one in particular.

Getting There & Away

Comodoro Rivadavia is a major transport junction on the coast with many bus and flight connections to other parts of the country.

Air Aerolíneas Argentina (tel 24781) is at San Martín 421. They have daily flights to Buenos Aires, Trelew, Río Gallegos and Ushuaia. They have flights two or three days a week to Río Grande, Esquel, Bariloche and Nuequén.

Austral is at San Martín 291. LADE is on Rivadavia, opposite the Hotel Comercio.

Bus The bus station is on Pellegrini.

Transportadora Patagonia has buses four days a week to Río Gallegos, and daily buses to Rawson, Trelew and Puerto Madryn.

La Puntual has daily buses to Buenos Aires and Puerto Madryn.

Transporte Don Otto has daily buses to Buenos Aires via Puerto Madryn.

Angel Giobbi SA has buses to Coyhaique in Chile three days a week. The same company has buses to Esquel two days a week.

Typical fares from Comodoro Rivadavia are: to Puerto Madryn US$13; Buenos Aires US$40; and Río Gallegos US$23.

Getting Around

Cars can be rented from National (tel 20334) at 9 de Julio 770.

Santa Cruz Province

The first European to set foot on Santa Cruz was probably a member of Ferdinand Magellan's expedition in 1520. Magellan's ships wintered at Puerto San Julian, before sailing south and entering the terrible straits which are now named after him. It was not until the 18th century that any exploration was carried out in the area (mainly by Jesuit missionaries) and not until the latter part of that century that the Spanish finally set up forts along its coast to guard against interloping foreign ships. The first attempts at establishing permanent settlements failed miserably due to the terrible weather and lack of food.

Numerous attempts in the second half of the 19th century to establish permanent settlements all failed until sheep-grazing (managed by British, Scottish and Australian grazers) was introduced from the Falkland Islands in the 1880s. The town of Santa Cruz was founded at the same time. Río Gallegos, now the capital, was founded in 1897. San Julián was founded in 1903.

Even so, the human population was ridiculously small. Only a thousand or so whites lived in Santa Cruz at the end of the 19th century. It was not until the 1920s that towns along the northern coast of the province were firmly established. After that development was rapid.

By the 1940s the population had grown to 25,000. In the 1950s the coastal highway, connecting Santa Cruz to the rest of Argentina, was paved. Coal was discovered at Río Turbio and a mine established and a railway built to carry the coal to the port at Río Gallegos.

Santa Cruz is extraordinary for its

geographical contrasts. The eastern part of the province is a series of grassy, rough plateaus, beaten by cold, savage winds that blow in ceaselessly from the Atlantic Ocean. Melting ice from the Andes feeds the rivers which flow through the plateaus into the ocean. The Andes fringe includes strangely coloured lakes like Lago Buenos Aires, surrounded by a landscape which would not look out of place in a Sci-Fi film set on another planet.

In the far south the grey-blue waters of Lago Argentino give rise to Río Santa Cruz. At the western extremity of this lake is one of the last great reminders of the Ice Age – the Moreno Glacier. Further north a string of glaciers, including the Upsala and Viedma glaciers, slide into Lago Argentino and Lago Viedma.

RIO GALLEGOS

Close to the southern tip of the Patagonian peninsula, Río Gallegos is the jumping-off point for trips to Calafate and to Ushuaia in Tierra de Fuego. There's nothing much to see in the town itself. The **museum** on Perito Moreno has a sizeable collection of fossils and Indian artefacts.

Information

Post The post office is at the corner of Roca and San Martín.

Telephone ENTEL is at Roca 631.

Banks US dollars cash and travellers' cheques, and Chilean pesos can be changed at the Cambio El Pingüino at Zapiola 469. There are other money changers and banks in the town centre.

Consulates The Chilean consulate is at Mariano Moreno 136.

Places to Stay – bottom end

Río Gallegos is a relatively expensive city for accommodation and like other towns in Patagonia the cheapest places are often permanently full. Accommodation is pretty basic, but even the cheaper hotels are usually in good condition.

One I'd highly recommend is the *Hotel Colonial* at the corner of Rivadavia and Urquiza. Clean, comfortable rooms are US$9 a single and US$11 a double, without private bathroom. There are hot showers, a bar, and the staff are friendly.

Similarly priced is the large *Hotel Central*, upstairs at Roca 1127. The rooms are fairly quiet because they're set back from the main street.

Other places worth trying for cheap rooms are the *Residencial Sachas* at Rivadavia 122; the *Residencial Internacional* on Federico Sphur near the corner with Roca; the *Hotel Ampeuro* at the corner of Roca and Federico Sphur; and the *Hotel Entre Ríos* on Entre Ríos between Zapiola and Libertad.

Places to Stay – middle

The *Hotel Río Turbio* (tel 2155) is at the corner of Zapiola and Entre Ríos. It has comfortable rooms from US$11 a single and US$17 a double without private bathrooms, and US$20 a single and US$25 a double with private bathroom.

Also try the *Hotel Covadonga* (tel 8190) at Roca 1244; the *Hotel Puerto Santa Cruz* on Zapiola near the corner with Rivadavia; and the *Hotel Punta Arenas* (tel 2743) at Federico Sphur 75 near the corner with Roca.

Places to Stay – top end

The *Hotel Alonso* (tel 2414) at Corrientes 33 has rooms with private bathroom for US$18 a single and US$27 a double. The *Hotel Comercio* at the corner of Roca and Estrada is slightly more expensive.

Places to Eat

Both the cosy *La Casa de Miguel* at Roca 1284, and the larger *Restaurant Díaz* at Roca 1157, serve very good and inexpensive seafood. Also try the cosy *Restaurant Montecarlo* at Zapiola 558.

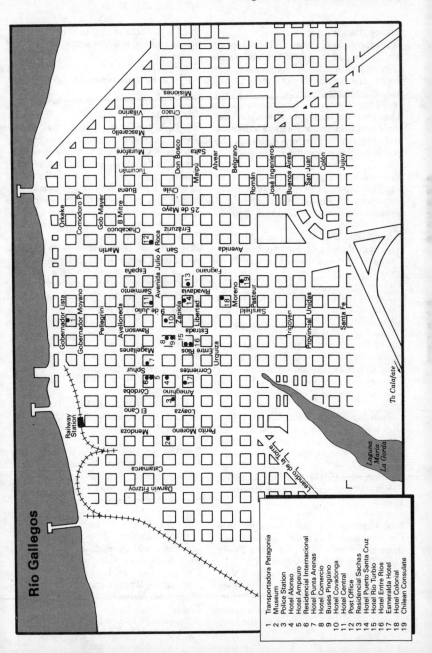

Río Gallegos

1 Transportadora Patagonia
2 Museum
3 Police Station
4 Hotel Alonso
5 Hotel Ampuero
6 Residencial Internacional
7 Hotel Punta Arenas
8 Hotel Comercio
9 Buses Pingüino
10 Hotel Covadonga
11 Hotel Central
12 Post Office
13 Residencial Sachas
14 Hotel Puerto Santa Cruz
15 Hotel Río Turbio
16 Hotel Entre Ríos
17 Esmeralda Hotel
18 Hotel Colonial
19 Chilean Consulate

Getting There & Away

From Río Gallegos you can head west to Río Turbio and then cross the mountains to Puerto Natales in Chile. Or head south-west to the Chilean city of Punta Arenas and cross the Straits of Magellan to Tierra del Fuego. The third alternative is to take a bus from Río Gallegos to Calafate, visit the Moreno Glacier and Fitzroy Mountains, and then bus to Puerto Natales via the Torres del Paine mountains in Chile.

Air Aerolíneas Argentinas (tel 8181) is at San Martín 545. They have daily flights to Comodoro Rivadavia, Río Grande and Ushuaia. Austral (tel 8038) is at Zapiola 122.

LADE (tel 2249) is at Fagnano 53. They have daily flights to Comodoro Rivadavia, Calafate, Río Grande and Ushuaia. They have flights three days a week to Río Turbio.

There's no bus for the 7½ km trip from the airport to the town centre. A taxi costs a few dollars.

Bus El Pingüino at Zapiola 445 has daily buses to Punta Arenas in Chile, and daily buses to Río Turbio and Calafate.

Buses San Ceferino at Entre Ríos 371 has buses to Río Turbio three days a week.

Transportadora Patagonia and Don Otto are both at Gobernador Lista 330 and have daily buses to Río Turbio, Calafate, Caleta Olivia and Comodoro Rivadavia.

Typical fares from Río Gallegos are: to Punta Arenas US$14; Río Turbio US$12; Calafate US$12; and Comodoro Rivadavia US$23.

Boat There are no direct buses between Río Grande and Río Gallegos although there is a ferry crossing between Punta Delgada and Primera Angostura.

The ferries are operated by the ENAP oil company. These generally leave every two hours between 7.30 am and 9.30 pm. There are no buses along this route so you have to hitch-hike. If you miss the ferry there is nowhere to stay in either of these places and you may get stuck.

Getting Around

Cars can be rented from A1 (tel 2453) at Entre Ríos 350.

RIO TURBIO

Río Turbio lies at the end of a long drive across the plains towards the mountains bordering Chile. This is a real frontier town with its drab collection of bungalows, hovels, converted army barracks and concrete bunkers. The only industry is coal mining and many Chileans work in the mines.

Places to Stay

The *Hotel El Gato Negro* is on Roque Sáenz Peña. Rooms with private bathroom are US$11 a single and US$18 a double. It's very clean, and by the standards of southern Argentina it's good value for money. Also try the *Hotel El Azteca* at the corner of Jorge Newbery and Castillo.

Getting There & Away

Air Aerolíneas Argentinas is on Castillo, at the junction with Hipólito Irigoyen. AUSTRAL is also on Castillo. LADE is at Mineros 375.

The only flights out of Río Turbio are with LADE, which has flights three days a week to Río Gallegos.

Bus The bus from Río Turbio to Puerto Natales takes about 1½ hours. One bus takes you to the Argentine customs post where you transfer to a Chilean bus which goes to Puerto Natales. The buses leave Río Turbio from the junction of Jorge Newbery and Puerto Ramón Castillo.

El Pingüino is on Jorge Newbery, near the corner with Avenida de los Mineros. They have daily buses to Río Gallegos. The trip takes six hours along a gravel road cutting through grassland grazed by sheep and dotted with large estancias. The fare is US$12.

Buses San Ceferino is on Castillo, at the

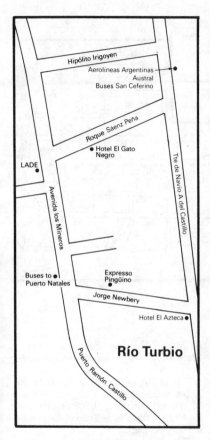

Chilean expansionism) by encouraging settlement.

Information
Tourist Office The tourist office is on San Martín and is worth visiting for lists of hospedajes and hotels.

National Parks The national parks office is at the corner of San Martín and Ezequiel Bustillo. They have good maps of the area.

Banks Cash and possibly travellers' cheques can be changed at the Banco de la Provincia de Santa Cruz at the corner of San Martín and 1 de Mayo.

Things to See
Calafate is an innocuous town set in a valley in the foothills of the Andes. It is, however, the jumping off point for three of the most dramatic sights in Argentina: the **Moreno Glacier**, the **Upsala Glacier**, and the **Fitzroy Mountains** (Cerro Fitzroy).

The Moreno Glacier is in the nearby *Parque Nacional de los Glaciares*. The glacier is a tremendous sight. It's four km wide, and descends to the surface of Lago Argentino where it rises 60 metres above the water level. The second mammoth glacier is the Upsala glacier, which can be visited by motor-boat.

In addition to the glaciers, there are many possibilities for walking and trekking in the mountains.

The tourist season in Calafate is between September and May, with most people flocking in during the Argentine holiday season in January and February. During winter the whole region is under snow and the roads to the glaciers are blocked. Even the road from Calafate to Río Gallegos is occasionally blocked by snow during this period and Calafate airport sometimes closes.

The best time to visit is late November and during December, when the roads are open and there are sufficient visitors for

junction with Hipólito Irigoyen. They have buses to Río Gallegos three days a week.

CALAFATE
Though it's one of the main tourist resorts of Argentine Patagonia, Calafate still has a touch of the pioneer feel. Standing amid half-completed houses with dust kicked about by the blustering winds tends to add to the illusion. The rate of construction is quite astonishing as the Argentine government strengthens its claims to Patagonia (against real or imagined

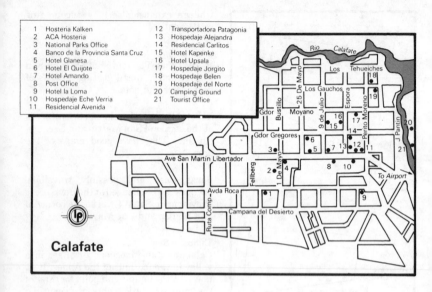

1	Hosteria Kalken	12	Transportadora Patagonia
2	ACA Hosteria	13	Hospedaje Alejandra
3	National Parks Office	14	Residencial Carlitos
4	Banco de la Provincia Santa Cruz	15	Hotel Kapenke
5	Hotel Glanesa	16	Hotel Upsala
6	Hotel El Quijote	17	Hospedaje Jorgito
7	Hotel Amando	18	Hospedaje Belen
8	Post Office	19	Hospedaje del Norte
9	Hotel la Loma	20	Camping Ground
10	Hospedaje Eche Verria	21	Tourist Office
11	Residencial Avenida		

Calafate

the tour buses to operate – but before the holiday season begins.

Something of the town's early history can be discerned in the **Museo Regional El Calafate**, which is on the road to the airport.

Places to Stay - bottom end

Apart from camping, the cheapest accommodation in Calafate is a room in a private house.

The best of the private houses is probably the *Hospedaje Eche Verria* at San Martín 989, which is a bright little house with friendly people. They charge about US$5 per person.

Other houses in Calafate which take guests include the *Hospedaje Belen* at the corner of Los Gauchos and Perito Moreno; the *Hospedaje del Norte* at the corner of Los Gauchos and Pantin; the *Hospedaje Alejandra* on Espora between San Martín and Gregores; and the *Hospedaje Jorgito*

on Moyano between Espora and Perito Moreno. All charge about US$5 or US$6 per person.

One of the better small hotels is the *Residencial Avenida* (tel 83) on San Martín with singles for US$9 and doubles for US$11. It's a neat little place run by friendly people.

There's a campsite in Calafate behind the tourist office. There are a number of refugios in the park which are free; the map in this book shows their locations.

Places to Stay - middle

The *ACA Hostería* (tel 04) overlooks San Martín; the entrance is on 1 de Mayo. Rooms with private bathroom are US$21 a single and US$31 a double. Similarly priced are the *Hotel La Loma* (tel 16) at the corner of Roca and Perito Moreno, and the *Hostería Kaiken* (tel 73) on Feilberg.

Other mid-range hotels are the *Residencial Carlitos* (tel 88) at Espora 991, and the *Hotel Amando* (tel 23) on San Martín near the corner with 9 de Julio.

If you'd like to stay at the Moreno glacier itself, the *Motel ACA* has a number of bungalows which will each sleep four people, but they're often booked out in summer.

Places to Stay – top end

Top of the list is the *Hotel Upsala* (tel 75) on Espora, between Gregores and Moyano. Singles are US$28 and doubles are US$40.

Places to Eat

There's not much choice of restaurants in Calafate. None are particularly interesting and few are cheap. Try the *Restaurant y Pizzeria O'Nelli* at Libertador 1197 which has very large servings; the *Parrilla La Tablita* by the tourist office; and the cheap *Restaurant Macios* on Los Gauchos opposite the Hospedaje del Norte.

Getting There & Away

Air LADE is at San Martín 1180. They have daily flights from Calafate to Ushuaia via Río Grande and Río Gallegos, though these tend to be heavily booked.

Calafate airport is a ten minute walk from the centre of town. Follow the road to Río Gallegos over the bridge and then turn left up the road opposite the museum.

Bus Transportadora Patagonia is on San Martín next to the Residencial Avenida. They have daily buses to Río Gallegos. The trip is 6½ hours of excruciating tedium through featureless plains. The fare is US$12.

Hitching might be possible during the height of the tourist season but forget it otherwise since there are few vehicles on the road. If you're hitching, you have a choice of coming from Río Gallegos or from Santa Cruz further north.

There's a new road connecting Calafate to Puerto Natales in Chile which runs through the Torres del Paine national park. Several tour organisers in Calafate have trips to Puerto Natales and the Torres del Paine during summer. The round-trip fare is around US$41 per person.

Getting Around

Interlago Turismo, Lake Travel Turismo and Gador Viajes, all on San Martín in Calafate, have tours to Cerro Fitzroy, Cerro Torre, Lago Viedma, the Moreno Glacier and the Torres del Paine National Park. Nova Terra on 9 de Julio has excursions to the Upsala Glacier. Typical prices per person are: Upsala Glacier US$35, Torres del Paine US$41, Moreno Glacier US$11.

PARQUE NACIONAL DE LOS GLACIARES

Almost 120 years ago an Argentine expedition, sent to find the source of the Río Santa Cruz in the far south of Patagonia, was about to give up and return home. Just then, so it is said, they heard a strange rumbling sound ahead of them. Their curiosity aroused, they continued onwards and became the first Europeans to set eyes on the deep blue lake now known as Lago Argentino, a large glacial lake which is the source of the Río Santa Cruz.

Branching off the western end of the lake is a channel of water presently cut in two by the Moreno Glacier. The glacier is one of the most awesome sights in South America. Further to the north the even larger Viedma Glacier slides down into Lago Viedma. The glaciers are located in the Parque Nacional los Glaciares. On the northern fringe of the park is one of the other great attractions of Patagonia, the jagged peaks of the Fitzroy Mountains.

The glaciers are reminders of the world's last great Ice Age, when huge sheets of glacial ice covered vast areas of the earth some 10,000 years ago. Glaciers are caused when thick layers of snow gradually recrystallise to form solid ice.

The thickness of the accumulated ice and snow increases until the pressure exerted by the weight of the accumulated ice becomes greater than the strength of

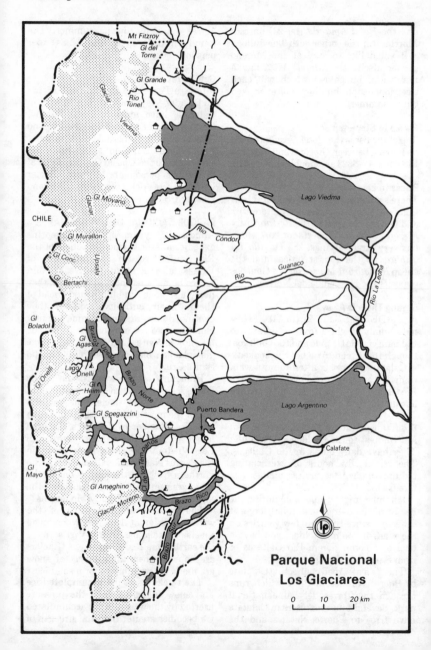

**Parque Nacional
Los Glaciares**

0   10   20 km

the ice mass. Because of pressure from above the ice mass starts to move, sliding down the slope of a mountain. Although small pieces of ice easily break, huge masses under enough pressure will flow like tar or molten plastic.

As glaciers flow down to lower altitudes they begin to lose ice due to melting and evaporation. If, as in the case of the Moreno and Upsala Glaciers, they slide into an ocean or lake, they lose ice by calving. When that happens, huge pieces will break off from the ice wall and float away as icebergs. The upper 30 to 60 metres of a glacier is actually brittle ice and does not flow, but is carried along by the layer of flowing ice beneath it.

If the bedrock beneath the glacier changes its slope suddenly, the mass of flowing ice is disrupted, causing the upper layer to break up into a chaotic mass of ice pinnacles. If different sections of the flowing ice start moving at different speeds, then crevices will appear in the upper layer. Standing in front of the Moreno Glacier's immense ice wall you might recall the lines from Samuel Taylor Coleridge's *The Rime of the Ancient Mariner*:

The ice was here, the ice was there,
The ice was all around:
It cracked and growled and roared and howled,
Like noises in a swound!

Not only does the glacier crack, growl, roar and howl, it shudders, grunts, groans and moans. Great pieces of it break off and tumble into the lake, producing huge waves and water sprays. Chunks of blue glacial ice wallowing in the lake suddenly crack and split in two. It is hard to see, and hear, such daunting animation without starting to think of the glacier more as a living organism than a huge river of dead ice.

The Moreno Glacier is 35 km long, 4½ km wide and rises about 60 metres above water level. It moves forward at a rate of just over 1½ metres per day. At the time of writing it has cut the lake in two, piling water up on one side five or six metres higher than the water level on the other side. Eventually the higher water will tunnel under the glacier and the wall of ice will collapse into the lake.

While you're in Calafate you should drop into the *Confitería Tío Cacho*, on 9 de Julio just down from San Martín. During the tourist season they have two showings daily of a film of the calving of the Moreno Glacier.

Despite its impressive dimensions, the Moreno Glacier is a midget compared to the giant Upsala Glacier to the north. The city of Buenos Aires will fit into the Upsala Glacier three times over. Like the world's other glaciers the Upsala is receding. The mountain slopes on either side of the lake, close to the front of the glacier, are almost bare of vegetation – indicating that the Upsala Glacier once extended much further than it does today.

Getting There & Away

The Moreno glacier is about 80 km from Calafate. In summer (November to February) there are daily tour buses to the edge of the glacier. It's a two hour trip and on the way you'll see a splendid array of bird life including cormorants, eagles and condors. For details of the tour companies see the 'Getting There & Away' section for Calafate.

In the winter you may be able to get local people to drive you out to the Moreno Glacier if the road is still open, although this will be quite expensive. The *Hotel La Loma* in Calafate has its own vehicles which can carry eight people and will arrange trips to the glacier. Staff members reportedly speak several foreign languages including English, Portugese, French and Italian.

In summer you can take a tour to the Upsala glacier by motor boat. The boats leave from Puerto Bandera, 45 km from Calafate, which you get to by bus. Although the glacier itself is not as impressive at first sight as the Moreno Glacier, getting there entails a boat ride through wild, untouched mountain country. After visiting the Upsala Glacier the boat docks briefly near Lago Onelli and you follow a trail through the forest to the lake. Onelli is clogged with icebergs which have broken off the Agassiz, Onelli and Bolado Glaciers. There is a refugio near here and you could get the launch one day, stay overnight and take it back to Calafate the next day.

THE FITZROY MOUNTAINS (CERRO FITZROY)

On the northern fringe of the Parque Nacional Los Glaciares stand the jagged peaks of the Fitzroy Mountain Range. Nearby stands a tall, pillar-like mountain called Cerro Torre, once thought to be unclimbable. Nowadays mountaineers clamber up and down this peak in two days, leaving the hostería at Chalten decorated with souvenir flags, posters and inscribed plaques of their expeditions.

If you're only here for a day head off along the path by the Fitzroy River. This trail leads to Lago Torre. At the half way point (where a small sign indicates that it's another 1½ hours to Lago Torre) you will get fine views of Cerro Torre and the Torre and Grande glaciers in the distance. The peaks of the Fitzroy range poke up over the ridge to the right. This is a gentle walk, apart from one point just near the start where you have to ease yourself along a narrow ledge of a cliff face.

Another path from Chalten leads to the base of the Fitzroy Mountains. This is a 3½ hour hike so you can't do it as a day-trip from Calafate. John Pilkington and Hilary Bradt's *Backpacking in Chile & Argentina* has a description of this hike. Aside from taking up with a mountaineering expedition, this is the best way to see the area. A day-trip from Calafate will whet but not satisfy your appetite.

The jumping off point for the Fitzroy Mountains is the tiny town of Chalten. This town was deliberately built to help consolidate, by virtue of colonisation, Argentina's claims to the area.

Places to Stay

There is a simple but comfortable hostería in Chalten which has rooms for US$13 per person, which includes breakfast. Meals are an additional US$7 each. It's a nice place to stay but you really need to trek and camp to make this region worth visiting. Room bookings can be made at the *Hostería Lago Argentina* in Calafate. There is a campsite near the hostería.

Getting There & Away

The company Al Chalten has buses from Calafate to Chalten three days a week and possibly more in the peak tourist season. The trip takes four hours, leaving in the morning and returning to Calafate the same day in the late afternoon. This is a regular bus service, not a tour bus, but you book tickets at the Interlagos agency in Calafate.

Hitching to the mountains in the off-season is virtually impossible as there is next to no traffic.

CALETA OLIVIA TO CHILE, VIA PERITO MORENO & LOS ANTIGOS

An interesting, and little explored way of entering Chile from Argentina is the overland route from Caleta Olivia to the border town of Los Antigos, via Perito Moreno. From Los Antigos you cross a river to the Chilean border town of Chile Chico, where you catch a ferry to Puerto Ibañez.

CALETA OLIVIA

Like Comodoro Rivadavia the first thing you notice about Caleta Olivia is the heavy stench of oil. The city has a backdrop of wall murals commemorating the Falklands War, monuments to the hardy oilmen, concrete block houses, ravaged footpaths, and fading political posters plastered up on crumbling brick walls. This is a town of few redeeming features.

Places to Stay

The moderately priced *Hotel Robert* is on San Martín, a few minutes walk from the bus station. Look for a large sign saying HOTEL. It's very clean and comfortable, but not cheap.

Places to Eat

There are many cheap restaurants in the vicinity of the bus station. The bus station has a café snack bar open until midnight.

Getting There & Away

The main bus station is in the centre of town at the junction of San Martín and Independencia, easily identified by the huge statue of the oilman.

Transportadora Patagonia has buses to Río Gallegos via Fitzroy, Puerto San Julián and Piedra Buena.

Transporte Co-mi has a bus every Monday and Thursday from Caleta Olivia to Perito Moreno and Los Antigos. It returns from Los Antigos to Caleta Olivia on Tuesday and Friday.

If you miss the bus or don't want to wait for the next one you'll have to hitch, which could be difficult as there are few cars on this route.

PERITO MORENO

The last reminders that Perito Moreno, a settlement of 2000 people, was once a frontier town are the elderly gauchos, dressed in their riding boots and enormous baggy trousers. Perito Moreno lies slap in the middle of the arid pampas, and is a stop-over on the route from Caleta Olivia to Los Antigos.

Information

Tourist Office The tourist office is at the corner of San Martín and 12 de Octubre.

Post The post office is on Buenos Aires.

Banks US dollars cash can be changed at the Hotel Belgrano.

Places to Stay – bottom end

The *Hotel Argentina* on Buenos Aires charges about US$5 per person. It has spartan rooms which are fairly clean

though the bathrooms leave much to be desired. There are no locks on the doors so don't leave valuables in your room.

Similarly priced is the *Hotel Santa Cruz* on Belgrano, and the rather nasty *Hotel Fénix* at the corner of San Martín and Mitre.

Possibly the best place to stay is the campsite in front of the Laguna de los Cisnes, on Mitre near the corner with San Martín. You can pitch a tent for US$1 or take a cabin for US$5.

Places to Stay – top end

The *Hotel Austral* on San Martín and the *Hotel Belgrano* at the corner of San Martín and Estrada are comfortable, modern buildings, with their own restaurants.

Getting There & Away

Air LADE is at the corner of Mariano Moreno and San Martín. They have flights to Ushuaia via Calafate, Río Gallegos and Río Grande.

Bus From Perito Moreno you can head west to Los Antigos and cross the border to the Chilean town of Chile Chico, or east to Caleta Olivia where you can turn north to Comodoro Rivadavia or south to Río Gallegos. For details of buses between Los Antigos, Perito Moreno, and Caleta Olivia see the section on Caleta Olivia. In Perito Moreno you can buy tickets for the buses from the Hotel Argentina.

LOS ANTIGOS

Los Antigos is a dusty settlement on the shores of Lago Buenos Aires. In the setting sun the soft colours on this vast lake, rimmed by the distant mountains, give it an eerie appearance.

Places to Stay

The *Hotel Argentina* is the only hotel. It's a modern building, spotlessly clean, moderately priced and has a bar and restaurant attached.

There's a campsite at the end of 11 de Julio by the beach; it's an attractive place

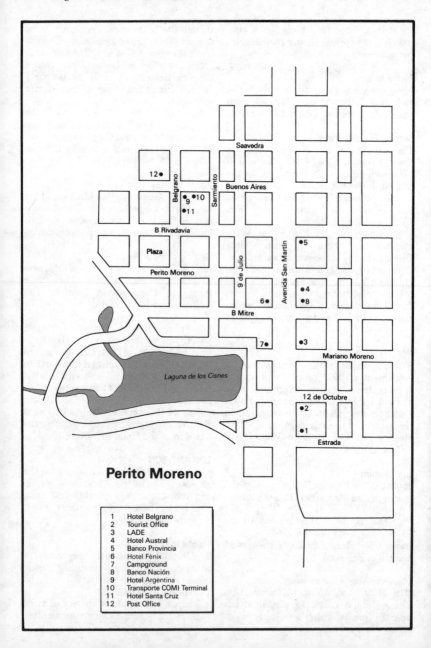

Perito Moreno

1	Hotel Belgrano
2	Tourist Office
3	LADE
4	Hotel Austral
5	Banco Provincia
6	Hotel Fénix
7	Campground
8	Banco Nación
9	Hotel Argentina
10	Transporte COMI Terminal
11	Hotel Santa Cruz
12	Post Office

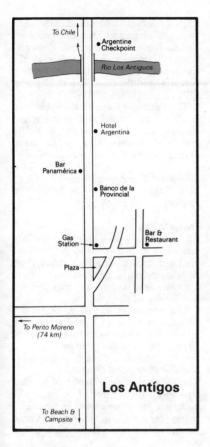

To Chile

Argentine
Checkpoint

Rio Los Antiguos

Hotel
Argentina

Bar
Panamérica

Banco de la
Provincial

Gas
Station

Bar &
Restaurant

Plaza

To Perito Moreno
(74 km)

Los Antígos

To Beach &
Campsite

and there are a few cabins if you don't have your own tent.

Getting There & Away
From Los Antigos you can take a bus to Caleta Olivia via Perito Moreno. For details of the buses on this route see the section on Caleta Olivia.

Chilean Patagonia

Chilean Patagonia includes the long slice of territory stretching all the way from the Straits of Magellan in the south to the Chilean lake district in the north. Geographically, this is a far more brutal land than the flat plains of Argentine Patagonia. The coastline of Chilean Patagonia is a jagged jigsaw of misshapen islands lashed by cold, howling winds. Much of it is uninhabited, but in the far south are the two sizeable towns of Punta Arenas and Puerto Natales.

Punta Arenas has its origins in the 1840s. Chile's brief civil war of 1831 was a victory for the conservative, landed gentry. At this time Chile was beginning to flex its muscles. Successful wars had been fought against Peru and Bolivia. Trade was expanding rapidly. Valparaíso was developing into the major port. Mines were being opened up.

In 1843 Chile's President Bulnes claimed the territory around the Straits of Magellan, Tierra del Fuego and even large areas of southern Patagonia. A fort (Fuerte Bulnes) was set up overlooking the Straits of Magellan. Five years later the city of Punta Arenas was founded nearby. Both the fort and the new settlement might have petered out had it not been for the discovery of gold in California in 1848.

The same metal which drove the Spanish to South America drove a new wave of fortune-seekers to North America. Since the Panama Canal was still many decades down the line, there were three methods of reaching the North American gold-fields from Europe. One was to land on the east coast of North America and endure a five month wagon ride across the continent. The other was to take a ship to Panama, cross the narrow isthmus and either travel overland by mule or take another ship to California. The cheaper and sometimes quicker route was round the tip of South America – a voyage which could take between three and seven months.

Giant sailing ships began pulling into Punta Arenas. When the age of steamships arrived the town became a coaling station. Ships would dispense their human cargo in America and then take Chilean nitrates, Australian meat and North American oil and wheat to Europe. Punta Arenas became a port of call on the trade route between Australia and Europe and between Europe and the west coast of the United States. It was only when the North Americans dug the Panama Canal that ships stopped using the southern route, and the golden age of Punta Arenas came to an end.

PUNTA ARENAS
Punta Arenas is located at the end of the Chilean mainland on the western shores of the Straits of Magellan. The discovery of oil in the region has turned Punta Arenas into a booming town of some 100,000 people. It once resembled Puerto Natales, with fragile-looking wooden buildings, but many of these have been replaced with concrete and brick. Punta Arenas is also an important Chilean naval base.

Information
Tourist Office The tourist office is at Waldo Seguel 689 (tel 24435) at one corner of the main plaza. They have maps of the city and the staff are friendly and helpful.

There's also a tourist information kiosk on the nature strip at the junction of Magallanes and Colón.

Post The main post office is at the corner of Menéndez and Bhories one block from the Plaza de Armas.

Telephone Long-distance phone calls can be made from Telex Chile at the corner of Fagnano and Nogueira diagonally opposite the plaza.

Banks There are several money-changers around the centre of town where you can change Chilean and Argentine currency. Try La Hermandad, corner of Roca and Lautaro Navarro; Sur Cambio at the corner of Pedro Montt and Lautaro Navarro; and the Casa Stop at Nogueira 1170.

The Banco de Chile on Roca, between Lautaro Navarro and 21 de Mayo, might change US dollars and US dollar travellers' cheques. Also try the Banco O'Higgins opposite the main plaza.

Consulates The Argentine consulate is at 21 de Mayo 1878. It's open Monday to Friday from 10 am to 2 pm.

Things to See
All around Punta Arenas there are reminders of bygone days. Monuments are lined up like beads on a string along Bhories, including memorials to the early Yugoslav settlers and to hardy farmers who pioneered the area.

The enormous cemetery on Bulnes contains many large family crypts and numerous tombstones and graves of early British and Yugoslav settlers.

Magallanes Regional Museum
Though once mainly a city of wooden buildings with corrugated tin roofs, the many gracious mansions of the city centre betray the early importance of Punta Arenas on the trade route round South America.

One of the finest mansions ever built, belonging to what was once one of the city's most important families – and whose name still crops up in the higher circles of both Chilean and Argentine society – is now referred to as the Centro Cultural Braun-Menéndez and houses the Museum Regional Magallanes. The owner of vast areas of Patagonia and Tierra del Fuego at the turn of the century, the family eventually moved to Buenos Aires due to a combination of expropriation and the opening of the Panama Canal.

The displays depict the European settlement of Punta Arenas and Tierra del Fuego. The front rooms of the house are preserved as they were when the family lived here, and the furnishings are the originals – almost every piece was imported from Europe (mainly France) to produce a house no less palatial than any in Santiago at the time.

The museum is situated on Magallanes just off the Plaza de Armas. It's open Tuesday to Saturday, 11 am to 4 pm, and holidays, 11 am to 1 pm.

Salesian College

A curious museum in the Colegio Salesiano describes the geography, fauna and flora of southern Patagonia, and harbours a collection of stuffed animals and the relics of dead Indians.

Large dioramas depict the Indian way of life before the coming of the white settlers, but depressing before-and-after photos (before the whites and after the whites) hardly require captions or explanations.

Ten thousand year-old droppings and unidentifiable fragments of the giant ground-sloth uncovered in the Milodon Cave near Puerto Natales are also on display. This is probably the best place to come if you want an overview of the natural history of southern Chile.

The museum is at the corner of Bulnes and Sarmiento. It's open Tuesday, Thursday and Saturday from 3 to 6 pm and on Sunday from 10 am to 1 pm and 3 to 6 pm.

Patagonian Institute

At the Instituto del Patagonia there's an extraordinary collection of old farming machinery, including steam tractors built in England or Europe and used in Tierra del Fuego and Magallanes in the 19th and 20th centuries. Other vehicles include a wooden wagon used by the early settlers before permanent houses were built, horse-drawn wagons and coaches, early petrol-engine farm tractors and vintage cars. More surprising are the simple wooden horse-drawn ploughs used in southern Patagonia and Tierra del Fuego until the 1930s. There is also a reconstructed settler's house from the Punta Arenas area dating back to 1875-80. There is a tiny zoo with several condors and pumas, sadly incarcerated in tiny cages.

The easiest way to get to the Institute is by taxi colectivo from the front of the Museum Regional de Magallanes, on Magallanes just off the plaza. They drop you off right in front of the institute.

The Penguin Colony

The best sight outside Punta Arenas is the *pingüineros*, the penguin colony, with burrows dug in the soft, sandy soil of the shoreline. They're surprisingly amiable, although they will bite if you prod them too closely. Penguin beaks, by the way, can inflict a nasty cut.

Try and go with only a small group of people if you visit the colony. Large groups frighten them and they'll hide in their burrows. Otherwise, they stand around in little herds and you can get to within a few feet of them. The drive to the penguin colony takes you through sheep-grazing country, also inhabited by wild guanacos, rhea and ibises.

For details of how to get there (you'll either have to hire a car or go on a tour) see the Getting Around section below.

Fuerte Bulnes

Although the Chileans may have planned to annex the southern tip of South America soon after independence from Spain, it was not until 1843 that they finally did so. In October of that year the first rude buildings of Fuerte Bulnes were slapped up from logs, thatch and mud. Cannons and a fence of pointed stakes were added for protection. The fort, 55 km from Punta Arenas, has been partly restored and is now a national monument. For details of how to get there see the Getting Around section below.

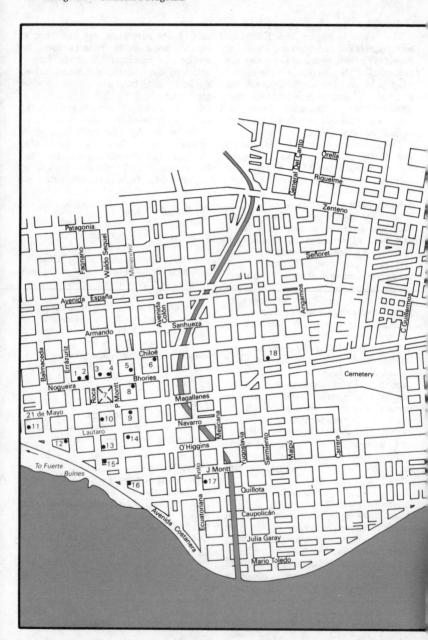

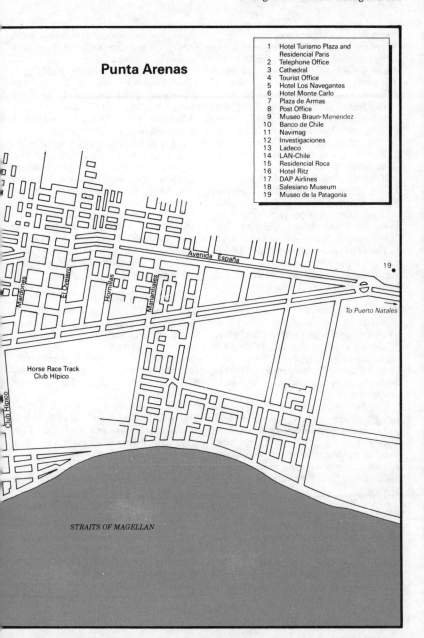

Punta Arenas

1 Hotel Turismo Plaza and
  Residencial Paris
2 Telephone Office
3 Cathedral
4 Tourist Office
5 Hotel Los Navegantes
6 Hotel Monte Carlo
7 Plaza de Armas
8 Post Office
9 Museo Braun-Menéndez
10 Banco de Chile
11 Navimag
12 Investigaciones
13 Ladeco
14 LAN-Chile
15 Residencial Roca
16 Hotel Ritz
17 DAP Airlines
18 Salesiano Museum
19 Museo de la Patagonia

Avenida España

19

To Puerto Natales

Marcones
El Ovejero
Hornillas
Manantiales

Horse Race Track
Club Hípico

Club Hípico

STRAITS OF MAGELLAN

Places to Stay - bottom end

There are two hotels on Nogueira in the same building a few doors up from the Plaza de Armas. These are the *Hotel Turismo Plaza* and the *Residencial París*.

The *Residencial París* (tel 23112) has rooms without bathrooms from US$6 per person, including breakfast. It's a very spartan place, but clean. There are no locks on the doors, so don't leave valuables lying around.

If these are full then try the *Residencial Roca* (tel 23803) at the corner of Roca and Emilio Korner, which is a decent place with rooms for US$6 per person including breakfast. They're friendly people and the hotel is popular with foreign visitors.

The *Hotel Monte Carlo* (tel 23448) at Colón 605, has been recommended. Single rooms are US$6 and doubles are US$11, both without private bathroom.

Places to Stay - middle

The *Hotel Ritz* (tel 24422) at Pedro Montt 1102 is recommended without hesitation. It's clean and comfortable, fairly quiet and is run by friendly people. Singles start from US$13 and doubles from US$20, both with private bathroom. It also has a restaurant.

The *Turismo Plaza* (tel 21300), in the same building as the Residencial Paris, has rooms without private bathroom from US$14 a single and US$17 a double. More expensive rooms have private bathrooms. It's spotlessly clean. The front rooms, if rather noisy, have good views overlooking the town.

Places to Stay - top end

The *Hotel Los Navegantes* (tel 24677) has single rooms for US$40 a single and US$50 a double. The *Hotel Cabo de Hornos* (tel 22134) faces the main plaza and has singles for US$63 and doubles for US$74 but is not as good as Los Navegantes.

Places to Eat

Since my favourite Italian restaurant is closed, and my favourite pizza shack was burned down, the pickings in Punta Arenas have been slim.

The *Bar Restaurant Solitos* at O'Higgins 1138 specialises in seafood. You can also investigate, if you dare, the effects of raw sea urchin on your digestive system. Otherwise it's a lively, if expensive restaurant with amiable waiters.

Other places worth trying include the *Nandu Café Grill* at Waldo Seguel 670, opposite the tourist office, which is more a bar than a restaurant – not bad. There are a number of sailors' bars along the harbour.

If all else fails there is a very cheap smorgasbord restaurant in the *Zona Franca*, which is the duty-free compound opposite the Patagonian Institute. The restaurant is in the first building on your right as you enter the compound.

Getting There & Away

The tourist office keeps a list of all road, sea and air transport out of Punta Arenas, Puerto Natales and Tierra del Fuego.

Air LAN-Chile (tel 23460) is at the corner of Pedro Montt and Lautaro Navarro. They have daily flights to Puerto Montt and Santiago.

DAP (tel 23958) is at Ignacio Carrena Pinto 1022. They have flights to Puerto Williams two days a week for US$57. They have daily flights to Porvenir for US$14. You may have to take the flight if the sea is too rough for the ferries.

Ladeco (tel 22665) is at Roca 924. They have flights to Concepción two days a week, and daily flights to Santiago and Puerto Montt.

Aerolíneas Argentinas used to have flights from Punta Arenas to Buenos Aires via Río Grande, Río Gallegos and Comodoro Rivadavia but these had been suspended at the time of writing. It may be worth asking about when you get there. Enquire at the Agencia Cabo de Hornos in the Hotel Cabo de Hornos.

The Aeropuerto Presidente Ibáñez is

Top: Upsala Glacier
Bottom: Parque Nacional Los Alerces

Top: Fitzroy Mountains
Bottom: Moreno Glacier

20 km out of Punta Arenas. DAP has its own bus to take passengers to the airport. Ladeco and LAN-Chile use one of the regular bus companies, so ask when you buy your tickets.

Bus Buses Sur is at Menéndez 565. They have daily buses to Puerto Natales. The trip takes four to 4½ hours and the fare is US$8. They have buses two days a week to Osorno and Puerto Montt, via Argentina. During summer they have buses three days a week to Calafate via the Torres del Paine National Park. The fare to Calafate is US$41.

Buses Fernández is at Chiloé 930. They have daily buses to Puerto Natales.

Buses Río Gallegos and El Pingüino are at Lautaro Navarro 971. Both have daily buses to Río Gallegos. The fare is around US$14.

For other buses to Puerto Montt try Buses Norte at Gamero 1039, and Turibus at Menéndez 647. The fare from Punta Arenas to Puerto Montt is about US$55. There are also sleeper coaches (coche cama) for US$68.

The bus trip from Punta Arenas to Puerto Montt is an excruciating journey of almost two full days. The route is: Punta Arenas, Río Gallegos, Comodoro Rivadavia, Rawson, San Antonio Oeste, Choele Choele, Nuequén, Picún Leufú, La Angostura, Osorno, Puerto Montt.

Boat For ships out of Punta Arenas enquire at Empremar (tel 211608) at Lautaro Navarro 1338, and at Navimag (tel 26600) at Independencia 830. Both these companies *may* have passenger accommodation on their ships but don't count on it.

If you want assured passages on ships going north then you'll have to go to Puerto Natales. Navimag have passenger/ cargo ships from Puerto Natales to Puerto Montt three times a month.

There are daily car and passenger ferries between Punta Arenas and Porvenir. The

crossing takes about three hours, and the fare is around US$2. The ferries are run by Transbordadora Austral Broom Ltda at Roca 924. Bring your passport when you buy your ticket. The ferries leave from Puerto Trente about one km past the Zona Franca – take a local bus or a taxi colectivo.

Getting Around

Taxi colectivos in Punta Arenas cost about US$0.30 per trip. Buses are about half that. Fares and destinations are posted on the outside of each bus and taxi. Although much of Punta Arenas is small enough to walk around you'll need the buses and colectivos to get to places further out like the Patagonian Institute and the Salesian College.

Cars can be rented from Hertz Rent-a-car at Lautaro Navarro 1064. Daily rates are about US$19 per trip plus US$0.15 per km plus tax. You can also rent for three-day periods for around US$120 including 600 km free.

Ask at the travel agents and the Hotel Cabo de Hornos about plane rides over Tierra del Fuego. They take you over the Marinelli Glacier, the Beagle Channel, Puerto Williams and even as far south as Cape Horn.

One of the best books on Patagonia is Bruce Chatwin's *In Patagonia*. Chatwin hangs his story off the experiences of his grandmother's cousin, Charley Milward. Milward had been the captain of a merchant ship which went down at the entrance of the Straits of Magellan. He survived the wreck, went to live in Punta Arenas and built a fine house there – a photo of which is included in Chatwin's book. The house, a peculiar Englishman's folly resembling a Victorian parsonage, still stands. It's at Avenida España 959, near the corner with Juez Waldo Sequel.

PUERTO NATALES

Puerto Natales is a cool, tidy town of timber and corrugated iron houses. While unspectacular in itself, the town is very popular with trekkers and climbers during the summer months as it's the gateway to the spectacular Torres del Paine National Park. It's also the jumping-off point for the Balmaceda Glacier and the Milodon Cave. Ships to Puerto Montt leave from Puerto Natales, and you can also take a bus over the mountains to Río Turbio in Argentina.

Information

Post & Communications The post office is on Eberhard, facing the main plaza. Telex Chile is in the same building.

Banks There are a number of money changers in Puerto Natales where you can change Argentine currency for Chilean currency (and vice versa). Try those at Encalada 266, Encalada 238 and Baquedano 180. You can only change travellers' cheques in Punta Arenas.

Things to See

Puerto Natales is the jumping off place for visits to the Milodon Cave, the old Meat-packing plant, the Balmaceda Glacier and, of course, the Torres del Paine National Park. Details are in the 'Around Puerto Natales' and 'The Torres del Paine National Park' sections below.

The Meat-Packing Plant

The miniature steam engine now set up in the Plaza de Armas was built in Bristol, Britain in 1920. It was used at the British-owned meat-packing and tanning factory, which was established early this century, just outside Puerto Natales. The meat and hides were taken from the factory along a railway line laid along a pier, and loaded onto ships.

The factory still operates, though the scale of operations is much smaller than it was during its heyday when several thousand sheep were being slaughtered weekly. At that time some of the sheep ranches in the area each ran as many as 80,000 to 120,000 sheep. Some of the land now included in the Torres del Paine park was once a sheep ranch, owned by a

Chilean-Italian up until the early part of the 1970s. No more sheep are grazed in the park now. Instead there are herds of guanaco and flocks of rheas and pink flamingo. Rheas are now a protected species; their meat is said to taste like turkey.

The meat processing plant is just outside Puerto Natales, by the road leading to Torres del Paine. Much of the original steam-driven machinery is still there but is no longer used. These days the compressors used to freeze the meat are electrically powered. The wooden buildings in front of the plant are used to dry the hides. Narrow spaces are left between the slats of their walls to allow air to circulate.

The Balmaceda Glacier

This impressive glacier slides down a mountain right into one of the many estuaries and fjords which make up the jagged southern Chilean coastline. Huge blocks of ice break off and wallow around in the lagoon in front of the glacier wall.

The glacier lies to the north-east of Puerto Natales. During January and February (and perhaps March) a boat called the *21 de Mayo* takes groups to the glacier almost every day; the cost is about US$16 per person. It leaves from the pier at the end of Bulnes around 8.30 am and returns in the late afternoon.

If the boat is not docked, enquire at the house of Señor Alvarez at Cadilleros 91, at the corner with Eberhard. You'll only be able to go when there are tour groups to fill up the boat. Bring something to eat – drinks are provided but no food unless you're with a tour group.

The tub is about 40 or 50 years old and the pioneering spirit is maintained by the provision of two inadequately sized life-boats and two life-preservers; there are no life-jackets. The winds that roar through the narrow channel leading to the glacier can be so strong that sometimes the boat has to turn back or does terrifying rolls in the choppy sea. Console yourself with the knowledge that it has done many successful trips.

Waterfalls, condors and bands of seals can be seen on the voyage. At the glacier the boat pulls into a small jetty and you can get off and walk up along a trail very close to the glacier itself. The Torres del Paine can be seen in the distance.

The Milodon Cave

The Milodon Cave of southern Patagonia, of which Bruce Chatwin includes a lengthy account of in his book *In Patagonia*, is a large cavity in a mountain on Last Hope Sound. The cave is not far from Puerto Natales, and is just off the road to Torres del Paine.

The area was first settled in 1893 by a Prussian, Herman Eberhard, who found his way to Chile after working on a pig farm in Nebraska, a whaling station in Alaska, and piloting ships in the Falklands. He came up the Sound with two British naval deserters and established a farm.

The story goes that in early 1895 Eberhard had a look inside the cave and found a human skull and a piece of skin sticking out of the floor. A year later a Swedish explorer visited the cave and found more skin as well as the eye-socket of an enormous mammal, a claw, a giant human thighbone and some stone tools. As pieces of the animal and other milodon bones were sent back to England and Europe, it was concluded that some species of giant sloth had survived into recent years. This idea was supported by Indian stories and traveller's tales of monstrous creatures inhabiting South America. In the hope of finding such a creature a British expedition was actually sent to the continent but had no success. The story of the expedition is told by its leader, H Hesketh Prichard, in his book *Through the Heart of Patagonia*.

Meanwhile the cave was excavated. In the uppermost layer were the remains of human settlement. In the middle were the remains of the now-extinct American horse. In the bottom layer were the remains of the milodon. One excavator even devised the bizarre theory that the milodon was a domesticated beast, kept by the Indians at the rear of the cave like a horse in a corral. He suggested that the creature should be called *Gryptotherium domesticum*. The modern conclusion is that the milodon lived about 10,000 years ago. Indians may have killed it in a battle for possession of the cave but, despite more fanciful theories to the contrary, they did not keep it as a pet.

The milodon was, in fact, a giant ground sloth. It was larger than a full-grown bull, and was of a type unique to South America. A life-size model of the milodon stands in the cave. Europeans first heard of such monsters near the end of the 18th century, when the bones of a similar but even larger milodon were found in Argentina and sent to Spain. The bones of that particular animal came from a creature which stood about five metres high and looked like a giant version of today's insect-eating sloths which hang upside down by their tails in trees.

Charles Darwin also found the bones of a milodon in South America and sent them back to England. The animal was so big that 19th century zoologists concluded that, since it would have been unable to clamber into the trees, it must have reared up on its enormous haunches and pulled the branches down to them so that it could feed on the leaves. Darwin, in his book *The Voyage of the Beagle*, gives a description of the milodon according to fossil evidence.

Places to Stay - bottom end

The *Residencial Burnier* is at the corner of Bulnes and Ladrilleros. It's always been a fairly spartan place, but it's now sad and run-down. It's around US$4 per bed. There are no locks on the doors, so don't leave valuables in your rooms.

Places to Stay - middle

The *Hotel Natalino* on Eberhard, near the corner with Tomas Rogers is one of the

1 Buses to Rio Turbio
2 Banco del Estado de Chile
3 Buses Fernández
4 Ladeco
5 Buses Sur
6 Post Office
7 Investigaciones
8 Hotel Natalino
9 Captain Eberhard Hotel
10 Hotel Palace
11 Residencial Burnier
12 Harbour Master's Office

Puerto Natales

best small hotels in Chile. It's very clean and comfortable, with heaters in the rooms, and has friendly staff. Rooms without private bathrooms are US$9 a single and US$14 a double. Rooms with private bathrooms are US$13 a single and US$18 a double.

Another fine place is the *Austral Hotel* at Valdivia 955. It has single rooms from around US$6. Doubles are twice that. Rooms with private bathroom cost a bit more. It's clean and comfortable and has a very good restaurant.

Places to Stay - top end

The *Hotel Palace* near the corner of Eberhard and Ladrilleros has singles for US$34 and doubles for US$45, which includes breakfast. The *Captain Eberhard Hotel* is on the waterfront at the corner with Senoret, and has rooms for US$36 a single and US$41 a double.

Places to Eat

The *Restaurant Midas* at Tomas Rogers 169, facing the main plaza, is a fine place for seafood. Despite its appearance it's surprisingly cheap. A few doors down is *Bianco's Pizza*. The *Café Tranquera* at Bulnes 579 is good.

Eduardo Scott's restaurant, in the Austral Hotel at Valdivia 955, specialises in fish and other seafood dishes such as crab and shellfish. Try his *sopa de marina* which is a piping hot, thick broth of seafood and is a meal in itself.

Getting There & Away

Air The nearest airport is at Punta Arenas. In Puerto Natales you can make bookings for Ladeco flights at their office at Bulnes 530. Buses from Puerto Natales to Punta Arenas will drop you off at the airport if you have to catch a flight.

Bus Buses Sur at Baquedano 534 and Buses Fernández at Eberhard 555 both have daily buses to Punta Arenas. The fare is US$8 and the trip takes about four hours.

For buses to Argentina try Buses Alvaro Gomez and San Ceferino at Baquedano 244. They have buses three days a week to Río Gallegos via Río Turbio.

You can go to Río Turbio and catch another bus from there to Río Gallegos. Buses to Río Turbio leave from the corner of Philippi and Baquedano, about every hour or half hour daily.

Boat The Navimag office is at the port of Puerto Natales. They have three passenger ships a month to Puerto Montt.

PARQUE NACIONAL TORRES DEL PAINE

The Torres del Paine are huge granite pillars which have been pushed up and folded by heat and pressure. From far away, across a windswept plain, you will see them rise up suddenly – so beautiful that superlatives will soon fail you.

The park is, despite the almost constant cold wind, some of the finest trekking country in Chile. It is not only endowed with mountains, lakes, waterfalls and glaciers, but also with herds of guanaco, flocks of pink flamingos,

graceful condors, and large Patagonian hares.

The park was originally established in 1959. Before this the area was sheep-grazing country and the shepherds' fires sometimes burned out of control. You can still see the devastation these fires cause near Lago Grey, where large areas of burnt-out forest and charred logs extend up the hillsides as far as the snowline. Even after all these years the land has still not fully recovered. More land was added to the park in 1962 and the name was changed to its present one. It's said that towers and park were named after a female climber or settler (or both) named Paine – although in an Indian language *payne* is the word for 'blue'. Estancia El Paine, a sheep grazing property, was added to the park around 1974.

With a bit of planning trekkers could spend weeks exploring the park, but it's possible to see a good deal of it on a day trip from Puerto Natales. A rough but motorable track extends up to Lago Grey, and you can see enormous blue icebergs which have broken off from the glacier at the other end of the lake and floated down. Some of the lakes are also accessible by road. The towers, when not shrouded by low cloud, are always present in the background.

Entry

There is a small entrance fee to the park – you pay at the entrance on the road up from Puerto Natales.

Maps

If you intend camping or trekking you'll need a map of the area to find out where the refugios are located. These are simple mountain huts, some of them with basic facilities, where you can find shelter for the night.

A good map to get hold of is the CONAF (Corporación Nacional Forestal) map called *Parque Nacional Torres del Paine*. This has all the refugios, roads, tracks, ranger stations and picnic areas marked

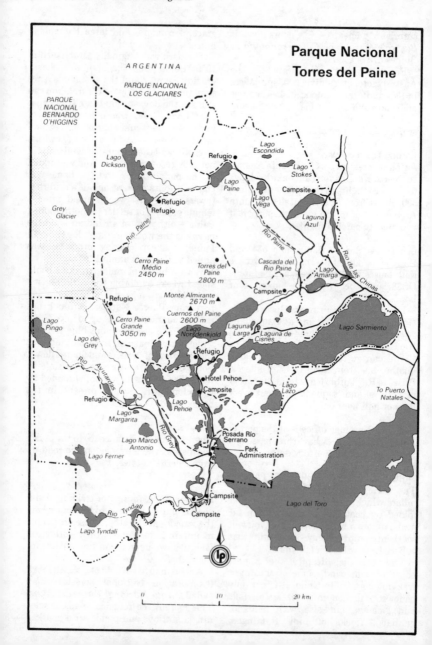

Parque Nacional Torres del Paine

ARGENTINA

PARQUE NACIONAL LOS GLACIARES

PARQUE NACIONAL BERNARDO O'HIGGINS

Lago Dickson

Grey Glacier

Refugio
Refugio

Río Paine

Lago Paine

Refugio

Lago Escondida

Lago Stokes

Campsite

Lago Vega

Laguna Azul

Cerro Paine Medio 2450 m

Torres del Paine 2800 m

Río Paine

Cascada del Río Paine

Lago Amarga

Río de las Chinas

Refugio

Monte Almirante 2670 m

Cuernos del Paine 2600 m

Campsite

Cerro Paine Grande 3050 m

Lago Pingo

Lago de Grey

Río Avutardas

Lago Nordenskjold

Laguna Larga

Laguna de Cisnes

Lago Sarmiento

Refugio

Lago Margarita

Río Grey

Refugio

Hotel Pehoe

Campsite

Lago Pehoe

Lago Lazo

To Puerto Natales

Lago Marco Antonio

Lago Ferrier

Posada Río Serrano

Park Administration

Río Tyndall

Campsite

Campsite

Lago del Toro

Lago Tyndall

0   10   20 km

on it. It used to be available from the CONAF office in Puerto Natales but this has closed. You can still get it from the CONAF hut at the park entrance.

The Austral Hotel, in Puerto Natales, sells good photostat copies of a map which is even clearer and more detailed than the CONAF map – definitely worth getting.

Books

If you intend trekking you should go to the park armed with a copy of Hilary Bradt's and John Pilkington's *Backpacking in Chile & Argentina* which includes a chapter on the park.

Warning

Take warm clothes with you even if you're not trekking! The weather can be stormy right through the summer months (though there are also beautiful days of warm sunshine and light wind). At Lago Grey, where the wind sweeps off the glacier, it can be very cold! You must have rain and wind protection and a change of clothing.

Places to Stay & Eat

There are two hotels in the park. The *Hotel Pehoe* is located on an island in Lago Pehoe and connected to the shore by a footbridge. It faces the towers across the lake – one of the most beautiful settings in the park.

The other is the *Posada Río Serrano* which is near Lago del Toro at the start of the road leading to Lago Grey. Single rooms are US$10 and doubles are US$15. Breakfast costs a few dollars per person. You can also camp in the hotel grounds for a few dollars per person. There is a small shop in the hotel where you can stock up on food but it's better to bring what you need from Puerto Natales.

There are refugios, campsites and shelters in the park. These are free. Their location is shown on park maps. If you intend trekking you must bring all your own food as there is none in the park other than what is available at the two hotels.

Getting There & Away

Getting to the park can be a bit of a haphazard affair, and what I've listed below are some of the possibilities worth investigating. Don't worry – you'll make it somehow!

If your time is limited or if you don't have the equipment or the urge to trek and camp, then take a tour to the park. Eduardo Scott, a Falklander who speaks both Spanish and English, makes day-trips to the park in his mini-van and can also arrange day and half-day horse-riding trips in the park. He also organises visits to the old meat-packing and tanning factory just outside of Puerto Natales. Contact him at the Austral Hotel in Puerto Natales. He used to work on the Estancia El Paine, so he knows a lot about that particular region. I've been on a tour with him to the park and recommend him highly! If you want to go trekking and camping in the park you can go up with one of his groups and get dropped off in the park.

Buses Fernández and Buses Sur in Punta Arenas have tours to the park in summer. These buses start in Punta Arenas and will probably be full, so don't expect to be able to get on board in Puerto Natales unless you've booked ahead.

A new road connects Puerto Natales with Calafate in Argentina and there are now buses and tour buses along this road in summer. Enquire at Buses Fernández in Punta Arenas.

If you're hitching there are very few vehicles outside summer and quite a bit of competition for rides during summer. If there's a group of you it's often cheaper and more convenient to hire a minibus or a taxi to take you from Puerto Natales to the park entrance.

A day-trip in a hired taxi from Puerto Natales to Torres del Paine will cost about US$70. This does have the advantage of being able to stop the vehicle and take photographs when you want to. You can also rent cars in Punta Arenas and drive yourself to the park.

Tierra del Fuego

When the Portuguese-born navigator Ferdinand Magellan came to the great island at the southern tip of the American continent, he saw the Indian campfires and called the island *Tierra del Humo*, the Land of Smoke. Later his patron, King Charles V of Spain, reasoned that there could be no smoke without fire and renamed the island *Tierra del Fuego* – the Land of Fire.

The Straits of Magellan separate Tierra del Fuego from the rest of South America. Tierra del Fuego is, in fact, not one island but a whole archipelago. The largest of the islands is the Isla Grande de Tierra del Fuego and is usually the one referred to when this region is mentioned.

The other inhabited parts of the archipelago are Navarino and Dawson islands, three islands at the mouth of the Beagle Channel, and the easternmost tip of Hoste Island.

History

When Magellan sailed through, Tierra del Fuego was home to four distinct groups of Indians. The oldest of these groups was the Haush who were pushed to the eastern tip of the island by the more numerous Ona and Yahgan. Like the Ona, the Haush dressed in guanaco skins, hunted guanaco with bows and arrows, and lived in huts made of sticks, branches and sometimes of skins. Like the Yahgan they used spears and harpoons to fish and also gathered mussels from the beaches at low tide. The nomadic Ona were similar to the Haush, but were much more numerous and ranged over most of Isla Grande in search of guanaco which provided them with all their needs.

Further south, along the beaches of the Beagle Channel and the islands southward to Cape Horn, lived the Yahgan. This group was also nomadic, but lived by hunting otter, fish and seals, with

harpoons and spears. They used slings and snares to catch birds, and clubs against each other. They used tree bark to make their canoes and seal skin for clothing.

The fourth group were the Alacaluf who ranged from Puerto Edén, in the forbidding fjords of southern Chile, to the Beagle Channel. They were similar to the Yahgan, but their language was different. They also used bows and arrows, and they had sails on their canoes. Unlike the Indians further north, none of the Fuegan Indians had chiefs or organised religion.

When Charles Darwin came to Tierra del Fuego in 1834 he described some Indians he found at Woollaston Island to the south of Navarino:

. . . naked and uncovered from the wind, rain & snow in this tempestuous climate, sleep on the wet ground, coiled up like animals. In the morning they rise to pick shell fish at low water; & the women, winter & summer, dive to collect sea eggs; such miserable food is eked out by tasteless berries & Fungi. They are surrounded by hostile tribes speaking different dialects; & the cause of their warfare would appear to be the means of subsistence. Their country is a

Magellan

broken mass of wild rocks, lofty hills & useless forests, & these are viewed through mists & endless storms. In search of food they move from spot to spot, & so steep is the coast, this must be done in wretched canoes . . .

Darwin found the Indians an unpleasant sight:

I never saw such miserable creatures; stunted in their growth, their hideous faces bedaubed with white paint & quite naked. One full aged woman absolutely so, the rain & spray were dripping from her body. Their red skins filthy and greasy, their hair entangled, their voices discordant, their gesticulation violent and without any dignity. Viewing such men, one can hardly make oneself believe that they are fellow creatures placed in the same world . . . how little must the mind of one of these beings resemble that of an educated man. What a scale of improvement is comprehended between the faculties of a Fuegan savage & a Sir Isaac Newton!

Today there are no 'pure-blooded' Fuegan Indians although there are some mestizos, such as those at Puerto Williams on Navarino Island. Many of the Indians were killed by the white settlers, in fights amongst themselves, or more commonly by measles, tuberculosis and other diseases brought by the whites. It is hard

to say when the last 'full-blooded' Fuegan Indians died. The latest any of them lived according to their old ways was around 1915 to 1920. Groups of 'full bloods' worked on the estancias in Chilean and Argentine Tierra del Fuego in the 1930s, but they knew or practised little of the old ways.

The string of events which brought the first Europeans to Tierra del Fuego, and resulted in the decimation of the native Indian population, began with Magellan's voyage in the 16th century. Contrary to popular belief Magellan did not circumnavigate the world, nor did he ever intend to. He was not even the first to sail through the straits which bear his name. Aside from the Fuegan Indians who had lived in the region since 7500 BC, Egyptian sailors may have come this way in the first and second centuries AD. It's possible that a Portuguese expedition preceded Magellan through the strait in 1514 but turned back.

In 1518 Magellan was awarded a charter by the King of Spain to command a Spanish fleet which would voyage to the legendary Spice Islands. These are known as the Maluku (Moluccas) Islands of Indonesia. Four hundred years ago they were the only source of several valuable spices. Magellan intended to get several ships into the Pacific Ocean, sail west to the Spice Islands, load up with spices and head back through the north Pacific to Panama. In Panama the cargo would be carried over the isthmus to the Caribbean and shipped to Spain. Magellan's ships would stay in the Pacific and form a permanent Spanish fleet for trade between the Spice Islands and Central America. It is hard to say how Magellan devised his plan. He had previously been in the East Indies and Malaya and he might have picked up some ideas from Chinese or Malay navigators about crossing the north Pacific using the Asian monsoon winds. If so, he had not revealed the secret to anyone else.

In October 1520, after sailing across the

Tierra del Fuegan Indian

Atlantic, the fleet entered the strait which is now known as the Straits of Magellan. It took five weeks to get through the nightmarish seas and into the Pacific. The fleet headed west and finally came to the Philippines where, as fate would have it, Magellan was killed in a skirmish with some of the native inhabitants.

Since no one else would dare return through the Straits of Magellan they pushed on westwards. Three years after the voyage had begun just one ship of the original five, the *Victoria*, limped into Spain. In a journey akin to Homer's *Odyssey*, they had inadvertently become the first people to sail around the world. Only about 30 men survived the expedition.

Magellan's voyage initiated what, for those days, was a veritable stampede. Spanish, Dutch, French and English ships passed through the strait or around Cape Horn. The toll on men and ships was formidable. In 1741 a British expedition under Commodore George Anson rounded the horn. Anson described the experience in his journal:

Heavy flaws and dangerous Gusts, expecting every moment to have my masts Carry'd away, having very little succor, from the standing rigging, every Shroud knotted, and not men able to keep the deck sufficient to take in a Topsail, all being violently afflicted with the Scurvy, and every day lessening our Number by six eight and Ten.

Four months later, after entering the Pacific, he wrote:

I mustered my Ship's Company, the number of Men I brought out from England, being Five hundred, are now reduced by Mortality to Two hundred and Thirteen, and many of them in a weak and Low condition.

To keep the interlopers out the Spanish contemplated building forts on the Straits of Magellan as early as 1580. Although this plan didn't come to fruition, in 1584 two colonies were established on the north side of the strait. Both were wiped out by famine. Voyages of exploration, scientific expeditions, English pirates sailing through the straits and up the west coast of South America to attack Valdivia, sealers and whalers (in increasing numbers by the end of the 18th century), all came this way, occasionally skirmishing with the Indians or introducing European diseases.

It was not until the early 19th century that the Europeans made any real attempt to settle Tierra del Fuego. In 1843 Chile (in the guise of the Englishman John Williams) officially took possession of the Straits of Magellan and founded Fuerte Bulnes on its western shore near the present-day city of Punta Arenas.

Had it not been for the discovery of gold in California this settlement might well have remained a distant outpost at the end of the earth. But the same metal that

drove the Spanish to South America now provoked an enormous migration to North America. Punta Arenas, which was founded on the west side of the strait, was suddenly an important port on one of the world's busiest shipping routes.

In 1843 Chile also laid claim to southern Patagonia. The renunciation of this claim and the division of Tierra del Fuego between Chile and Argentina was made in 1881 when Chile was fighting the War of the Pacific with Bolivia and Peru. This war made it imperative for Chile to keep the peace and finalise her borders with Argentina. However, it was not until 1902 that the boundaries were finalised. This 'perpetual accord' inspired the famous statue of Christ which was erected on Mount Aconcagua to celebrate the decision and symbolise peace between the two countries.

The first farms were opened on Tierra del Fuego in the 1880s and from there on the history of the island is one of who owned the turf. The first white residents were English missionaries who stayed on as farmers to be followed by Germans, Argentines, Chileans, Yugoslavs, Italians and other immigrants. For a few years the island even had a Rumanian dictator, who printed his own money and stamps, and maintained his own goldmines and a private army until his death in 1893.

The Indians, meanwhile, were forced to prey on the settler's livestock as the herds of guanaco and other animals which they hunted became increasingly scarce. The settlers placed bounties on Indian heads and they were hunted down like animals. Others were wiped out by imported diseases. An epidemic in 1864 killed half the Yahgans. A measles epidemic in 1884 reduced their numbers to just a few hundred. More died in 1891 during an epidemic of typhoid, smallpox and whooping cough. Many Ona were rounded up and placed in missions, but were almost exterminated in 1925 by a measles epidemic.

Sawmills, meat-salting, tallow-making

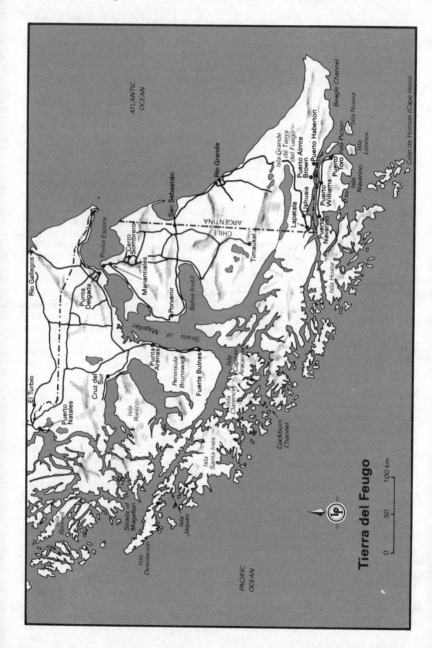

Tierra del Feugo

plants, whaling stations, meat warehouses, and crab and mussel canning industries were all established from the 1880s to the 1920s. By the middle of the second decade of the 20th century there were 800,000 sheep on the island, outnumbering humans by 300 to one. Ushuaia and Río Grande (with just 150 people) were the only towns. The rest of the population lived on the estancias. Sheep farming is still the main industry on the island. Cattle grazing and oil extraction are also big business.

The San Sebastián refinery was completed in 1975 and produces liquefied petroleum gas. Oil prospecting began in 1938 but it wasn't until 1959 that the first commercial well was drilled by the Tennessee Argentina Company. During the last decade tourism has also boomed in Tierra del Fuego. Aided by its magnificent trekking country and the duty-free status of the biggest town, Ushuaia, the island is a favoured holiday resort for Argentines.

Geography & Climate

Altogether the archipelago of Tierra del Fuego covers an area slightly smaller than Ireland. About 70% belongs to Chile. The border between Chile and Argentina on the Isla Grande is a straight line running north to south and then along the Beagle Channel.

The northern part of the island is a windswept land of vast treeless plains where sheep grazing and oil extraction are important. The central region is covered in snow from April to November, and is too mountainous for farming or grazing.

The Beagle Channel separates Isla Grande from Navarino. The narrow strip of land on Isla Grande bordering the channel has a comparatively mild climate with cool summers and snow in winter.

The eastern part of the island has less snow and ice, but much more rain and cloudy weather. In the west the climate is sub-Antarctic with fierce winds and heavy rain.

These distinct climatic areas influence the type of fauna and flora found on the island. The northern plains are treeless. The mountains and shores of the Beagle Channel are covered in forest and swampland. In the east and west are dense forests. Cape Horn and the other outer islands have tough bog plants and dwarf trees and bushes.

Tierra del Fuego is home to several of the world's largest birds, including the rhea (which is akin to an ostrich or emu), the condor and the albatross. Large animals include guanacos, otters, seals and sea lions.

Travel in Tierra del Fuego

The chief settlement on the Chilean side is Porvenir. From there you can get a ferry across the straits to Punta Arenas. On the Argentine side Río Grande and Ushuaia are the two largest towns. The main crossing point between Chilean and Argentine territory is at San Sebastián on the road between Río Grande and Porvenir. Immediately south of Tierra del Fuego, separated by the narrow Beagle Channel, is the Chilean island of Navarino. The only settlement on Navarino is Puerto Williams, a Chilean naval base, which can be visited.

PORVENIR

With some 4500 people Porvenir is the only settlement of any size in Chilean Tierra del Fuego. Its predominant ethnic group is Yugoslav. As a sign by the ferry dock points out, Yugoslavia is only 18,662 km away.

Places to Stay & Eat

Try the *Residencial Camerón* and the *Hotel Central y Gran Tienda*. Ask around for others as it's a very small town. Try the *Yugoslav Club* for lunch. The *Restaurante Puerto Montt* is also good for seafood. Most pensiones offer full board.

Getting There & Away

Air If rough weather forces the cancellation

of the ferries to Punta Arenas, there is the possibility of flying. DAP has daily flights to Punta Arenas for US$14.

Bus Transporte Senkovic is at Carlos Bories 201, at the opposite end of the harbour from where you catch the ferry to Punta Arenas. This company runs buses between Porvenir and Río Grande two days a week. The fare to Río Grande is US$14. The trip takes about 7½ hours.

Boat There is a daily car and passenger ferry from Porvenir to Punta Arenas, departing Porvenir in the afternoon. The crossing takes two to three hours depending on the weather. The fare is US$2 – buy your ticket on the ferry. The ferry is operated by Transbordador Broom Ltda at Roca 924.

RIO GRANDE

On the east coast of Tierra del Fuego, Río Grande sits on a flat, windswept plain. This is a shepherds' town and oil refinery centre. There's not much of interest here to the visitor and it's really just a stop-over between Porvenir and Ushuaia.

Things to See

If you have some spare time it's suggested you visit the old **Salesian Mission** 11 km north of Río Grande. It's now used as an agricultural boarding school and museum, with some interesting exhibits which include Ona Indian artefacts. There are also displays on local flora, fauna, palaeontology and geology.

Places to Stay

It's not always easy to find a room in Río Grande. Most of the cheap places are occupied by men working on the oil installations. You may have to check quite a few hotels before you find something and even then, if you want

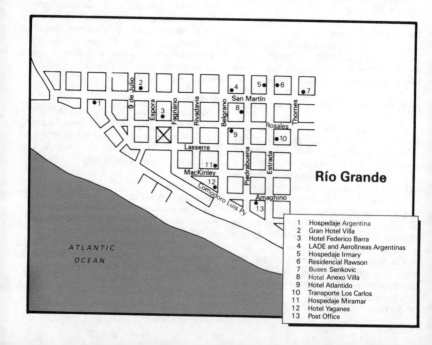

1	Hospedaje Argentina
2	Gran Hotel Villa
3	Hotel Federico Barra
4	LADE and Aerolíneas Argentinas
5	Hospedaje Irmary
6	Residencial Rawson
7	Buses Senkovic
8	Hotel Anexo Villa
9	Hotel Atlantido
10	Transporte Los Carlos
11	Hospedaje Miramar
12	Hotel Yaganes
13	Post Office

somewhere cheap, you may have to take a dormitory bed.

Places to Stay – bottom end

One of the cheapest places is the *Hospedaje Argentina* at 64 San Martín, between 11 de Julio and Comodoro Luis Py. Dormitory beds are a few dollars a night. However, your chances of getting accommodation here are slim.

The *Hospedaje Irmary* at Estrada 743, near the corner with San Martín, is very clean. Rooms are US$6 per person.

The *Hotel Anexo Villa* at Piedrabuena 641 is a decent place but it's often full. Beds are US$6 per person.

The *Residencial Arboleas* at the corner of Rosales and Rivadavia has also been recommended.

Places to Stay – middle

The *Residencial Rawson* at Estrada 750 is rather sterile but worth trying. Rooms with private bathroom are US$14 a single and US$18 a double.

One of the city's better hotels is the *Hospedaje Miramar* at the corner of MacKinley and Belgrano. Rooms without private bathroom are US$9 a single and US$14 a double. The hotel is very clean and has heating. Since it's a bit more expensive than the other places there's a good chance they'll have a room available.

The *Gran Hotel Villa* at San Martín 281 is also good. Rooms with private bathroom are US$15 a single and US$20 a double. Rooms without private bathroom are US$13 a single and US$16 a double. It's clean, quiet, and has friendly staff. There's a good, cheap restaurant downstairs.

Places to Stay – top end

The *Hotel Yaganes* is on Py, at the junction with Belgrano. Singles are US$31 and doubles are US$40, which includes breakfast. Similarly priced is the *Hotel Federico Barra* on Rosales, facing the main plaza. The city's newest hotel is the *Hotel Atlantido* at the corner of Belgrano and Rosales, with single and double rooms for US$40.

Places to Eat

The *Restaurant El Porteñito* on Lasserre, near Belgrano, is worth checking out. Also try the *Restaurant El Castor* which is a parrillada on Lasserre near the corner with Fagnano. The meals at the *Gran Hotel Villa* are cheap and very filling.

Getting There & Away

Air LADE and Aerolíneas Argentinas (tel 22749) are at the corner of San Martín and Belgrano. LADE has daily flights to Calafate, Río Gallegos and Ushuaia. Aerolíneas has daily flights to Ushuaia and to Buenos Aires via Río Gallegos, including stop-overs some days of the week in Comodoro Rivadavia, Trelew, Viedma, Bahía Blanca and Mar del Plata.

Bus Transporte Los Carlos is at Estrada 568. During summer they have daily buses to Ushuaia. Buses are less frequent in winter. The trip takes about four to 4½ hours. The fare is US$10.

Buses Senkovic is at San Martín 959. They have buses to Porvenir at 6 am every Wednesday and Saturday. The trip takes about 7½ hours. The fare is US$14. The bus connects with the ferry to Punta Arenas.

Getting Around

Cars can be rented from A1 (tel 22657) at the corner of Belgrano and Ameghino.

USHUAIA

Ushuaia, the world's southernmost town began, not with a brave band of hardy colonisers, but with a prefabricated mission hut put up in 1869 by an Anglican bishop. He lived there for six months alongside the huts of the Yahgan Indians.

The following year an Anglican minister named Thomas Bridges, together with his wife, set up a mission and became Tierra del Fuego's first permanent white settlers.

Perhaps his greatest achievement was the compilation of a large dictionary of the Yahgan language which described the incredible complexity and use of metaphor which the Yahgan used in everyday speech. Sixteen years later the Argentine navy paid a visit to the settlement, bringing with it pneumonia and measles which killed the Indians. Ushuaia was then used as a naval base, and then as a convict station.

Today, Ushuaia is a resort town, a sort of Antarctic version of Cairns or Brighton, and a good place to base yourself to explore the many lakes and mountains of Tierra del Fuego. There is also a ski run above the town; the season is May to October. Some people find the area reminiscent of parts of Canada, while others liken the mountains, the drizzle and the biting wind to Scotland. You can forget any images you have of some isolated backwoods town inhabited by weather-beaten frontiersmen. This city at the end of the world is a modern, duty-free port of concrete houses, sprawling up hills overlooking the Beagle Channel and whipped by cold winds that sweep in from every side.

Information

Tourist Office The tourist office is at San Martín 524, near the corner with Lasserre. The staff are friendly and speak some English, and there's plenty of hotel information available. If you're stuck for accommodation they'll telephone families who put lodgers up and try and find a room or a bed for you.

Post The post office is at the corner of San Martín and Godoy.

Banks The Banco de la Nación Argentina at the corner of San Martín and Rivadavia will change American Express and Thomas Cook travellers' cheques.

Consulates The Chilean consulate is at the corner of Malvinas Argentinas and Jainen.

National Parks The *Intendencia Parque Nacional Tierra del Fuego* is on San Martín near the corner with Patagonia.

Books For a round-up of Tierra del Fuego get *Tierra del Fuego* by Rae Natalie which is in both English and Spanish and can be bought in the book shops in Ushuaia. *Backpacking in Chile & Argentina* by Hilary Bradt and John Pilkington (Bradt Enterprises) has an excellent description of the treks in the area.

Things to See

About 150 years ago, Charles Darwin wrote the following description of the Beagle Channel, on whose shores Ushuaia now stands:

The scenery here becomes even grander than before. The lofty mountains on the north side compose the gigantic axis, or backbone of the country, and boldly rise to a height of between three thousand and four thousand feet .... they are covered by a wide mantle of perpetual snow, and numerous cascades pour their waters, through the woods, into the narrow channel below. In many parts, magnificent glaciers extend from the mountain side to the water's edge. It is scarcely possible to imagine any thing more beautiful than the beryl-like blue of these glaciers ...

Most of what there is to see around Ushuaia demands time, a reasonable supply of money and, to make the most of it, trekking and camping equipment. Ushuaia is a trekker's paradise which never fails to impress even experienced walkers. For details of trekking possibilities, enquire at the tourist office and at Onas Tours at the corner of 25 de Mayo and Maipú. During summer there are buses twice daily to the entrance of the Tierra del Fuego National Park leaving from San Martín 56. The return fare is US$6. If you don't intend trekking there are tours available to places of interest in the surrounding area. Try

Rumbo Sur tourist agency at San Martin 342, and Tiempo Libre at San Martín 152.

During the summer months, there are daily ferry trips to the sea lion colony on the Isla de los Lobos. The ferry is a large catamaran with catwalks around the hull. It skirts the coastline of Tierra del Fuego before cutting across the channel to the Isla de Pájaros (Bird Island) where many different species of bird roost. The catamaran then pulls up within a few feet of the Isla de los Lobos (Island of the Seals) which is a cluster of rocks in the middle of the channel where you'll see shaggy-necked sea-lions. The last stop, before heading back to Ushuaia, is another rock cluster where hundreds of cormorants perch. The six hour trip costs US$13.

There are day-trips which include the Isla de Pájaros, Isla de los Lobos, Haberton Ranch, Gable Island at the mouth of the Beagle Channel and the penguin colonies on Martello Island. These cost US$38. There are day trips to Río Grande which include visits to an estancia and a meat-processing plant. There are also day-trips to Lapatia and Ensenada Bays and to the bird and seal colonies on Bridges Island. These cost US$22.

There are tours to the Martial Glacier above Ushuaia but it's just as easy and much cheaper to do it yourself. There is a regular bus which leaves from outside the Rumbo Sur travel agency to the Martial Glacier chairlift. You take the chairlift to the top and then walk uphill to within sight of the glacier. Take good walking boots and warm clothes as it's likely to be snowing at this altitude, even during the summer months.

Summer yacht cruises are run by Ksar Tours. Contact Jean Paul Bassaget at the corner of Gobernador Paz and Lasserre. They have seven day cruises to Cape Horn, 10 day cruises to the Mitre Peninsula and 15 day cruises to Staton Island.

Places to Stay – bottom end
It's worth trying to find somewhere to stay in a private house, especially during January and February. The tourist office has a list of these places and will telephone around to try and find a room or a bed for you. Don't expect too much. The chances are that at the height of the tourist season you'll wind up sharing someone's bunk bed in a matchbox-sized attic. It may not be palatial but it's certainly better than sleeping out!

A good place is the Pensión Rosita on Paz between 9 de Julio and Triunvirato. It costs US$6 per bed and is run by a friendly woman.

There is a hospedaje above the Restaurant Los Canelos at the corner of Maipú and 9 de Julio. A bed in a four-bed room is US$6. There is a similarly priced hospedaje above a restaurant at San Martín 845.

In desperation try the Las Goletas at Maipú 857 (there's no sign) which is one of the cheapest places in town. It's a real flophouse.

Two other places worth trying are the unfortunately named Kau-pen at Piedrabuena 118, and Hilda Sanchez's house at Deloqui 786.

Places to Stay – lower middle
One of the cheaper hotels is the Residencial Capri (tel 91833) at San Martín 720, between 9 de Julio and Solis. It has bunk beds and hot water, is fairly clean, but is often full. Singles are US$13 and doubles are US$15.

Places to Stay – upper middle
The Hospedaje Fernández (tel 91453) at Ochanaga 68, is very friendly and serves meals. Singles are US$25 and doubles are US$32.

The Hospedaje Malvinas (tel 92626) at Deloqui 609, with doubles from US$30 has been recommended.

Other places in this price range include: the Hospedaje César (tel 91460) at San Martín 753; the Hostería Mustapic (tel 91718) at Piedrabuena 230; and the Hotel Maiten (tel 92745) at 12 de Octubre 140.

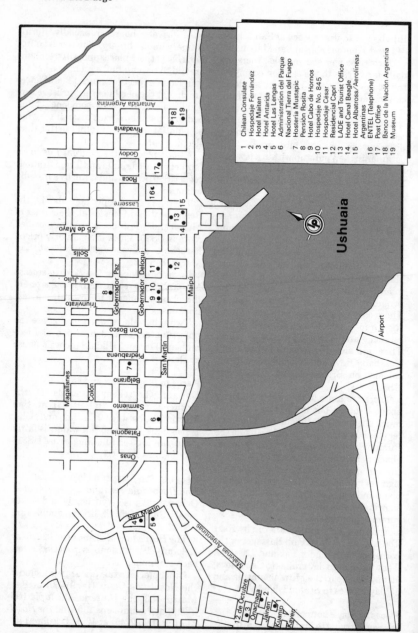

1 Chilean Consulate
2 Hospedaje Fernández
3 Hotel Maiten
4 Hotel Antarida
5 Hotel Las Lengas
6 Administration del Parque Nacional Tierra del Fuego
7 Hostería Mustapic
8 Pensión Rosita
9 Hotel Cabo de Hornos
10 Hospedaje No. 845
11 Hospedaje Cesar
12 Residencial Capri
13 LADE and Tourist Office
14 Hotel Canal Beagle
15 Hotel Albatross/Aerolíneas Argentinas
16 ENTEL (Telephone)
17 Post Office
18 Banco de la Nación Argentina
19 Museum

Ushuaia

Places to Stay – top end

The *Hotel Canal Beagle* (tel 91117), on the waterfront at the corner of Maipú and 25 de Mayo, has singles for US$31 and doubles for US$40. The *Hotel Albatross* (tel 92504) at the corner of Maipú and Lasserre is slightly cheaper. Also cheaper is the *Hotel Cabo de Hornos* (tel 92187) at the corner of San Martín and Triunvirato.

Places to Eat

The *Restaurant Los Canelos* at the corner of Maipú and 9 de Julio is a cosy place with a wide range of seafood. The servings are very large and moderately expensive. The *Sloggert Pub* on Godoy between Maipú and San Martín is worth trying.

The appropriately-named *Cafetería Ideal* at the corner of San Martín and Roca is an ideal place to eat. A main course of giant mussels (*cholga*) with potatoes plus drinks and dessert makes a filling, moderately priced meal. They also have pretty good pizzas – served whole or by the portion.

Getting There & Away

From Ushuaia you can take the ferry to Puerto Williams in Chile and then fly to Punta Arenas. Or take a bus to Río Grande and carry on by bus and boat to Punta Arenas via Porvenir. Or fly from Ushuaia to Río Grande and beyond.

Air LADE is at San Martín 542. They have daily flights to Calafate via Río Grande and Río Gallegos. These carry on to Perito Moreno. There are connections three days a week from Río Gallegos to Río Turbio.

Aerolíneas Argentinas (tel 91218) is at the corner of Maipú and Lasserre. They have daily flights from Ushuaia to Buenos Aires, via Río Grande and Río Gallegos. There are stop-overs some days of the week in Comodoro Rivadavia, Trelew, Viedma, Bahía Blanca and Mar del Plata.

Ushuaia's airport is on the other side of the harbour to the town. To get there take a local bus or a taxi. A taxi will cost a few dollars. You can get a local bus to the airport from Maipú.

Bus Transporte Los Carlos is at the corner of San Martín and Triunvirato. In summer they have daily buses to Río Grande. The fare is US$10. The trip takes four to 4½ hours.

Boat There used to be a once weekly ferry from Ushuaia to Puerto Williams but this appears to have been discontinued. There may be ferries taking tour groups across during the summer. Ask at the tourist office when you get to Ushuaia.

PUERTO WILLIAMS

For over 35 years the naval base of Puerto Williams on Navarino Island has been waving the Chilean flag at the toe-nails of Argentina. The forerunner of this settlement was the world's most southerly sawmilling concern. Spread along the shores of the Beagle Channel it's an admirable setting. The last people of identifiable Yahgan Indian descent can be found here and there is a fine museum. Trekking on the island is limited since there are few trails and only two roads. The flight from Punta Arenas is spectacular on a clear day with brilliant views of the archipelago.

Information

The settlement has a central block of shops and offices. The Agencia de Viajes Avenoger Loda will change US dollars for Argentine and Chilean currency. There is also a post office and a supermarket.

Things to See

The **Museo Martín Gusinde** has some fine exhibits on the natural history of the region, the Indians who once lived here, and on European exploration and settlement.

The last people of identifiable Yahgan Indian descent live in a small enclave of houses called Ukika, by the road a short distance east of the town.

On a clear day there are good views

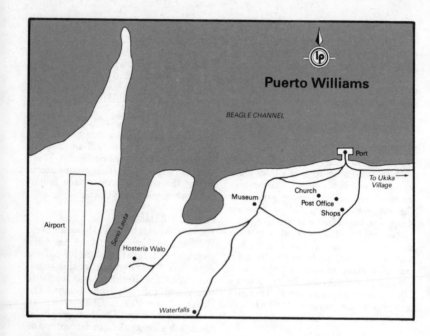

across the Beagle Channel to Gable Island and the mountains to the north. West of town, a branch road runs about four km to a waterfall.

Places to Stay & Eat

In the central block just behind the gymnasium (a large green building) is a small hotel which also has a restaurant. It's a spartan place but clean and decent. Rooms are about US$7 per person with full board.

The *Hostería Walo* is on the airport road. It's surprisingly comfortable, with a good restaurant and blazing fireplace. Rooms are US$25 a single and US$30 a double. The food is quite expensive; *curanto* for lunch will set you back US$10 and even a simple breakfast is around US$4. They have tours to the museum, waterfalls and the Ukika village.

Getting There & Away

Air DAP flies from Puerto Williams to Punta Arenas three days a week. The fare is US$57. Tickets are available in Puerto Williams from the DAP agent at the Casa Stop in the central block of shops and offices.

Boat There used to be a weekly ferry from Ushuaia to Puerto Williams but this appears to have been discontinued. There may be ferries taking tour groups across during summer. In Puerto Williams enquire at the Agencia de Viajes Avenoger Loda. In Ushuaia ask at the tourist office.

The ship *M/N Argonauta* runs from Punta Arenas to Puerto Williams once a month. The fare is around US$80. Tickets and information are available from the Agencia de Viajes Aventour in the Hostería Walo in Puerto Williams.

Index

MAPS

Temperature

To convert °C to °F multiply by 1.8 and add 32

To convert °F to °C subtract 32 and multiply by ·55

Length, Distance & Area

	multiply by
inches to centimetres	2.54
centimetres to inches	0.39
feet to metres	0.30
metres to feet	3.28
yards to metres	0.91
metres to yards	1.09
miles to kilometres	1.61
kilometres to miles	0.62
acres to hectares	0.40
hectares to acres	2.47

Weight

	multiply by
ounces to grams	28.35
grams to ounces	0.035
pounds to kilograms	0.45
kilograms to pounds	2.21
British tons to kilograms	1016
US tons to kilograms	907

A British ton is 2240 lbs, a US ton is 2000 lbs

Volume

	multiply by
Imperial gallons to litres	4.55
litres to imperial gallons	0.22
US gallons to litres	3.79
litres to US gallons	0.26

5 imperial gallons equals 6 US gallons
a litre is slightly more than a US quart, slightly less
than a British one

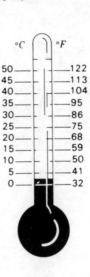

Guides to the Americas

Alaska – a travel survival kit
A definitive guide to one of the world's most spectacular regions – including detailed information on hiking and canoeing.

Canada – a travel survival kit
Canada offers a unique combination of English, French and American culture, with forests mountains and lakes that cover a vast area.

Chile & Easter Island – a travel survival kit
Chile has one of the most varied geographies in the world, including deserts, tranquil lakes, snow-covered volcanoes and windswept fjords. Easter Island is covered, in detail.

Ecuador & the Galapagos Islands – a travel survival kit
Ecuador is the smallest of the Andean countries, and in many ways it is the easiest and most pleasant to travel in. The Galapagos Islands and their amazing inhabitants continue to cast a spell over every visitor.

Mexico – a travel survival kit
Mexico has a unique blend of Indian and Spanish culture and a fascinating historical legacy. The hospitality of the people makes Mexico a paradise for travellers.

Peru – a travel survival kit
The famed city of Machu Picchu, the Andean altiplano and the Amazon rainforests are just some of Peru's attractions. All the facts you need can be found in this comprehensive guide.

South America on a shoestring
An up-dated edition of a budget travellers bible that covers Central and South America from the USA-Mexico border to Tierra del Fuego. Written by the author the *New York Times* called "the patron saint of travellers in the third world".

Baja California – a travel survival kit
Mexico's Baja peninsula offers a great escape, right at California's back door. This comprehensive guide follows the long road south from raucous border towns like Tijuana, to resorts, untouched villages and deserted villages.

Colombia – a travel survival kit
Colombia is the land of emeralds, orchids and El Dorado. You may not find the mythical city of gold, but you will find an exotic, wild and beautiful country.

Bolivia – a travel survival kit
Bolivia offers safe and intriguing travel options – from isolated villages in the Andes and ancient ruins to the incredible city of La Paz.

Lonely Planet Guidebooks

Lonely Planet guidebooks cover virtually every accessible part of Asia as well as Australia, the Pacific, Central and South America, Africa, the Middle East and parts of North America. There are four main series: 'travel survival kits', covering a single country for a range of budgets; 'shoestring' guides with compact information for low-budget travel in a major region; trekking guides; and 'phrasebooks'.

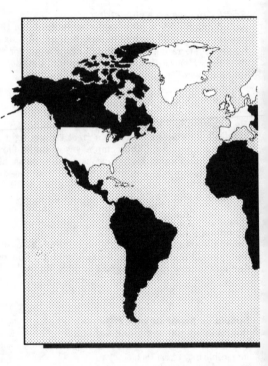

Mail Order

Lonely Planet guidebooks are distributed worldwide and are sold by good bookshops everywhere. They are also available by mail order from Lonely Planet, so if you have difficulty finding a title please write to us. US and Canadian residents should write to Embarcadero West, 112 Linden St, Oakland CA 94607, USA and residents of other countries to PO Box 617, Hawthorn, Victoria 3122, Australia.

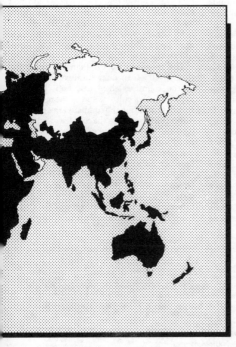

Eastern Europe
Eastern Europe

Indian Subcontinent
India
Hindi/Urdu phrasebook
Kashmir, Ladakh & Zanskar
Trekking in the Indian Himalaya
Pakistan
Kathmandu & the Kingdom of Nepal
Trekking in the Nepal Himalaya
Nepal phrasebook
Sri Lanka
Sri Lanka phrasebook
Bangladesh
Karakoram Highway

Africa
Africa on a shoestring
East Africa
Swahili phrasebook
West Africa
Central Africa
Morocco, Algeria & Tunisia

North America
Canada
Alaska

Mexico
Mexico
Baja California

South America
South America on a shoestring
Ecuador & the Galapagos Islands
Colombia
Chile & Easter Island
Bolivia
Brazil
Peru
Argentina
Quechua phrasebook

Middle East
Israel
Egypt & the Sudan
Jordan & Syria
Yemen

Lonely Planet

Lonely Planet published its first book in 1973. Tony and Maureen Wheeler had made a lengthy overland trip from England to Australia and, in response to numerous 'how do you do it?' questions, Tony wrote and they published *Across Asia on the Cheap*. It became an instant local best-seller and inspired thoughts of a second travel guide. A year and a half in South-East Asia resulted in their second book, *South-East Asia on a Shoestring*, which they put together in a backstreet Chinese hotel in Singapore in 1975. The 'yellow book', as it quickly became known, soon became *the* guide to the region and has gone through five editions, always with its familiar yellow cover.

Soon other writers came to them with ideas for similar books – books that went off the beaten track with an adventurous approach to travel, books that 'assumed you knew how to get your luggage off the carousel,' as one reviewer put it. Lonely Planet grew from a kitchen table operation to a spare room and then to its own office. Its international reputation began to grow as the Lonely Planet logo began to appear in more and more countries. In 1982 *India – a travel survival kit* won the Thomas Cook award for the best guidebook of the year.

These days there are over 70 Lonely Planet titles. Over 40 people work at our office in Melbourne, Australia and another half dozen at our US office in Oakland, California.

At first Lonely Planet specialised in the Asia region but these days we are also developing major ranges of guidebooks to the Pacific region, to South America and to Africa. The list of walking guides is growing and Lonely Planet now has a unique series of phrasebooks to 'unusual' languages. The emphasis continues to be on travel for travellers and Tony and Maureen still manage to fit in a number of trips each year and play a very active part in the writing and updating of Lonely Planet's guides.

Keeping guidebooks up to date is a constant battle which requires an ear to the ground and lots of walking, but technology also plays its part. All Lonely Planet guidebooks are now stored and updated on computer, and some authors even take lap-top computers into the field. Lonely Planet is also using computers to draw maps and eventually many of the maps will be stored on disk.

The people at Lonely Planet strongly feel that travellers can make a positive contribution to the countries they visit both by better appreciation of cultures and by the money they spend. In addition the company tries to make a direct contribution to the countries and regions it covers. Since 1986 a percentage of the income from each book has gone to aid groups and associations. This has included donations to famine relief in Africa, to aid projects in India, to agricultural projects in Central America, to Greenpeace's efforts to halt French nuclear testing in the Pacific and to Amnesty International. In 1989 $41,000 was donated by Lonely Planet to these projects.

Lonely Planet Distributors

Australia & Papua New Guinea Lonely Planet Publications, PO Box 617, Hawthorn, Victoria 3122.
Canada Raincoast Books, 112 East 3rd Avenue, Vancouver, British Columbia V5T 1C8.
Denmark, Finland & Norway Scanvik Books aps, Store Kongensgade 59 A, DK-1264 Copenhagen K.
India & Nepal UBS Distributors, 5 Ansari Rd, New Delhi – 110002
Israel Geographical Tours Ltd, 8 Tverya St, Tel Aviv 63144.
Japan Intercontinental Marketing Corp, IPO Box 5056, Tokyo 100-31.
Kenya Westland Sundries Ltd, PO Box 14107, Nairobi, Kenya.
Netherlands Nilsson & Lamm bv, Postbus 195, Pampuslaan 212, 1380 AD Weesp.
New Zealand Transworld Publishers, PO Box 83-094, Edmonton PO, Auckland.
Singapore & Malaysia MPH Distributors, 601 Sims Drive, #03-21, Singapore 1438.
Spain Altair, Balmes 69, 08007 Barcelona.
Sweden Esselte Kartcentrum AB, Vasagatan 16, S-111 20 Stockholm.
Thailand Chalermnit, 108 Sukhumvit 53, Bangkok 10110.
Turkey Yab-Yay Dagitim, Alay Koshu Caddesi 12/A, Kat 4 no. 11-12, Cagaloglu, Istanbul.
UK Roger Lascelles, 47 York Rd, Brentford, Middlesex, TW8 0QP
USA Lonely Planet Publications, PO Box 2001A, Berkeley, CA 94702.
West Germany Buchvertrieb Gerda Schettler, Postfach 64, D3415 Hattorf a H.
All Other Countries refer to Australia address.